# The Natural Eye

## Art Book One

The Society of Wildlife Artists

Published by Red Hare Publishing Ltd in association
with The Society of Wildlife Artists

Red Hare Publishing Ltd, c/o Pinkfoot Gallery,
High Street, Cley, Norfolk NR25 7RB
Tel: 01263 740947
info@redharepublishing.co.uk
www.redharepublishing.co.uk

ISBN 978-0-9569976-7-8



Printed in Britain by Swallowtail Print, Norwich, UK
www.swallowtailprint.co.uk

*Common Seals,* Bruce Pearson

# The Natural Eye

## Art Book One

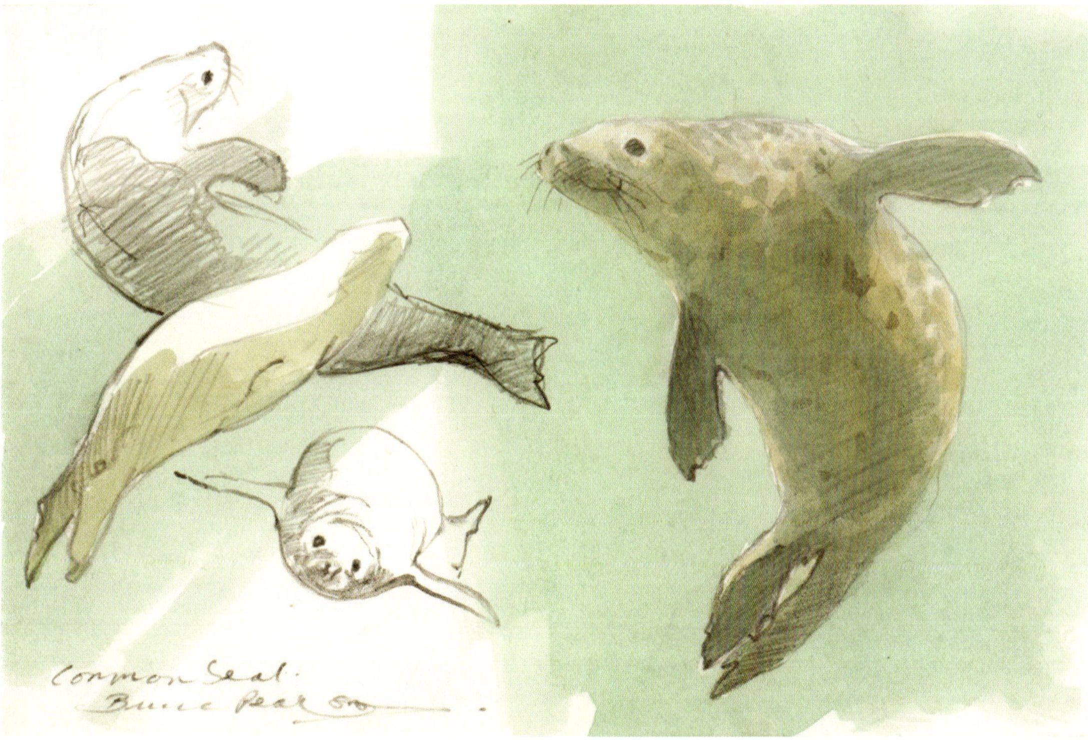

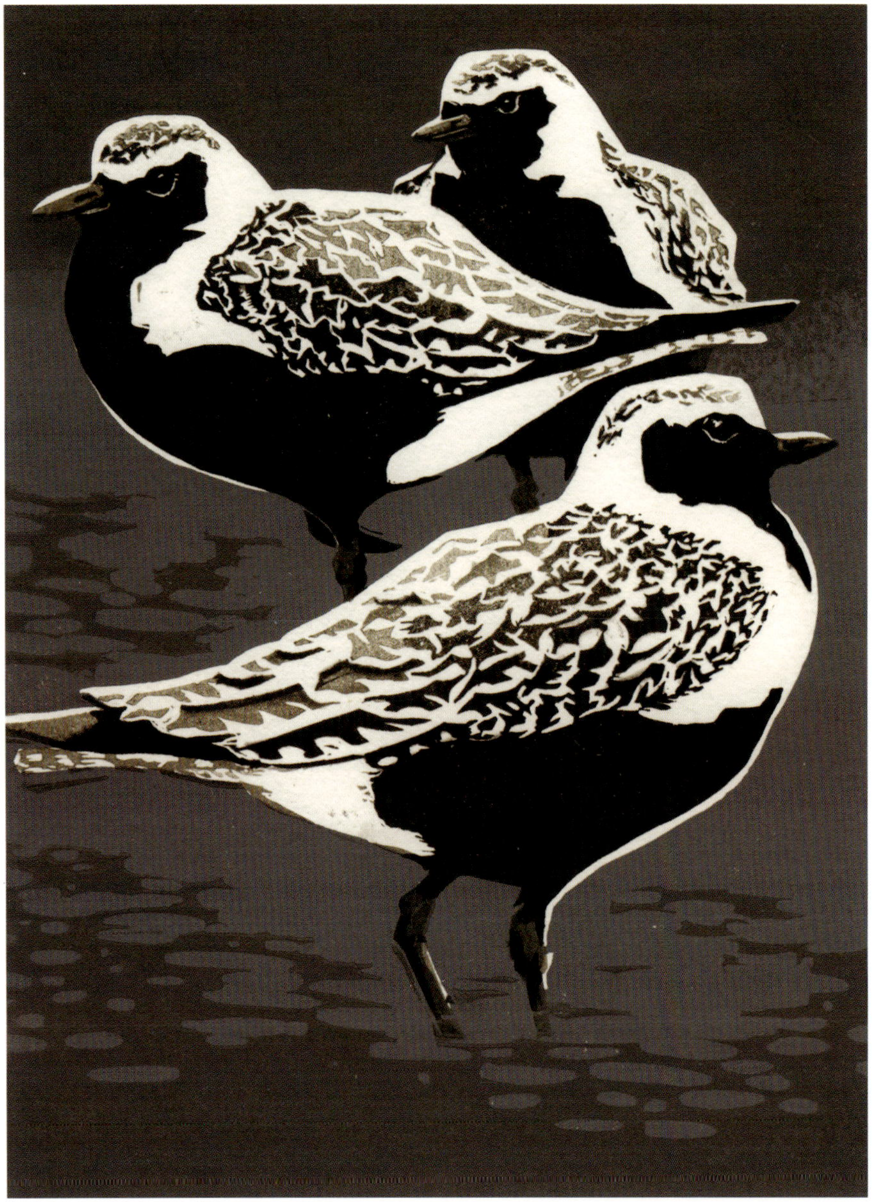

*Grey Plovers*, linocut, Thelma Sykes

# Foreword by Chris Packham

Nature is perfect. Or so very nearly perfect. Maybe only its overall complexity manifests the slight flaws that allow evolution to act to constantly change it, sometimes slowly, sometimes rapidly, but ultimately for the better. But any organism in artificial isolation is essentially perfect. Certainly physically but of course also behaviourally, and when in the context of its wider community, it is ecologically perfect too. And this is what makes it beautiful. Absolutely beautiful, beyond compare or corruption.

Brave then is any artist who tries to harness this beauty, to transform or transpose elements of it and offer it up to connoisseurs for appraisal and appreciation. Braver still those who do not only seek to illustrate it but actually modify it through their personal response and emotional connection to it. These folk are playing with nature's perfect fire and any slip, any betrayal of its simple beauty will result in disaster. They will be found out unless their use of shape, form, colour or texture conforms to life's wonderful conventions in some recognisable fashion, which allows their audience to respond positively to their manipulated stimulation. And what about those who pare down their subjects into the most fundamental aspects of the organism? Here simplicity becomes the cruellest of critics because nature's design has to be rigorously observed and represented. The very success of an artist's work can hang on the subtle nuances of a single line. The flexing of their hand or fingers for a fraction of a second during their process will eternally mark their skill and expose their sensitivity to their subject's total existence in form and context.

For me the immense difficulty of this task is what most stirs awe when I peruse these works. Their styles and attitudes cover a vast range of techniques and methods, but their objectives are unified. I also revel in the wonder of what made each artist choose each species or scene, what passion was fired by it to elicit the desire to respond creatively. I like to unravel my imagined stories to construct a route from blank space to finished work. Sometimes as an exercise, I dissect each fraction of the form or process to try to understand its origin or motivation. But this can be destructive because it's the 'bigger picture' that contains the purpose - murdering to dissect art can have a miserable end!

The SWLA has a rich legacy of our finest wildlife artists' involvement and this volume shows that condition prevails today. It is an exciting collection which will be dispersed for charitable purpose to fortunate folk but it also serves as a lasting testament to a remarkable and valuable skill set and to that irresistible and enduring beauty and perfection of nature.

# The Birth of The Society
## by Robert Gillmor (President 1984–1994)

I was extremely fortunate to attend schools where art and natural history were regarded as seriously as academic subjects and sport. The 'Bird Group' met every Friday evening, under the benevolent eye of Duncan Wood, a first-rate ornithologist with a reputation which led him to being asked to take on the editorship of *British Birds*, then the only monthly magazine devoted to birds, when its senior editor, Bernard Tucker, was too unwell to continue.

Through Duncan, and the regular meetings, often addressed by leading bird-men of the day, we had a unique contact with the wider world of ornithology.
We kept detailed daily records of the birds in the school grounds and were enthusiastic ringers. Birdwatching trips included stays on Skokholm Island, where school parties had helped Ronald Lockley establish his bird observatory and build a Heligoland trap.

My friend Nick Jones and I were extremely keen on wildfowl and joined what was then the Severn Wildfowl Trust: Nick in its first year, me in the second! We stayed at Slimbridge during the winter holidays and, through Nick's studies of Canada Geese in the Kennet Valley, got to know Peter Scott. My first illustrations appeared in *British Birds* in 1952 and I became hugely interested in bird art and artists. At that time it was very difficult to see original work by wildlife artists. There was one gallery in London, Rowland Wards in Piccadilly, where the (remarkably few) leading artists exhibited and, as a youngster, I always asked to go there on rare visits to London. Those first drawings in *British Birds* illustrated an article by Max Nicholson on Shearwaters in the English Channel. As a result he invited me to be his guest at a special meeting of the British Ornithologists' Club devoted to bird

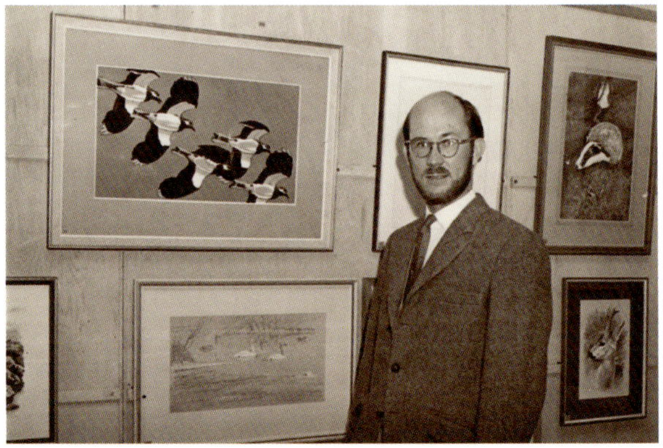

Robert Gillmor with his *Migrating Lapwings* linocut at the second SWLA exhibition in 1965, at the Galleries of the FBA, 6 1/2 Suffolk Street, London

art. Members had been encouraged to introduce bird artists and so I found myself in exalted company. The occasion started to crystalise an idea I'd been considering – why couldn't the bird artists get together for a joint exhibition? As I already had contacts with a few, I wrote to see what they thought of the idea and the answers were all very positive. I had become secretary of the Reading Ornithological Club and knew the director of Reading Museum & Art Gallery, who was keen to put on the exhibition. So I compiled a list of all the artists I could think of – in the end just 28, including three from aboard! A committee was formed, including Eric Ennion, Peter Scott and his close friend Keith Shackleton. Peter persuaded Lord Alanbroke, a keen naturalist and wildlife film-maker, to open the exhibition, which took place on 26 November 1960. By then the Art Exhibitions Bureau, run by Maurice Bradshaw, had got involved and he took the show on a provincial tour for a year; extended to two by popular demand.

Eric Ennion and I got together to ensure that this initial enthusiasm and success was not wasted. Maurice Bradshaw also ran the Federation of British Artists, a loose federation of seven art societies, and he could see that a body of wildlife artists would fit well into his organisation. We started to collect names and a correspondence developed with Eric when we swapped lists and ideas for a constitution etc. I well remember a BOU weekend conference at Chester Zoo when Eric and I cut lectures to sit in the grounds in the sun opposite the chimps, to go over our ideas and plan the future society. We were joined on a steering committee by R B Talbot-Kelly and Maurice Wilson, who both brought wisdom and practical help to our meetings. The inaugural exhibition was planned for August 1964, which James Fisher was invited to open. By then we had 35 founder members, ten of which are still with us and able to help celebrate our 50th Anniversary.

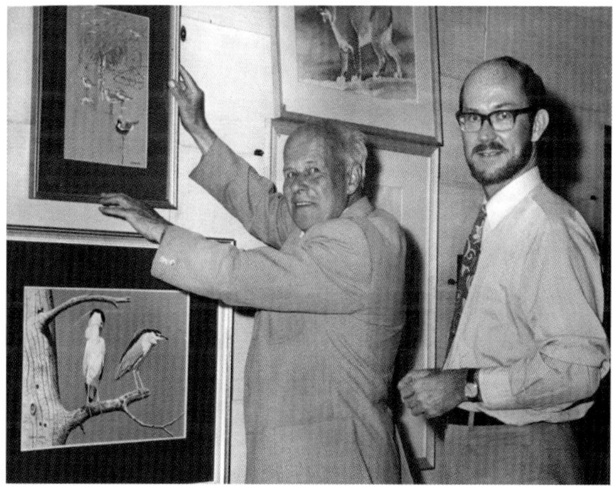

Eric Ennion and Robert Gillmor hanging their pictures at the 1973 SWLA exhibition, Mall Galleries, London.

# Here And Now by Harriet Mead

## Current President of the SWLA

The Society of Wildlife Artists celebrates its 50th anniversary this year. I first showed my work at the SWLA in 1990 when I was a student. I had not visited the show before and was thrilled to have my sculptures, which were made of unconventional materials, exhibited among so much 'proper' art by such skilled and established artists. The sheer range of approaches, subjects and methods was inspiring and made a deep impression on me. The experience definitely encouraged me to carry on creating and gave me confidence to continue making art. That rather awestruck teenager would be astonished to learn that her much older self would have the honour of being at the helm of the Society that continues to help other young artists on their path to creating work inspired by the natural world.

So what is Wildlife Art? Is it about the majesty of nature? The drama of life and death as prey and predator meet? Is it about the colour and texture of mass migration or the moments of solitude of a lone Polar Bear in the vast Arctic landscape that captures the fragility of our planet? Is it a way of documenting the natural world or a celebration of an individual animal? I believe it can be any one of those things but what I feel is important is that the artist understands their subject. Many of our artists choose to work in the field so that when they create their work either directly 'plein air' or later back in the studio using their sketches, there is a depth of knowledge that is obvious in the piece. Whether depicting a wasp or an albatross, a bear or a beetle, at the beating heart of The Society of Wildlife Artists is the quest to capture the essence of that creature and its place in the world. What connects this art is the celebration of the natural world and the love of the subject.

Art can be a powerful tool for conservation. It can breathe life onto the bones of research by reminding us exactly why we should care about the increasingly gloomy news of habitat loss, climate change and extinction. Indeed many of our artists work closely with conservation charities which realise the value of using the artists' view to help spread their message. The work in this book, like the work that we exhibit at our annual show 'The Natural Eye', celebrates the natural world and I like to think it helps encapsulate why the environment needs conserving, whether it be the big issues of disappearing rainforests and melting ice caps or the quieter issues closer to home like the decline of farmland birds or scarcity of amphibians.

This book was born from the generosity and talents of the members of the SWLA. It contains examples from the majority of our membership, from the recently elected to some of the founding members from our first exhibition 50 years ago. We have deliberately chosen not to use it as a portfolio of key pieces made by our artists. Instead it is a celebration of work on a smaller scale, whether it is field sketches or mono-prints, oil paintings or watercolours, collages or sculpture. For the past few years we have held the Original Art Work Draw at the British Bird Watching Fair and had a tremendous response from our members. The collected works were a glorious patchwork of our members' talent and the idea of gathering the pieces in a book accompanied by the artists' own words was born.

I must thank all the artists who have made this book possible and thank you for buying it. The funds raised from the sale of this book, and indeed the sale of the artwork within, will assist the SWLA in providing opportunities through our bursary scheme and other projects for artists young and old to continue their artistic journeys. We hope to build on our relationships with conservation organisations so that we can help preserve the creatures that inspire us.

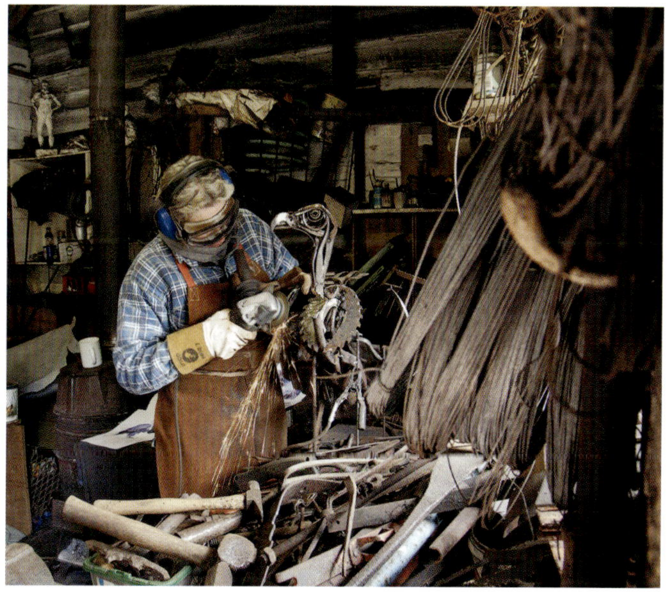

Harriet Mead angle grinding in her Norfolk studio.

## The Society's Future
## by Bruce Pearson (President 1994–2004)

When asked what does the SWLA do, a spontaneous formal response is to say that it is a gathering of about 80 passionate artist-naturalists who exhibit together annually, sometimes sharing creative adventures together in smaller groups. But a more reflective answer that considers the Society's progress over the past 50 years and its potential to grow and develop in the future creates a far more interesting picture.

The principal focus for the Society has always been the annual exhibition at the Mall Galleries, a prime space in central London that is the natural home of the SWLA and the other eight member societies that make up the Federation of British Artists (FBA). The inaugural 1964 SWLA exhibition showed 149 works by 35 artists. In the 2012 'Natural Eye' exhibition there were over 400 works in a many different media from 109 artists - mainly members from the UK, but also some from Europe, North America and Russia - as well as a selection of paintings, sculptures, prints and drawings from non-members and successful bursary winners.

Every artist taking the natural world as their creative starting point has their own way of responding and method of expression - from photo-realism to abstract, from found object sculpture to casting in bronze, and from video installation to hand-burnished relief print, with so much else in between. All of those kinds of responses - to everything from freshwater fish and tropical birds to polar mammals and oceanic reptiles - have featured in

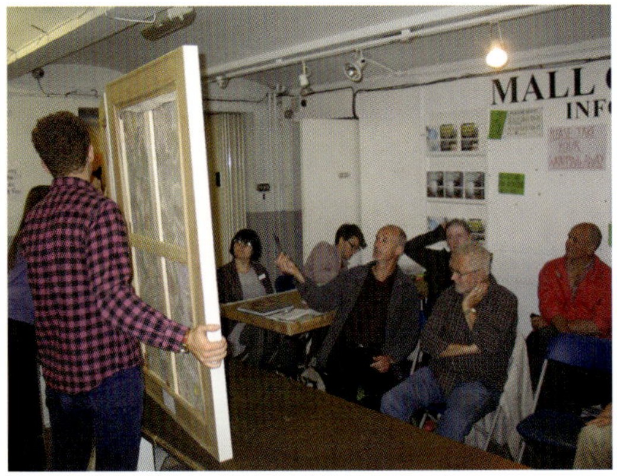

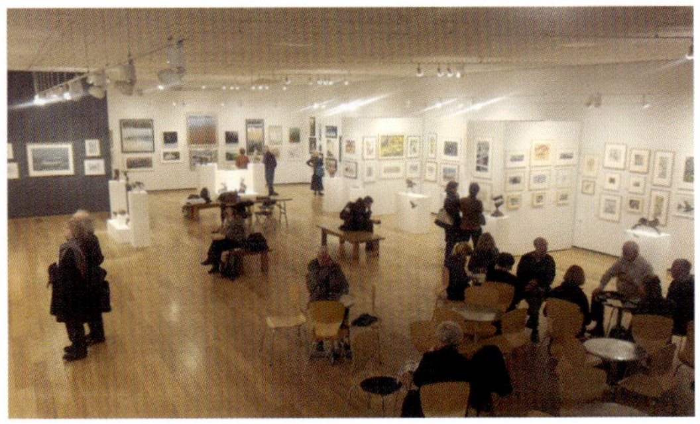

Top: SWLA Selection day for the annual exhibition. Below: The Natural Eye exhibition at the Mall Galleries, London.

the annual exhibition over the past 50 years. But it was when the SWLA became a registered charity in 1990 and established a bursary scheme in 1993 that its creative breadth increased greatly and accelerated the Society's ability to reach beyond the confines of its annual exhibition.

Charitable status formalised the Society's purpose of encouraging all forms of visual art-based on or representing the world's wildlife, and of supporting and promoting arts based objectives of other conservation and wildlife charities. It also opened the door for commercial sponsorship. With generous funding from Lloyds Private Banking, the SWLA Bursary Scheme was established to help young artists develop their knowledge and skills in wildlife art by contributing to travel expenses or the cost of materials in pursuance of a challenging and succinct project proposal. Over the years further sponsorship and support from CAPMARK Europe, the Artists for Nature Foundation, RSPB, Wildfowl and Wetlands Trust, British Trust for Ornithology and a number of other conservation and arts organizations has been fed either directly into the bursary scheme or into awards, events and projects which have all successfully increased the reach and enhanced the profile of the Society. Support has been provided for aspiring artists wanting to join a renowned seabird drawing course in Scotland. More recently a new partnership with The Wildlife Trusts provided for a unique Underwater Art Award, a bursary for artists of any age and experience offering the

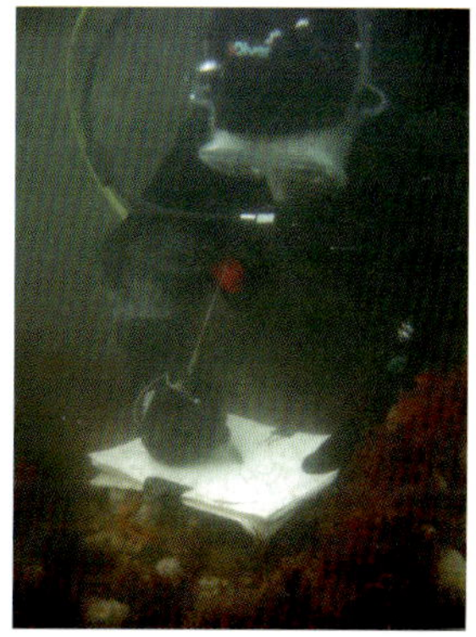

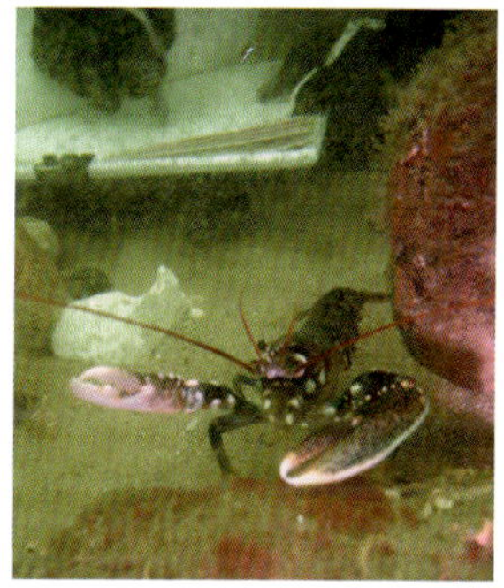

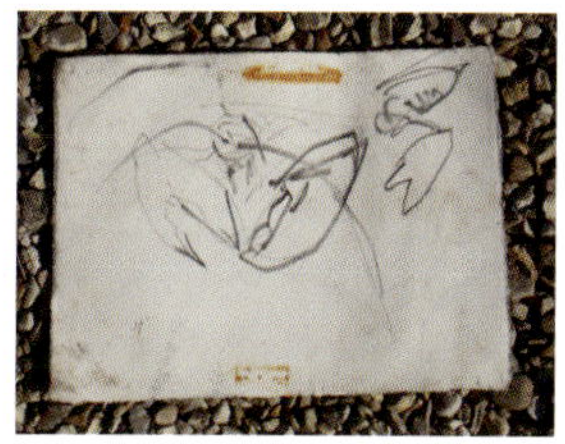

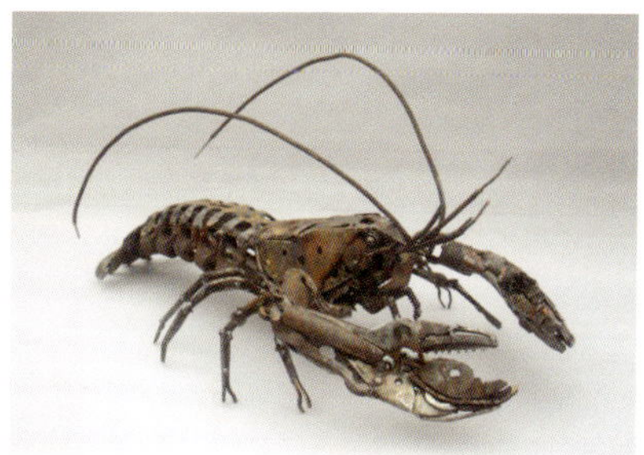

The making of *Mole Grip Lobster* by Harriet Mead for the 2011 Wildlife Trusts' Diving Bursary.

opportunity to learn to dive in order to portray the beauty and fragility of the UK's marine environment. At the annual exhibition there are many awards and prizes on behalf of conservation charities and publishers that recognize a range of artistic talents, skills and ideas.

With wildlife artists working mostly on their own, both in the field and in studio settings, the projects the SWLA has developed through a range of partnerships and collaborations have been hugely beneficial for the Society. They have also raised the bar creatively as each project has presented new opportunities for members and other artists to collaborate and share experiences, as well as contribute to wider reaching environmental education and awareness programmes. Collaborating with the RSPB at their Minsmere reserve in 1998 and 1999, a small number of artists worked together for only a few days to produce two wonderful handmade books, each limited to 50 copies. Perhaps the most ambitious projects were collaborations with The Forestry Commission in 2000 and 2005. The first was *Drawn to the Forest* a book and exhibition that showed the biodiversity, ecology and cultural landscape of the New Forest. The second Aig an Oir project was an opportunity for SWLA artists, bursary winners and others to collaborate in creating a unique portrait of Scotland's Atlantic oakwoods.

The overall aim of the annual exhibition, and the books, exhibitions and outreaching of creative energy beyond the Mall Galleries, has been so that as many people as possible can experience the natural world through artists' eyes, and in so doing enhance their enjoyment and understanding of it. And the bursary awards have become one of the most important aspects of the Society's activities; they nurture new talent which feeds the Society's roots, and the work of the award winners in a dedicated section adds a distinctive character to the exhibition. Without the bursary scheme the SWLA would lack a clear charitable focus and purpose.

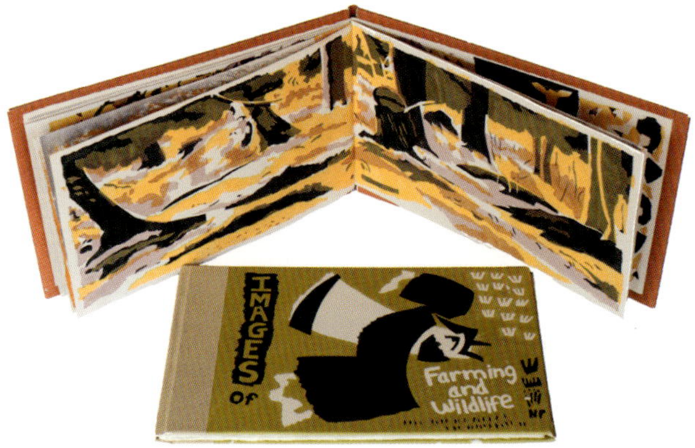


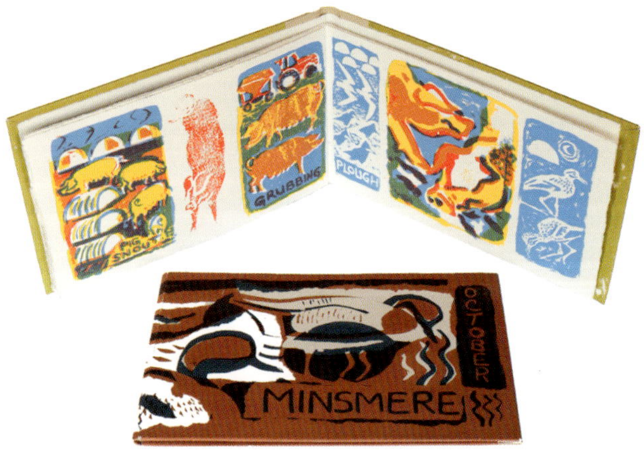


Handmade books with original art by SWLA artists for a collaborative scheme with the RSPB.

The SWLA is at a very exciting stage in its 50 year evolution from a smaller and slightly more narrowly focused gathering of like-minded artists to a larger and more established grouping of contemporary artists drawn together around a broad central theme. The potential for it to evolve further is enormous, but challenging. It requires considerable effort from the president and council, and support from sponsors, friends and members. The immediate effort must be on securing sufficient funding to enable the bursary fund to go on rewarding talent, ingenuity and creativity, and at the same time, just as important, seeking new project initiatives that will stretch our creative potential. This book of postcard images reflects the urgency of those two imperatives – successful sales will result in funds going to support the Society's charitable activities in the future, and the enthusiasm for this project shown by the many people who have helped make this book indicate that the SWLA is a positive creative force with an exciting future.

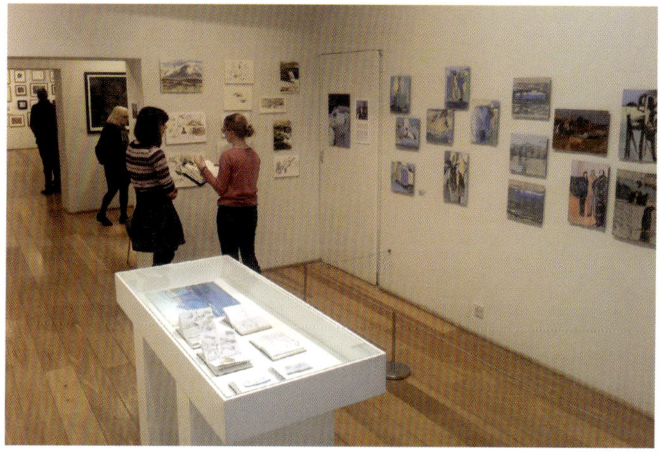

The Out of the Frame room at the Natural Eye annual exhibition showcases three projects from our members which encapsulates our ethos of artists working in the field.

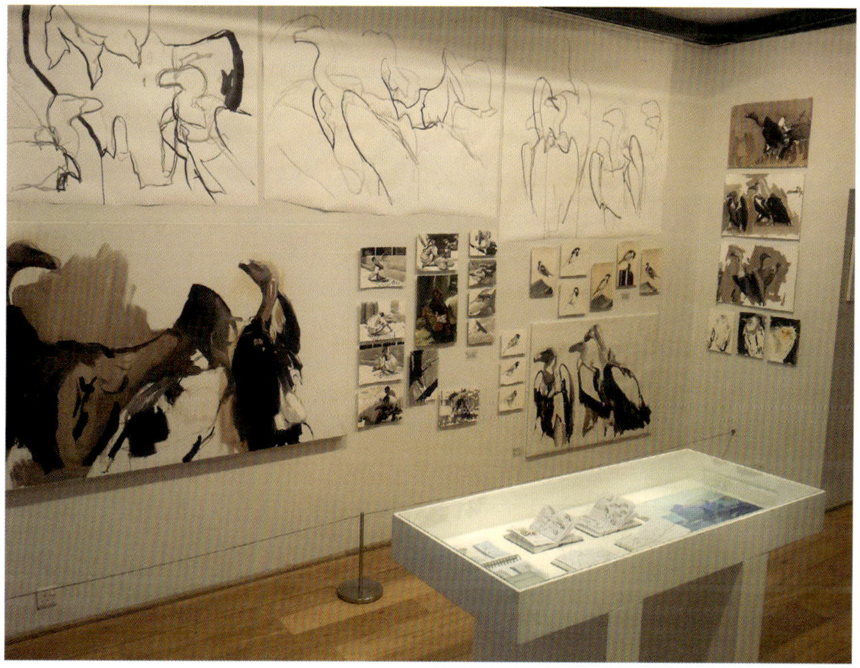

Esther Tyson's work from the Nepal Vulture Project (BirdLife International) in the Out of the Frame room at the annual exhibition.

# Artists At Work

Many of our artists work in the field or spend time just watching their subjects. The following pictures show a variety of approaches our members use when creating art inspired by the natural world and have got up close and personal with wildlife.

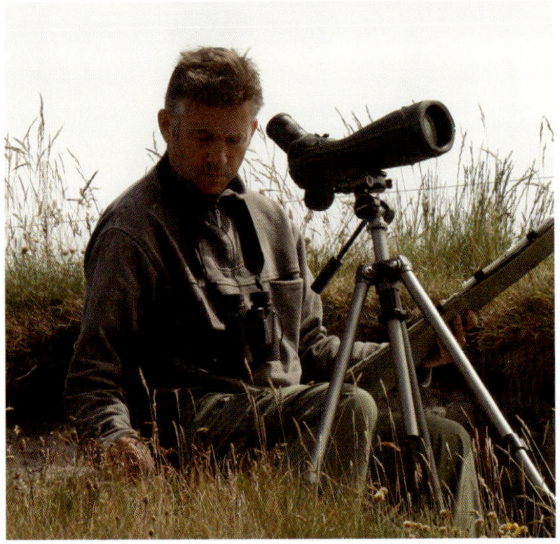

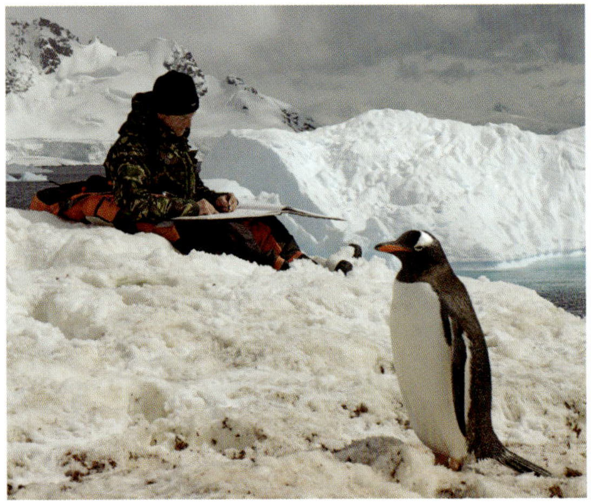

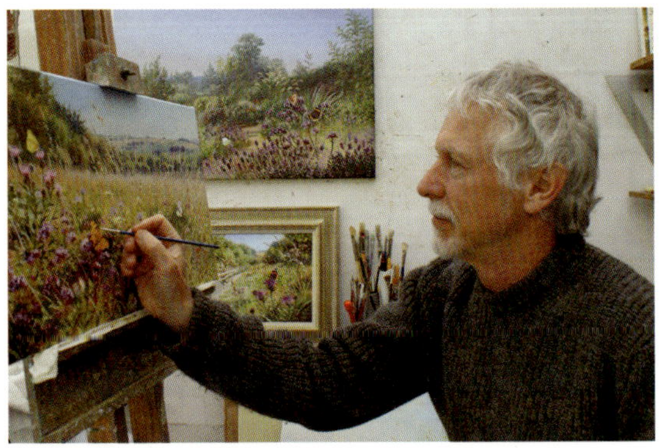

*Top: John Threlfall*
*Middle: Andrew Stock*
*Bottom: Richard Tratt*

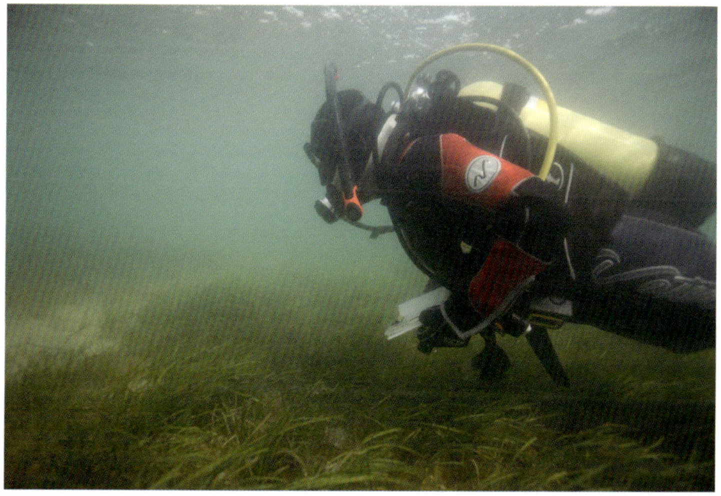

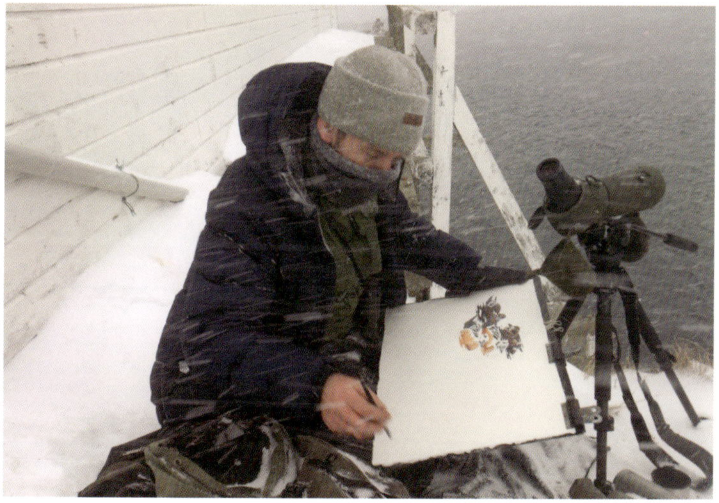

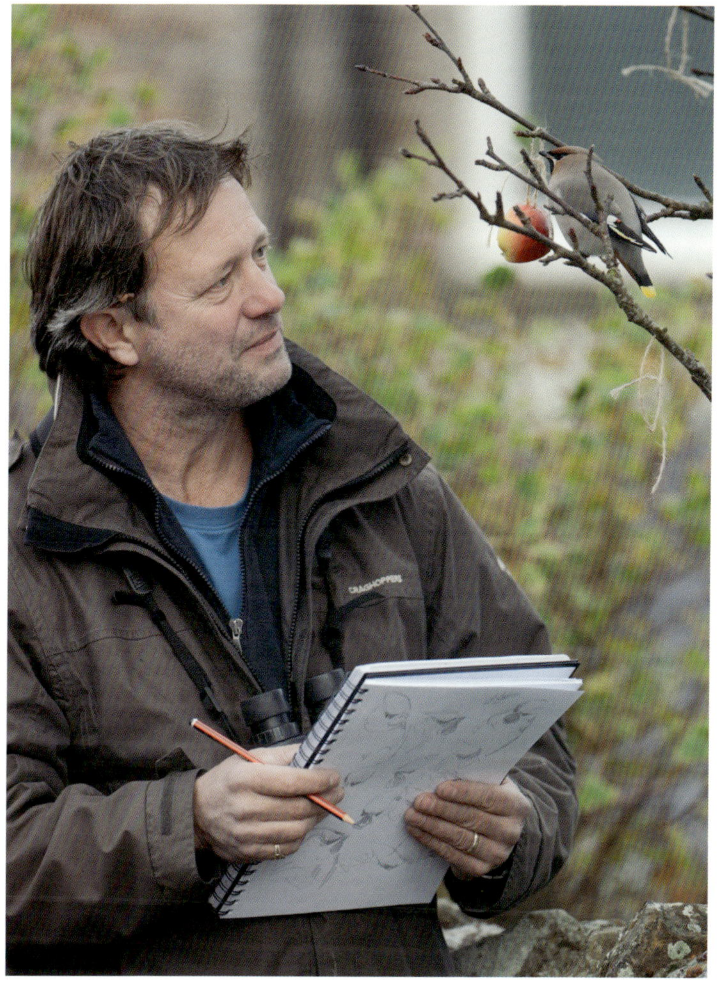

*Top: Esther Tyson*
*Bottom: Darren Woodhead*
*Right: Tim Wootton*

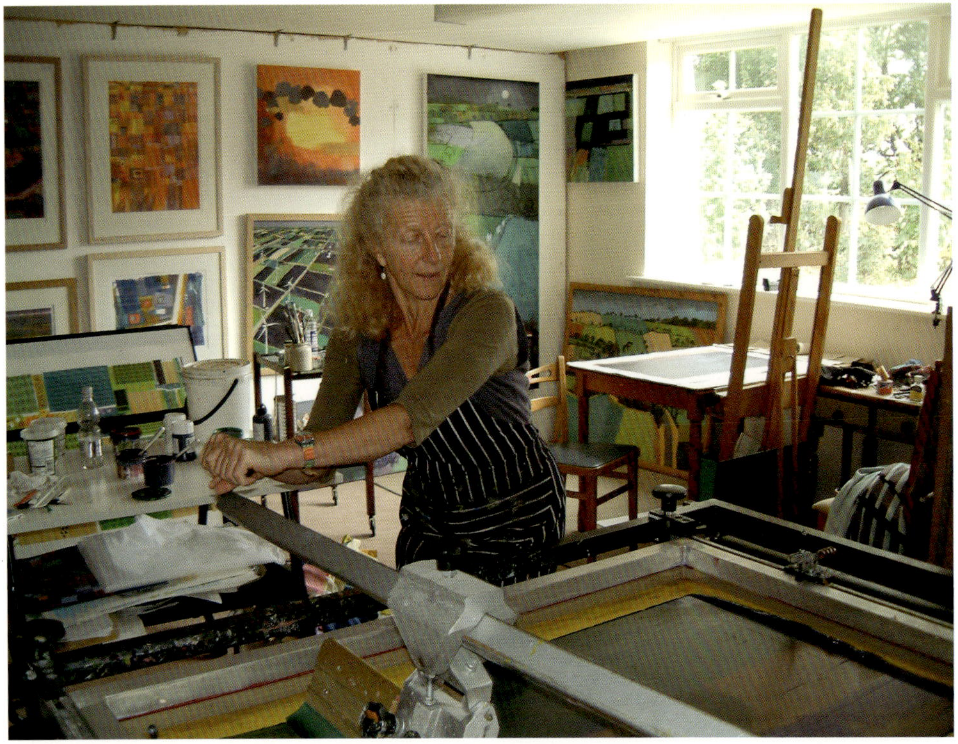

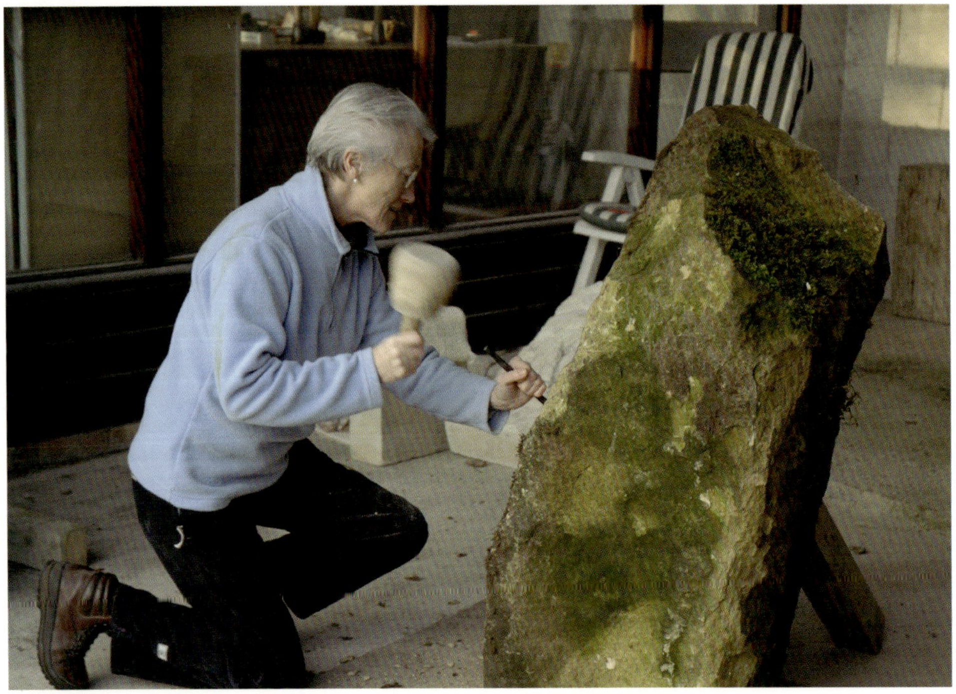

*Top: Carry Akroyd*
*Bottom: Madeline Goold*

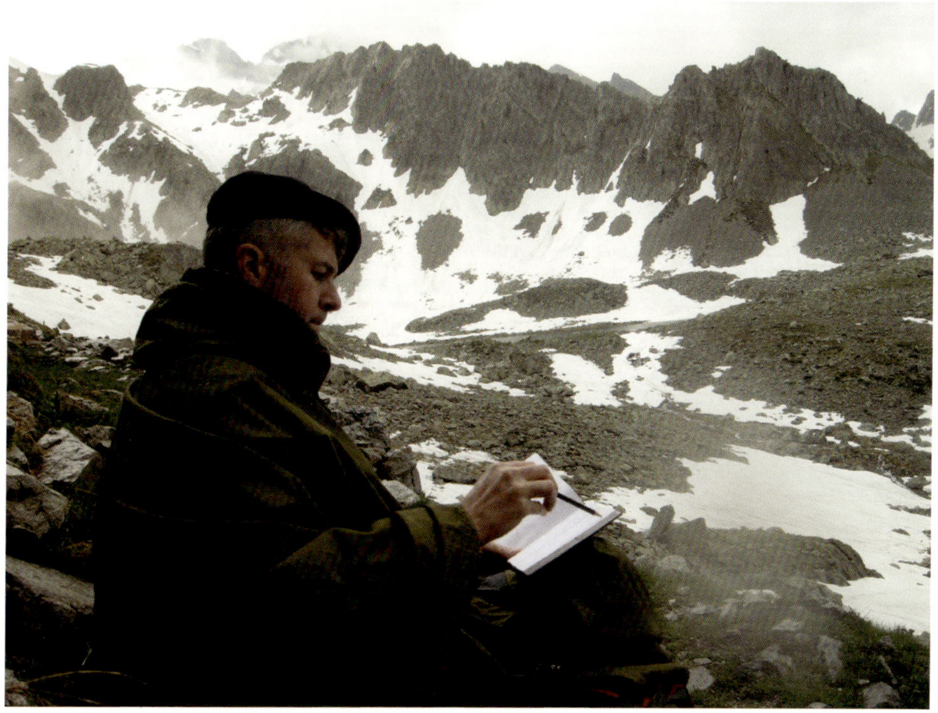

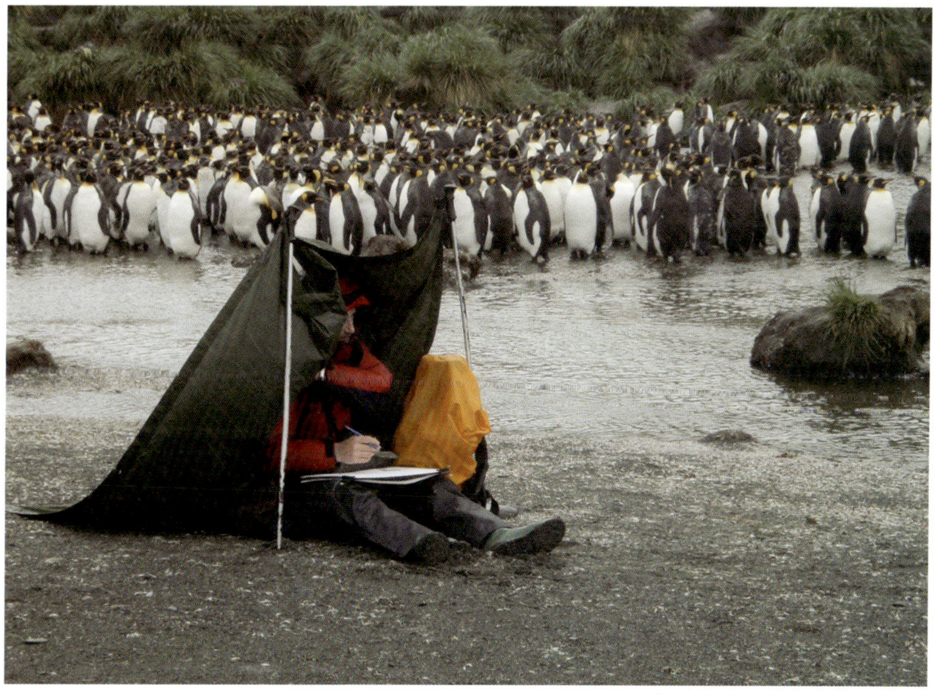

*Top: Matt Underwood*
*Bottom: Chris Rose*

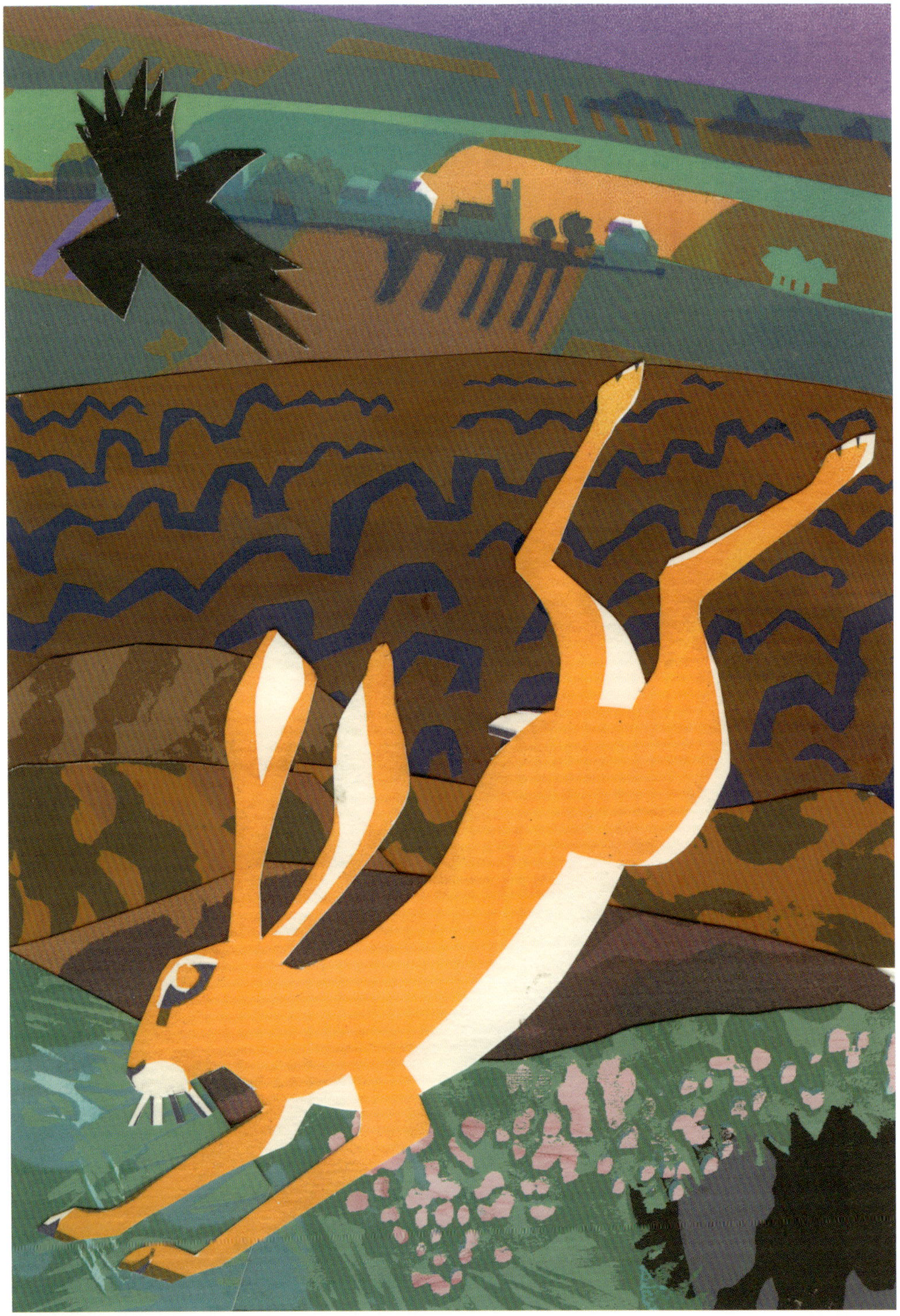

# Carry Akroyd

*Bouncy Hare,* screen print collage

Sometimes, when shuffling through a pile of old reject screen prints, I find a subject that I return to from time to time. These days, pictures of hares are almost a cliché but nevertheless sometimes I feel a dancing hare of some sort wants to appear. This one was originally doing a handstand by moonlight but the sky got smeared, so I cut it out.

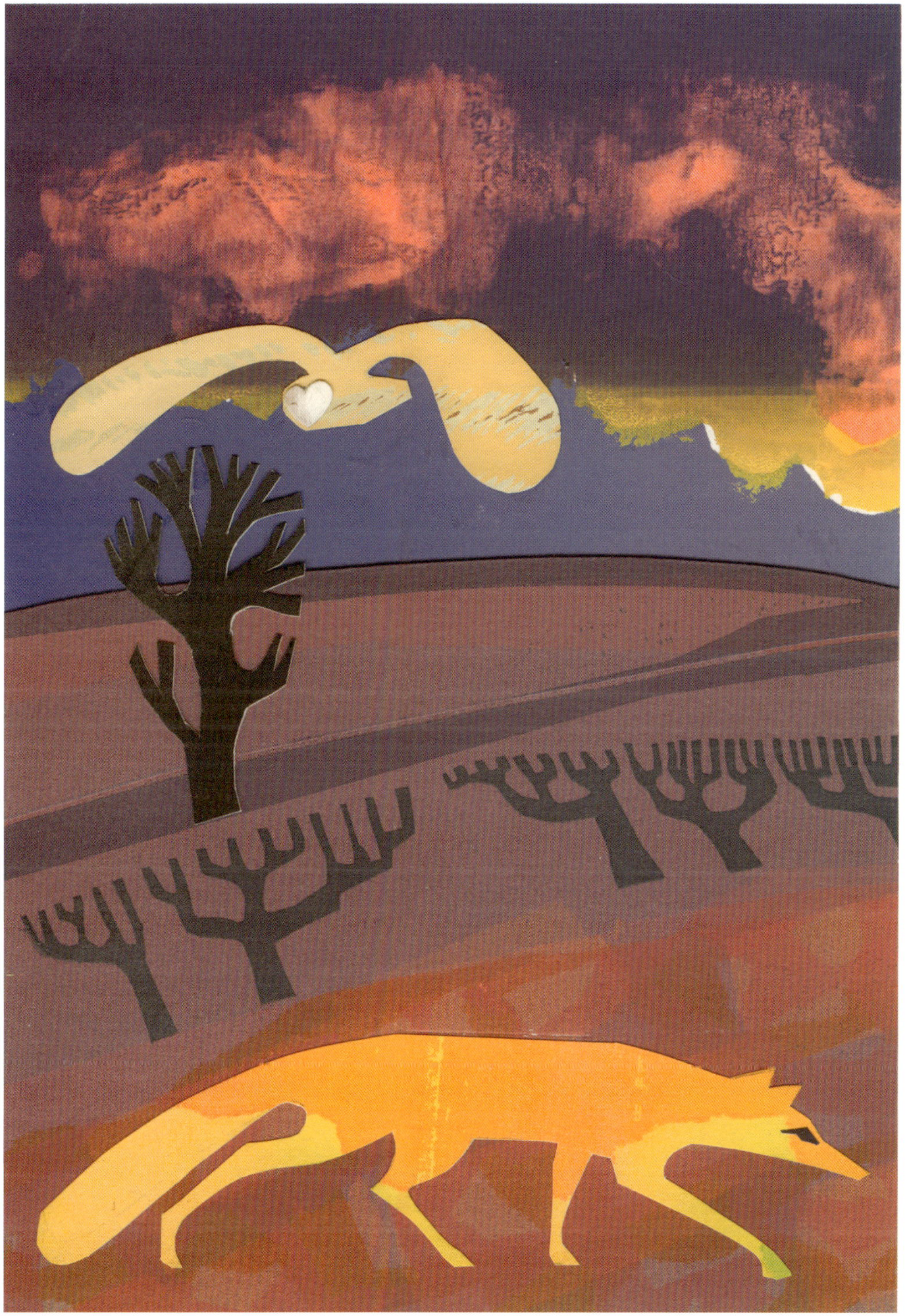

*Fox and an Owl,* screen print collage

I keep a drawerful of some of my handmade screen prints or serigraphs that 'went wrong'. I like to rummage through them from time to time to make collages or birthday cards, and rediscover some forgotten ideas. Foxes are a favourite device for me, they symbolize a bit of wildlife that survives on the margins despite everything.

# Max Angus

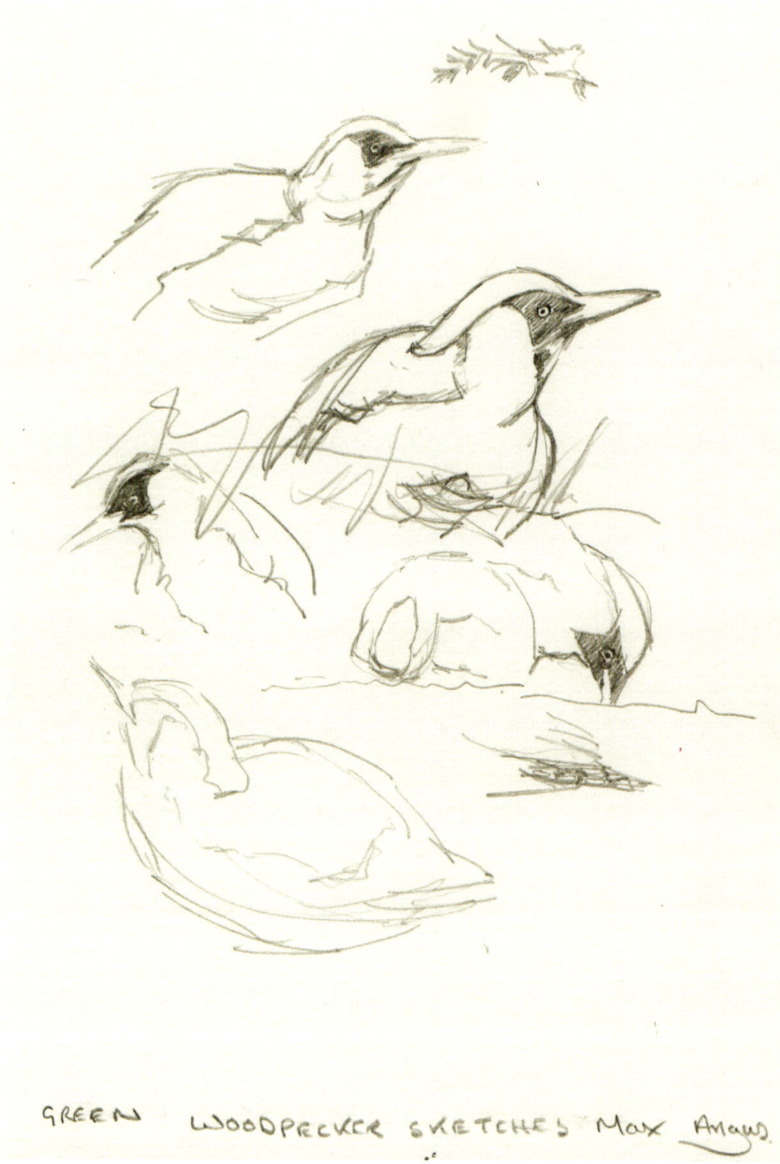


*The Green Woodpecker*, pencil

This winter has been very hard for the birds to find food with so much frequent snow. Along with a determined Fieldfare the female woodpecker has taken favour with the food available in the back garden. It has been bliss being able to sit on a comfortable chair by the patio door in the warm and sketch.

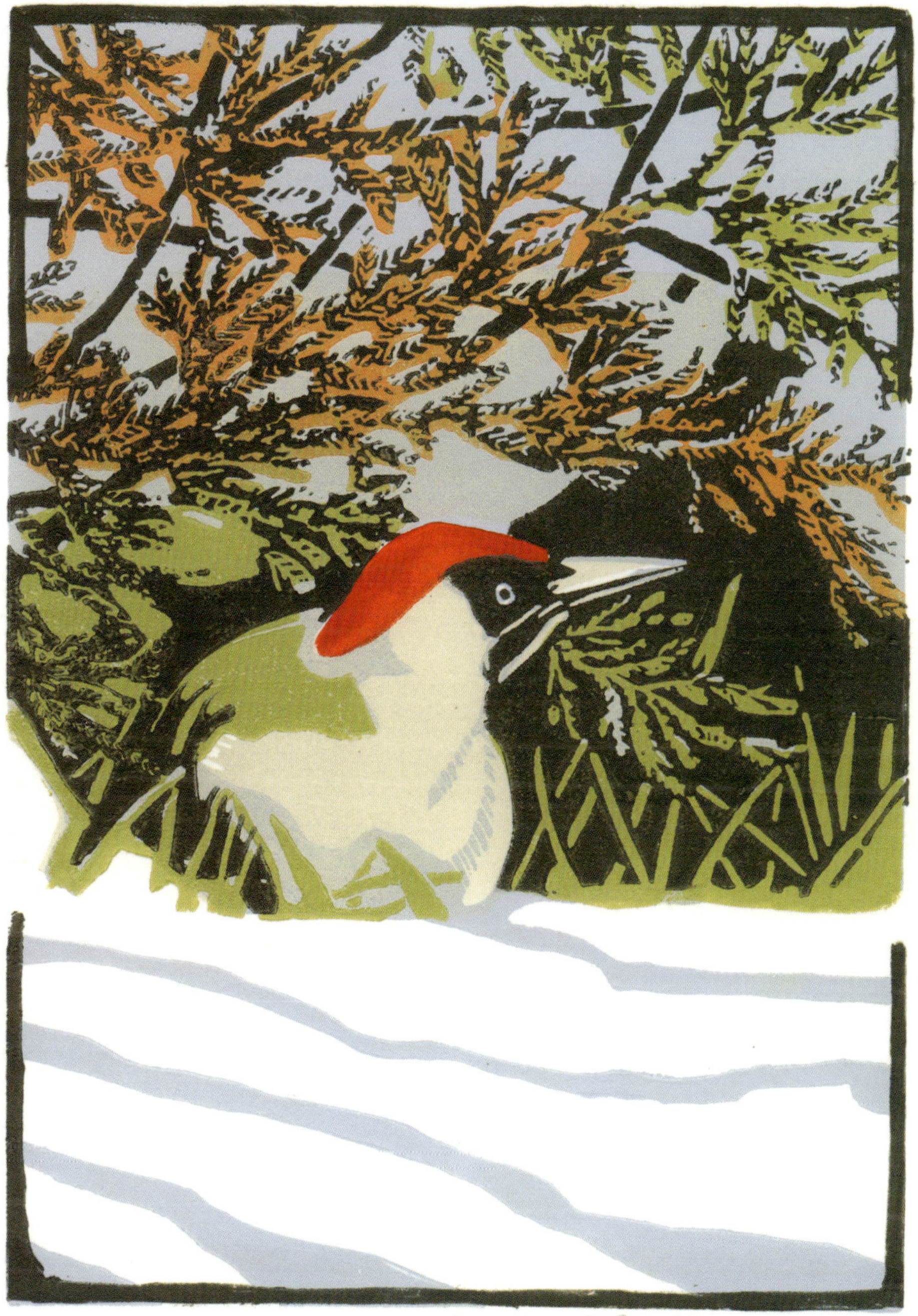

*The Green Woodpecker,* linocut

For the last couple of years I'd hoped to create a linocut of a Green Woodpecker. They are such shy birds. As soon as you see them, they see you. Then they're gone.

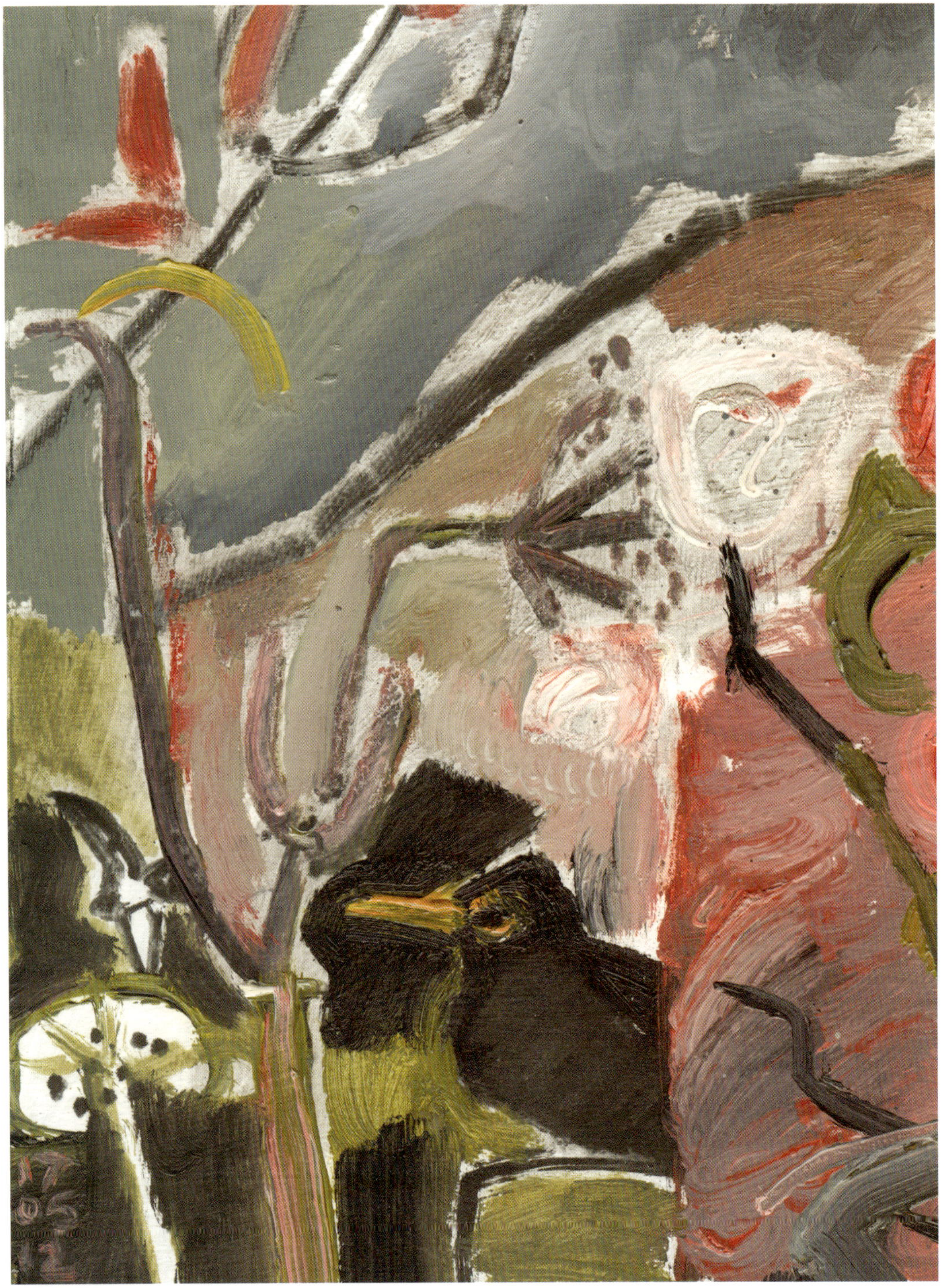

# Kim Atkinson

*Blackbird & Blossom*, oil on gesso ground

The phrases of song rich and varied and generous as umbels of cow parsley and apple blossom; charcoal drawn on graining gesso ground, then oily paint marks put down in phrases and sentences; arabesques of sound before the rain.

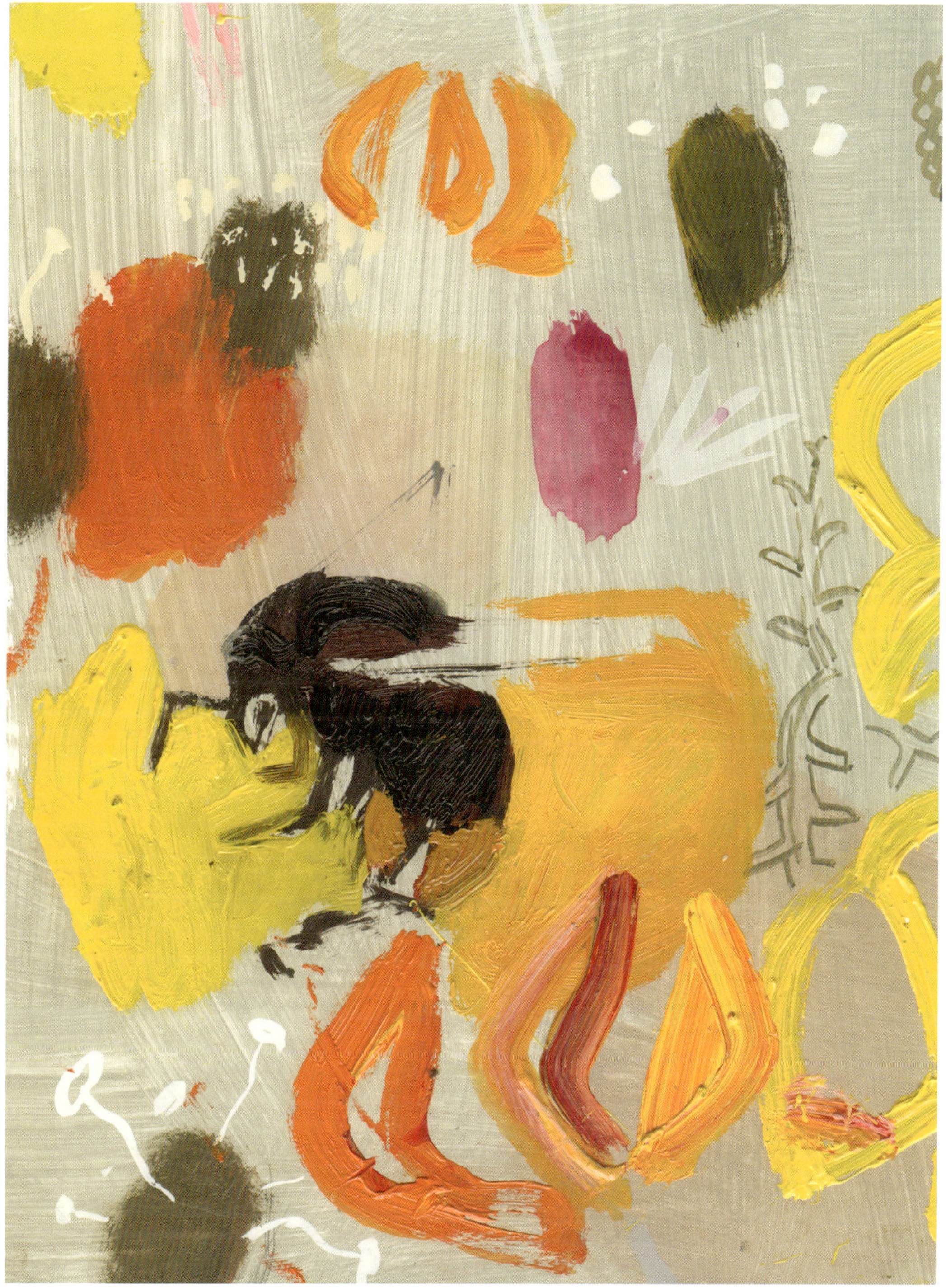

*Bombus lapidarius Rummaging Among Birds-foot Trefoil*, watercolour and oil on gesso ground

I spent some time in the summer on the cliff top turf near home, peering through the close-focusing binoculars. Where grazing is restricted there were flowering Sea Campion, Thrift, Trefoil, Buckthorn Plantain, which attracted Rose Chafers, the bumblebees and most excitingly of all, a Thrift Clearwing laying eggs on the clumps of Thrift.

# Paul Bartlett

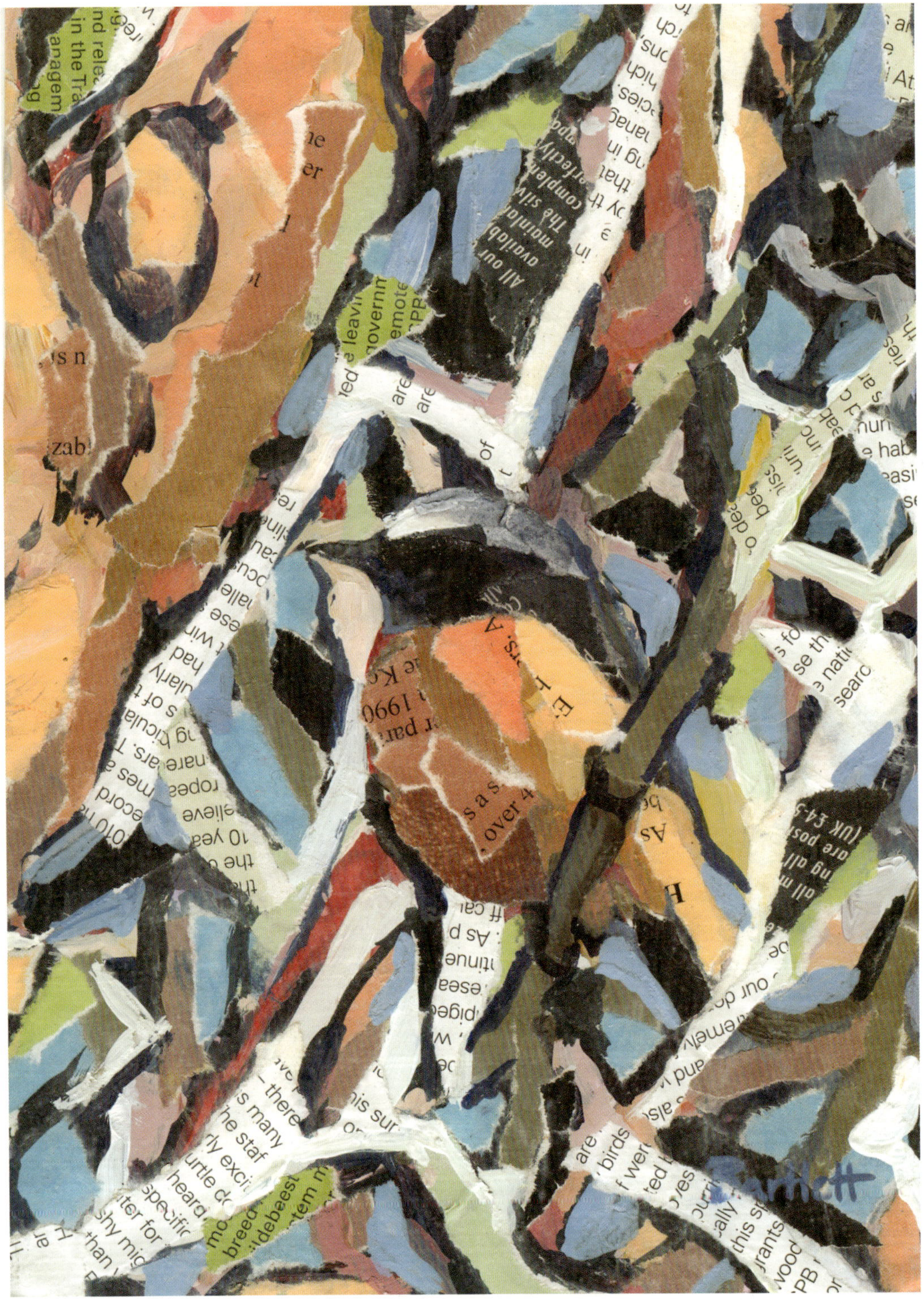

*Redstart,* collage and acrylics

In 2010 I took my family to live in La Rochelle for a year. This Redstart was one of the first local garden birds I met. Perched literally outside the window, I marvelled at how lucky I was to sketch It from the comfort of the studio. Later I realized that they are as common as Robins out here.

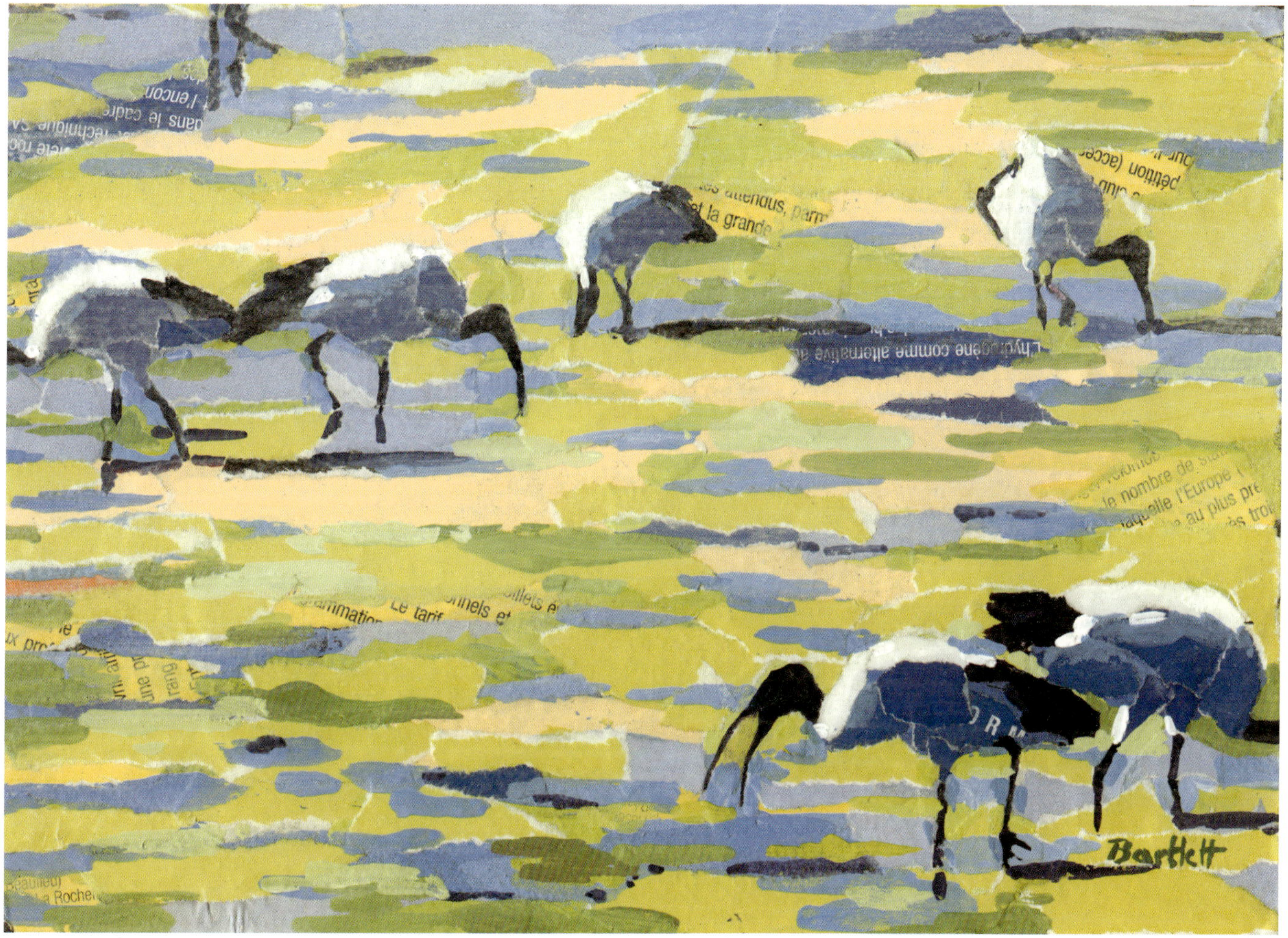


*Sacred Ibis,* collage and acrylics

This species, and the closely related White Ibis are birds I've seen in Southern Africa and Australia respectively, so I was a little surprised to find a flock feeding on a marsh close to La Rochelle. The text in this collage is recycled from the local newspaper, which adds a French authenticity to the picture.

# David Bennett

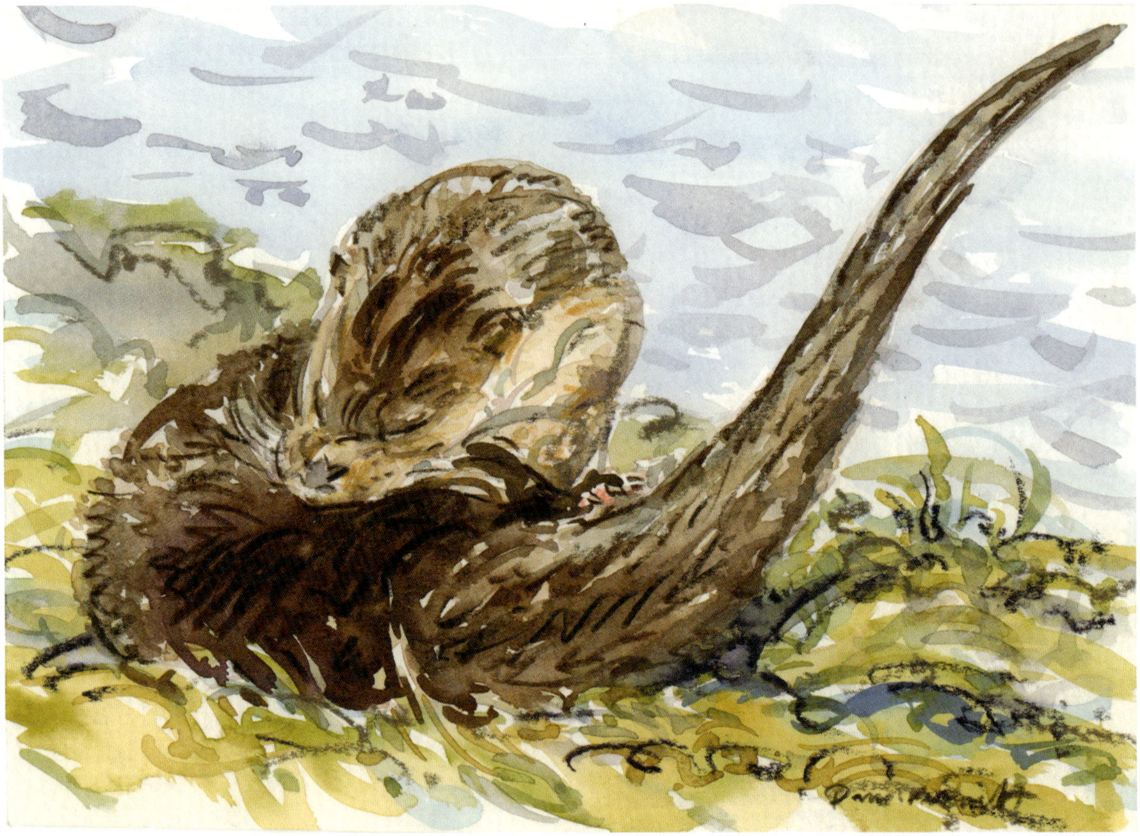

*Curled Otter, Mull,* watercolour

On a blanket of wrack the Otter grooms before snoozing. My vantage point puts me at the same level as the Otter. Rising through the weed with a fuzzy crackle, water infiltrates my hiding spot. The Otter's couch slowly begins to lift with the incoming tide disturbing its doze. I see it wake and slip away.

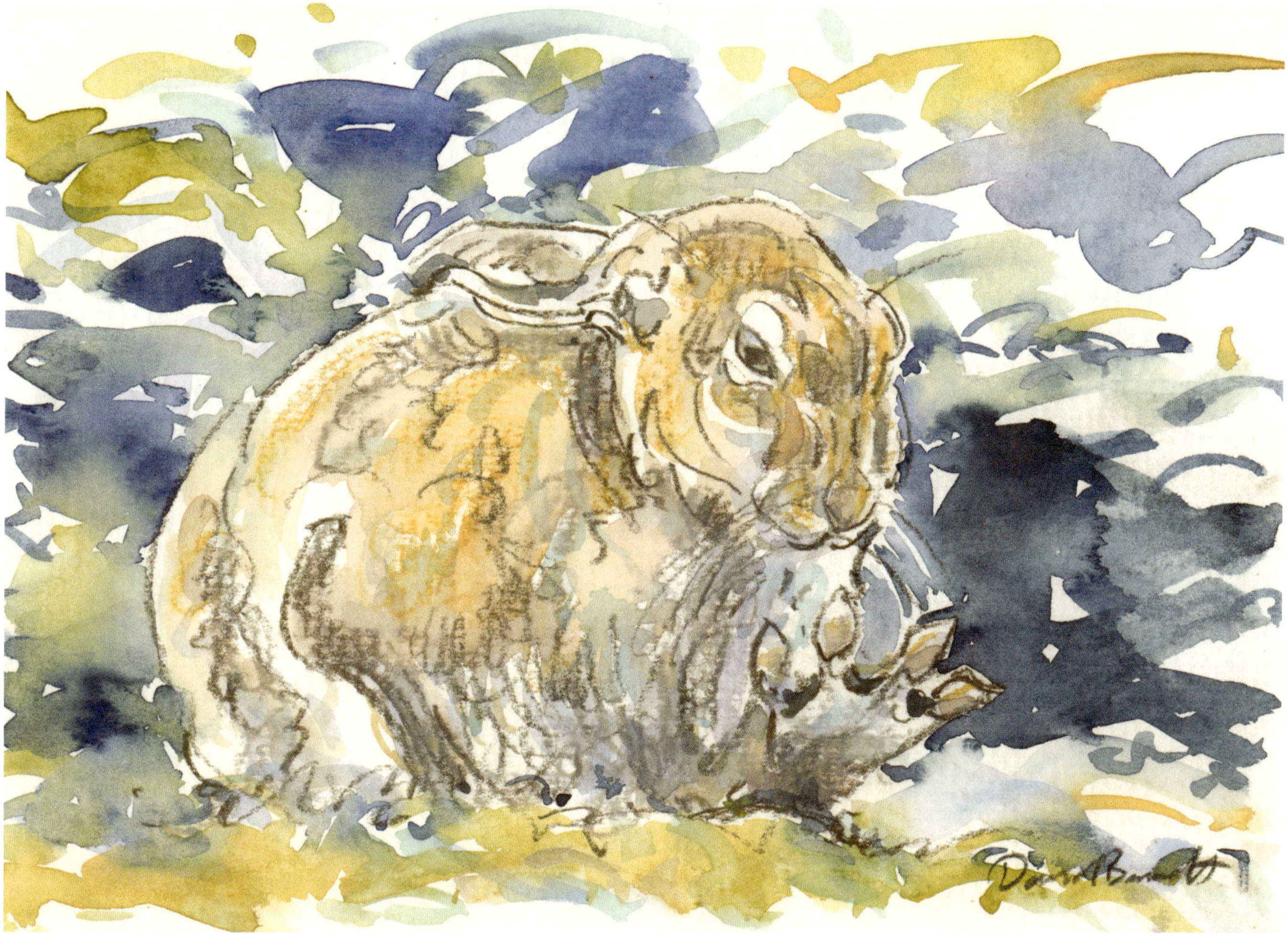

*Mountain Hare, Mull,* watercolour

Tempted by seaweed, Mountain hares are drawn to the shore. Relying on stillness and their coat of buff and grey for camouflage, their presence goes unnoticed, but venture too near and they spring into action, bounding over boulders towards the cover of the foreshore.

# Madeline Goold

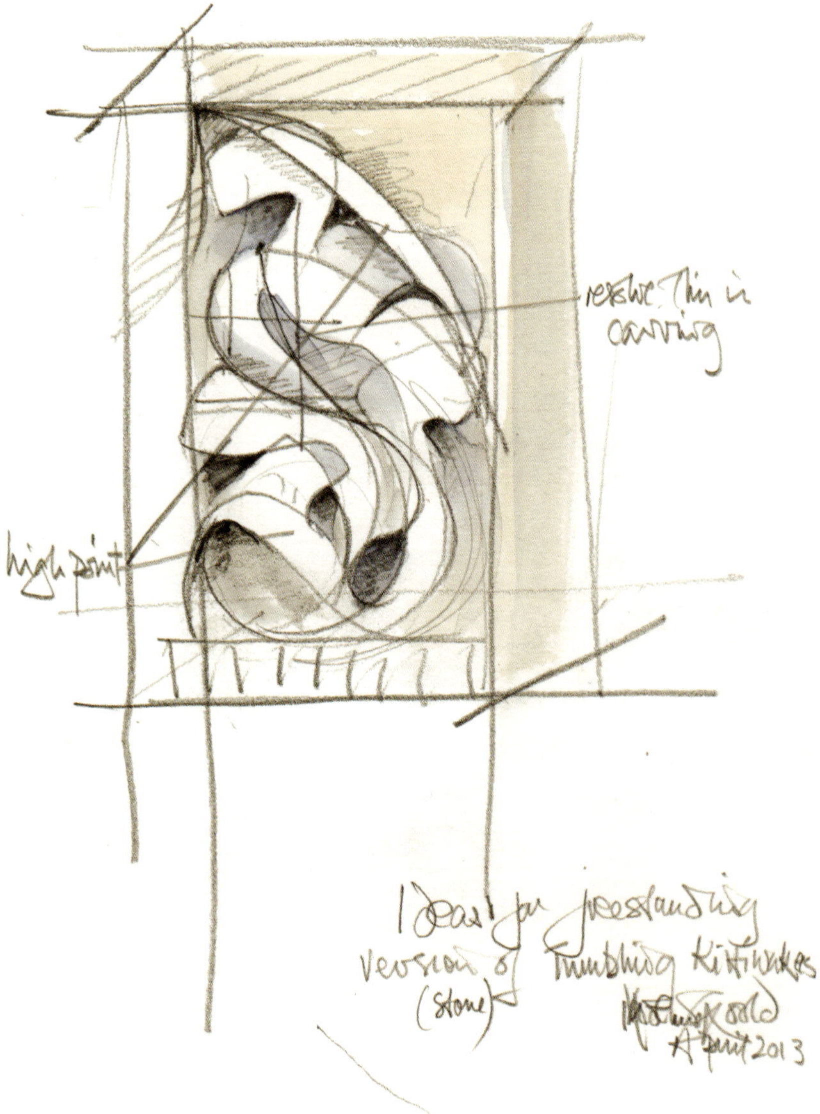


*Twisting Kittiwakes,* working drawing

This working drawing for a carved stone sculpture is made from several swift sketchbook notes of the characteristic turning, twisting forms of Kittiwakes as they squabbled and tumbled down the cliff-face at Dunbar. My first thoughts were for a deep relief piece in limestone, but as the drawing emerged, it suggested a fully three-dimensional sculpture.

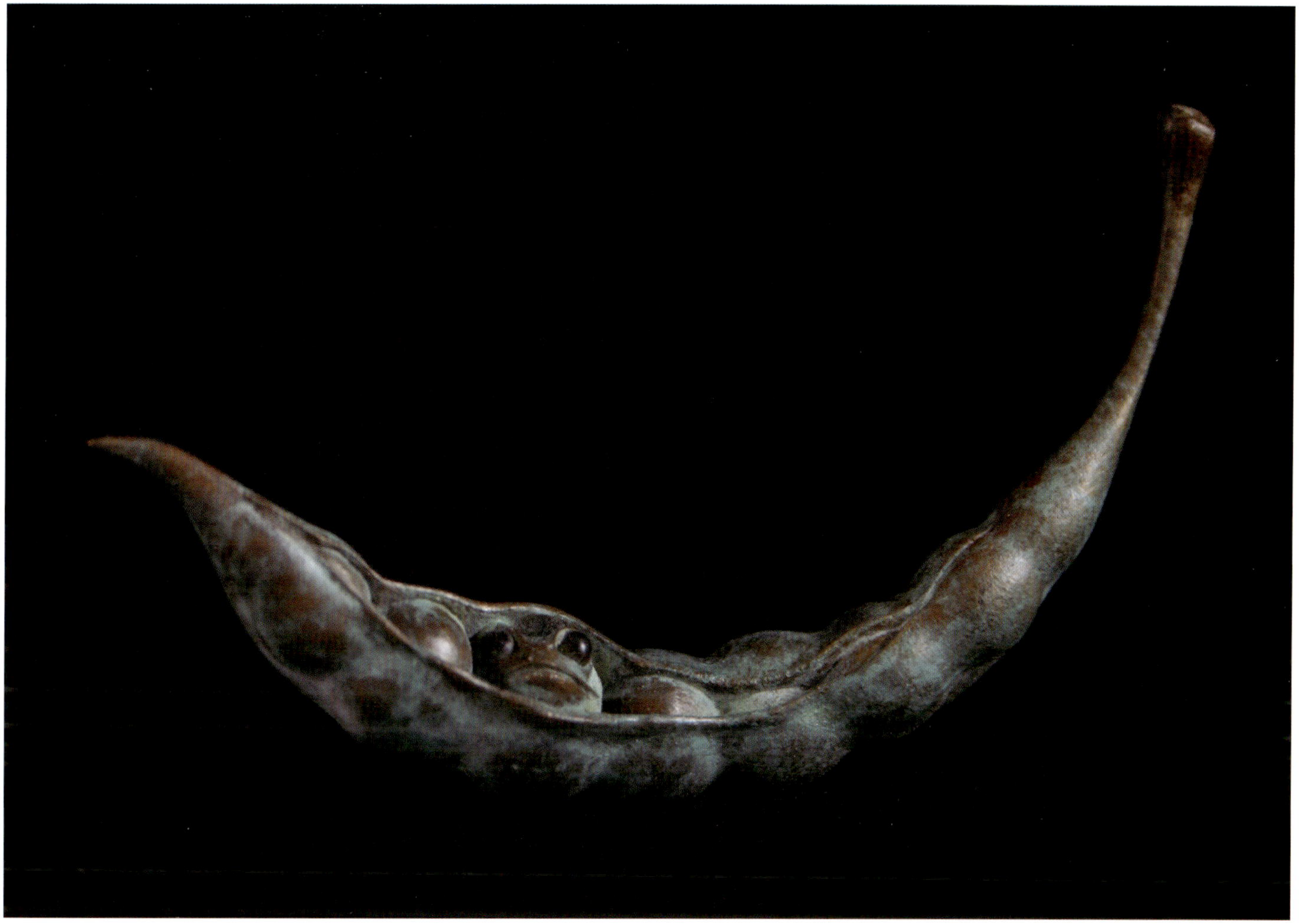

# Adam Binder

*Frog in a Pod,* bronze

Every now and then the inspiration behind a piece is hard to ignore. I love the immediacy of carving nature's miniature encounters, as was the case with *Frog in a Pod.* The delight of the unexpected frog peering up from a discreet little hiding place always puts a smile on my face.

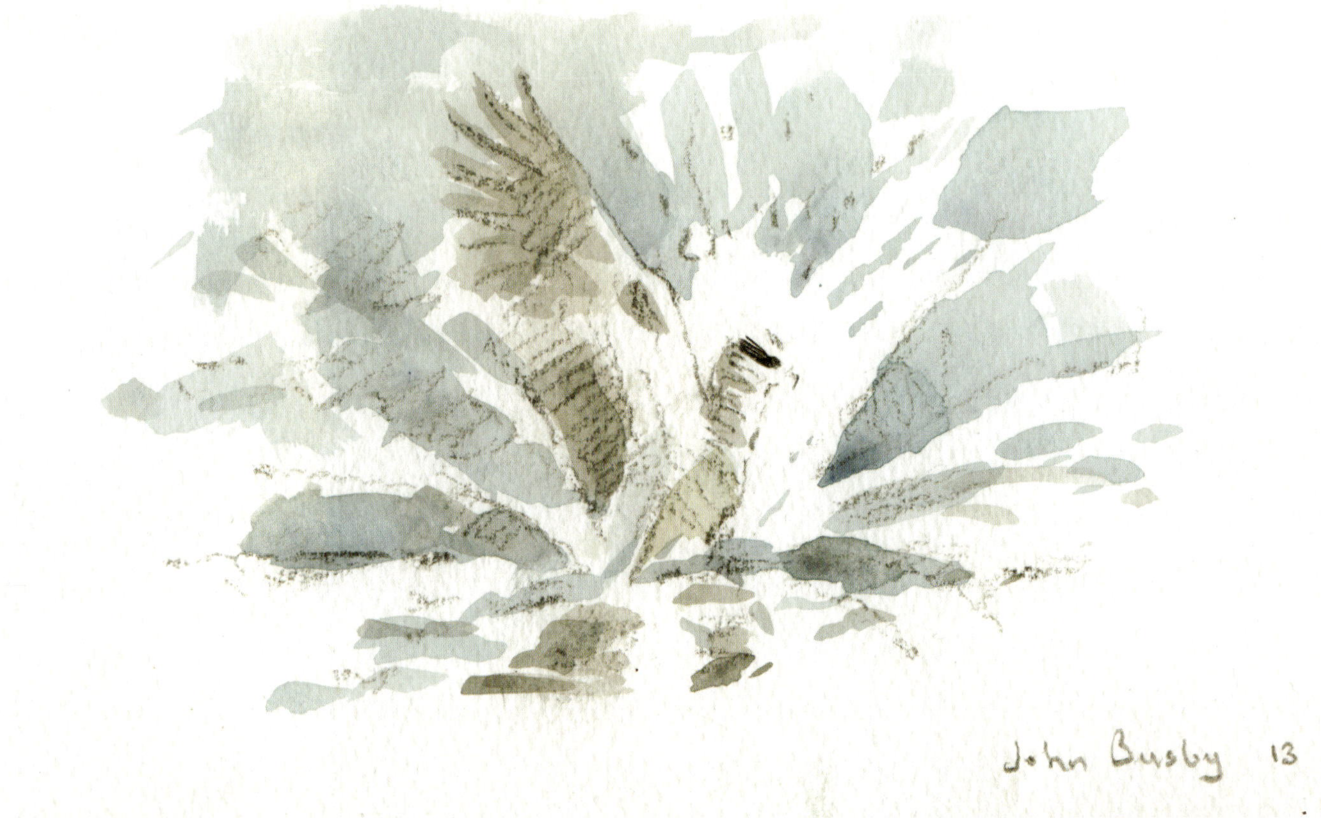


*Osprey,* watercolour

# John Busby

It is always an exciting moment when an Osprey appears, especially if it is actively fishing. I find myself as interested in the size and shapes of the splashes the bird makes on its dives into the water as the bird itself. My closest look at Ospreys was from a photographer's hide in Speyside. When a male parent returned with a fish, it was given to the female at the nest, who then fed each chick mouthful by mouthful in a calm and ordered way– no clamour to be fed.

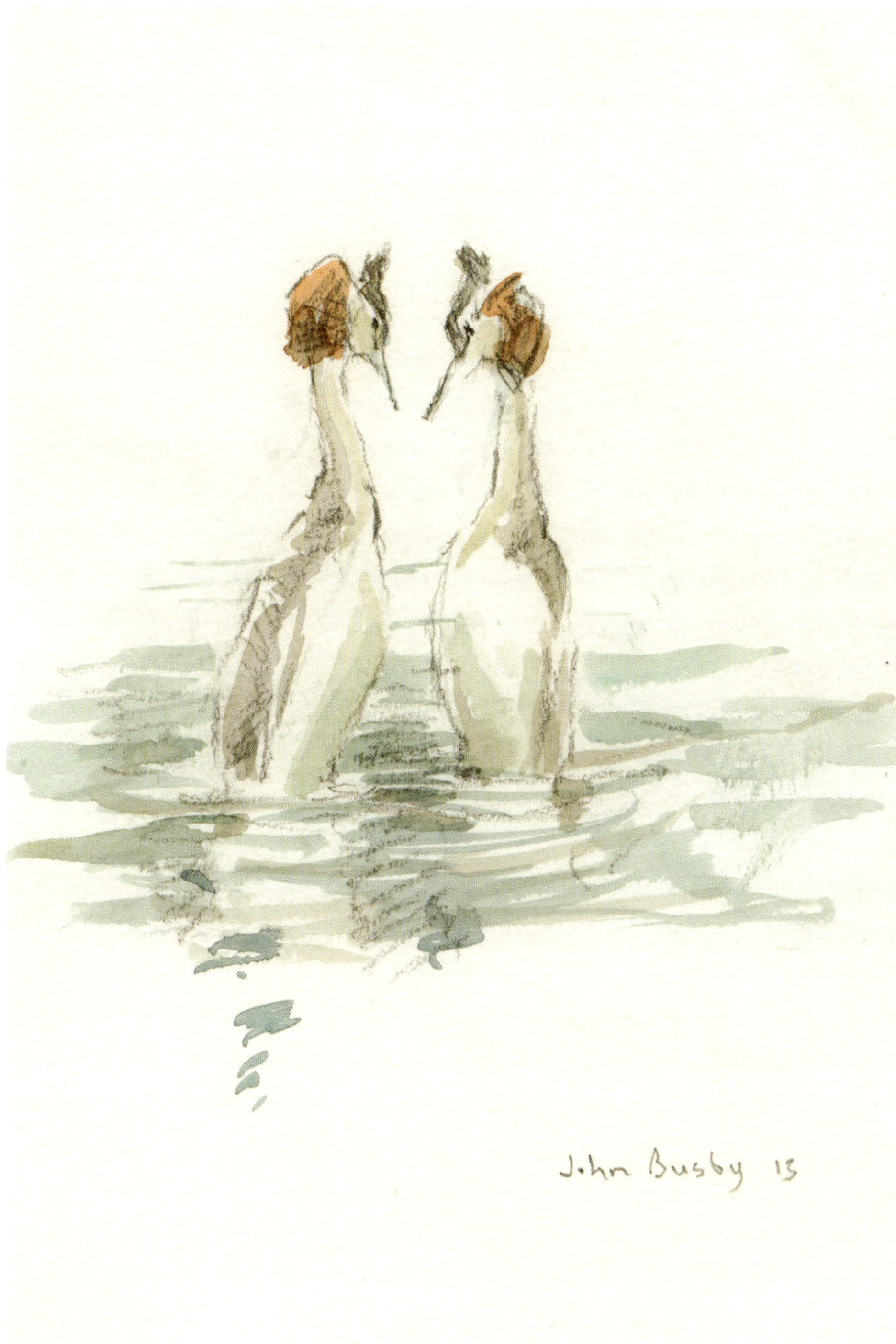

*Great Crested Grebes Courting*,
watercolour

Grebes are among my favourite birds.
The Great Crested has such elegance.
It can preen on the water with open wings,
and as its bill probes breast and flanks and
even tail feathers it is always beautifully poised.
Reflections add greatly to the bird's beauty
in still water, but even in winter plumage on
an equally grey sea amid bouncing waves, the
Great Crested is a dashing streamlined figure
at one with its environment.

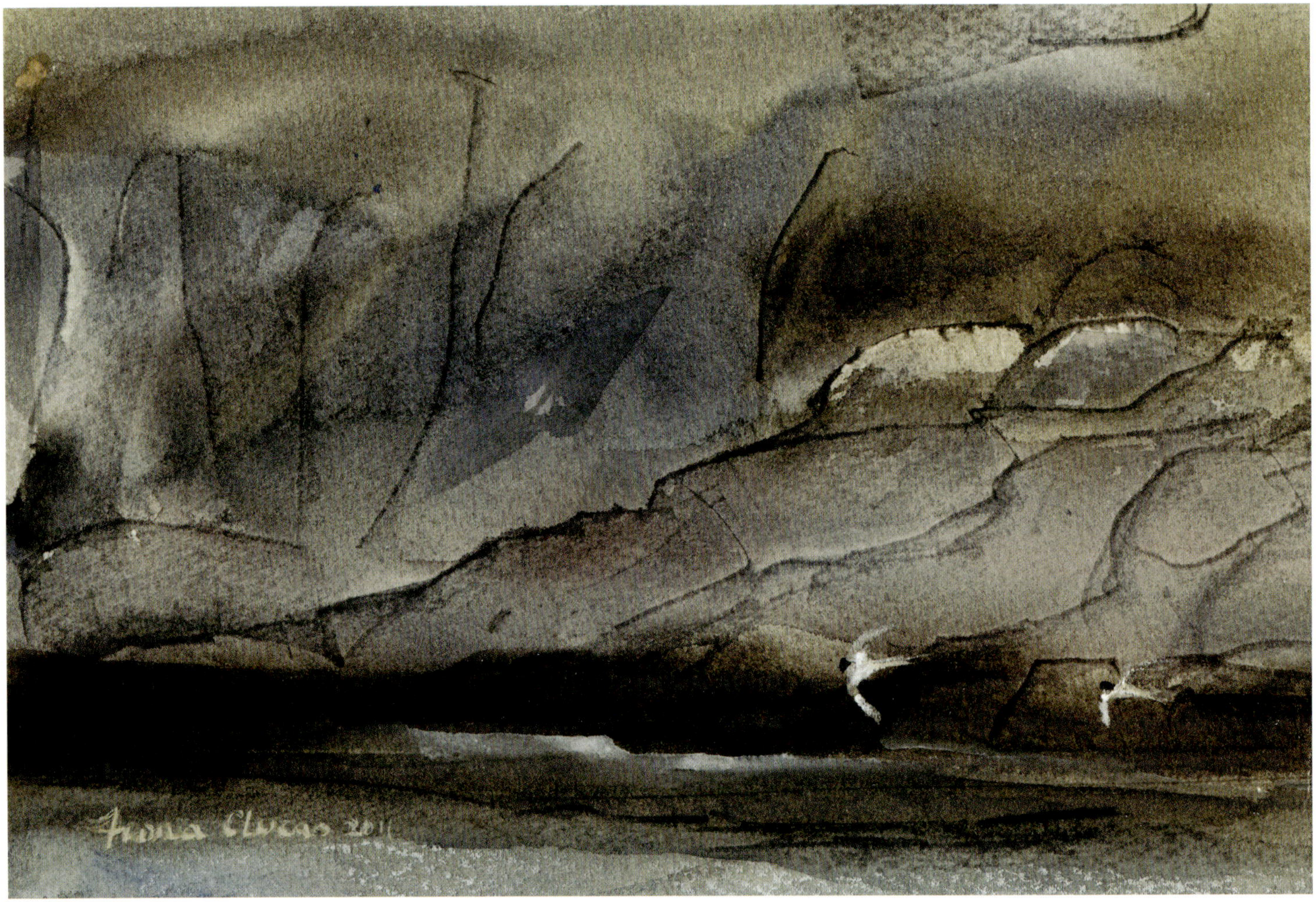

# Fiona Clucas

*Arctic Terns, Deepdale, Shetlands*, mixed media on paper

This is just one of several gouache studies made during a midsummer trip to Shetland. Very lucky with the weather; long sunny days. These Arctic Terns were flying, circling the rocks and cliffs at ten o'clock at night. The contours and pinks and mauve colours of the rocks were a beautiful backdrop to the fast and playful flight of these terns.

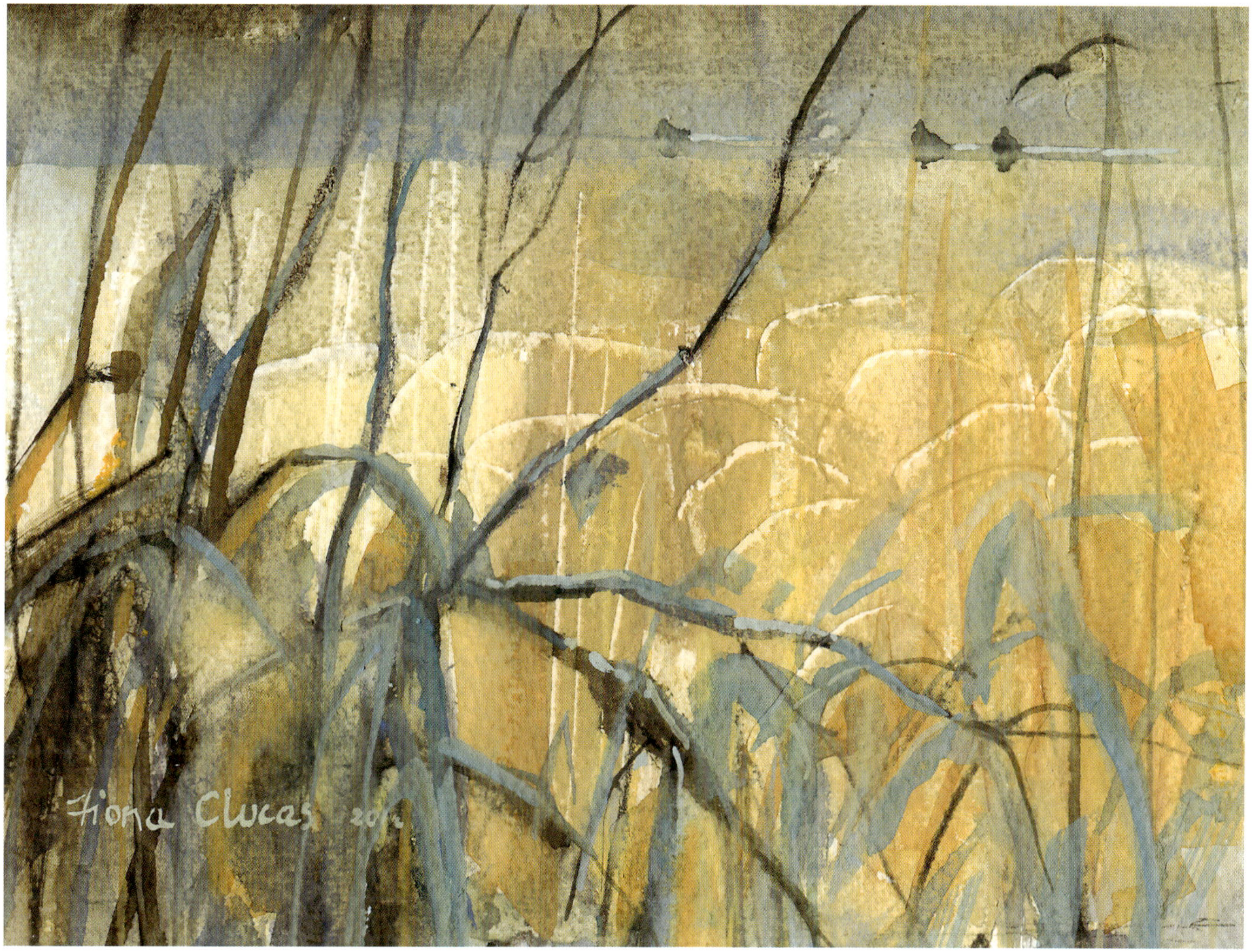


*Winter, Hawes Water, Silverdale,* gouache

This gouache study was made on a bright and very cold morning in February. It had been a very hard frost, the golden reeds were laced with a cool blue, the air was so still and clear. The grainy effect on the left of this painting was the rather magical result of the pigment separating as my colour washes froze instantly on the paper.

# Daniel Cole

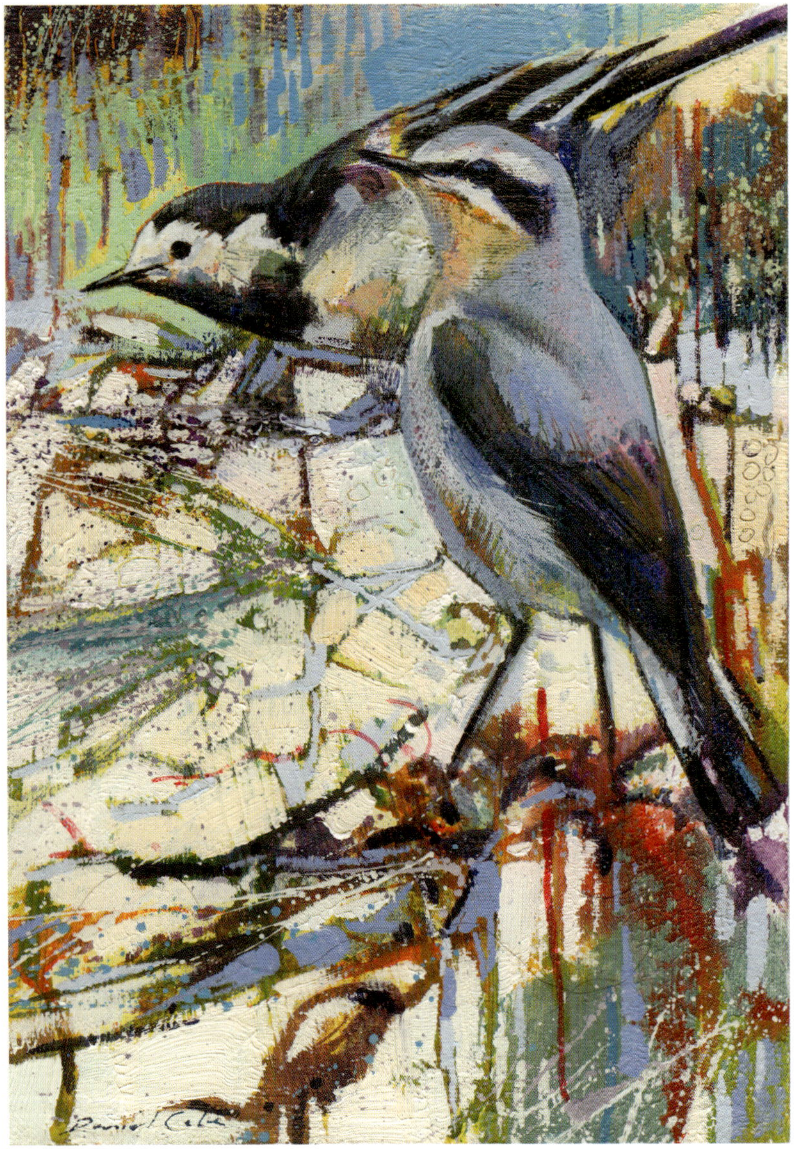

*Pied Wagtail and Wheatear,* oil on board

Looking along the strandline of Par Beach in Cornwall, I came across a party of Pied Wagtails feeding in the seaweed. As I watched they were joined by a beautiful cock Wheatear, my first of the year. So this picture shows two of my favourite birds together on that cold March morning.

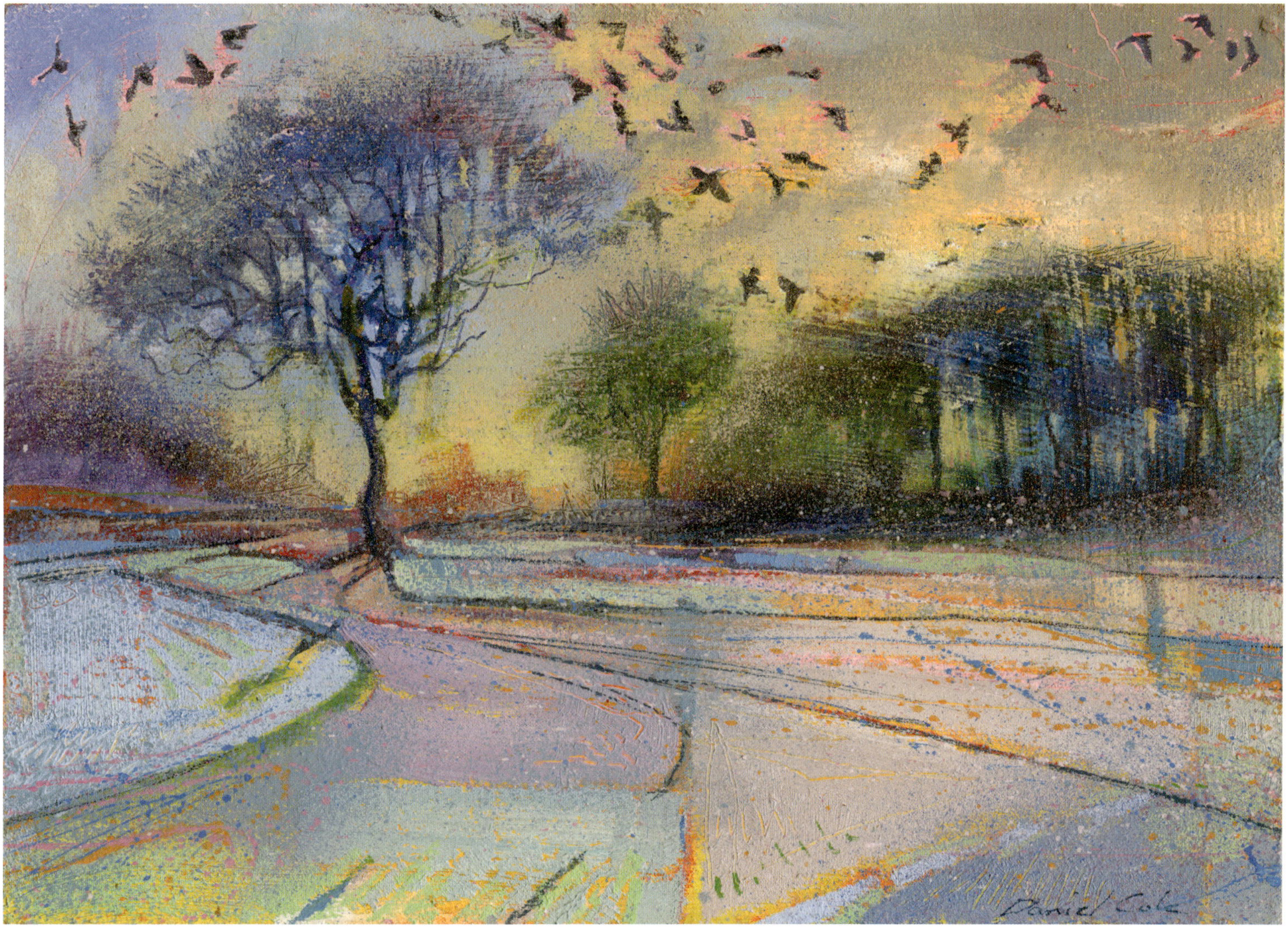

*Winter Crows*, oil on board

I drive through some beautiful countryside on my daily journey to my studio, and regularly see big flocks of corvids rising out of the trees or off the fields. This painting recalls one such moment.

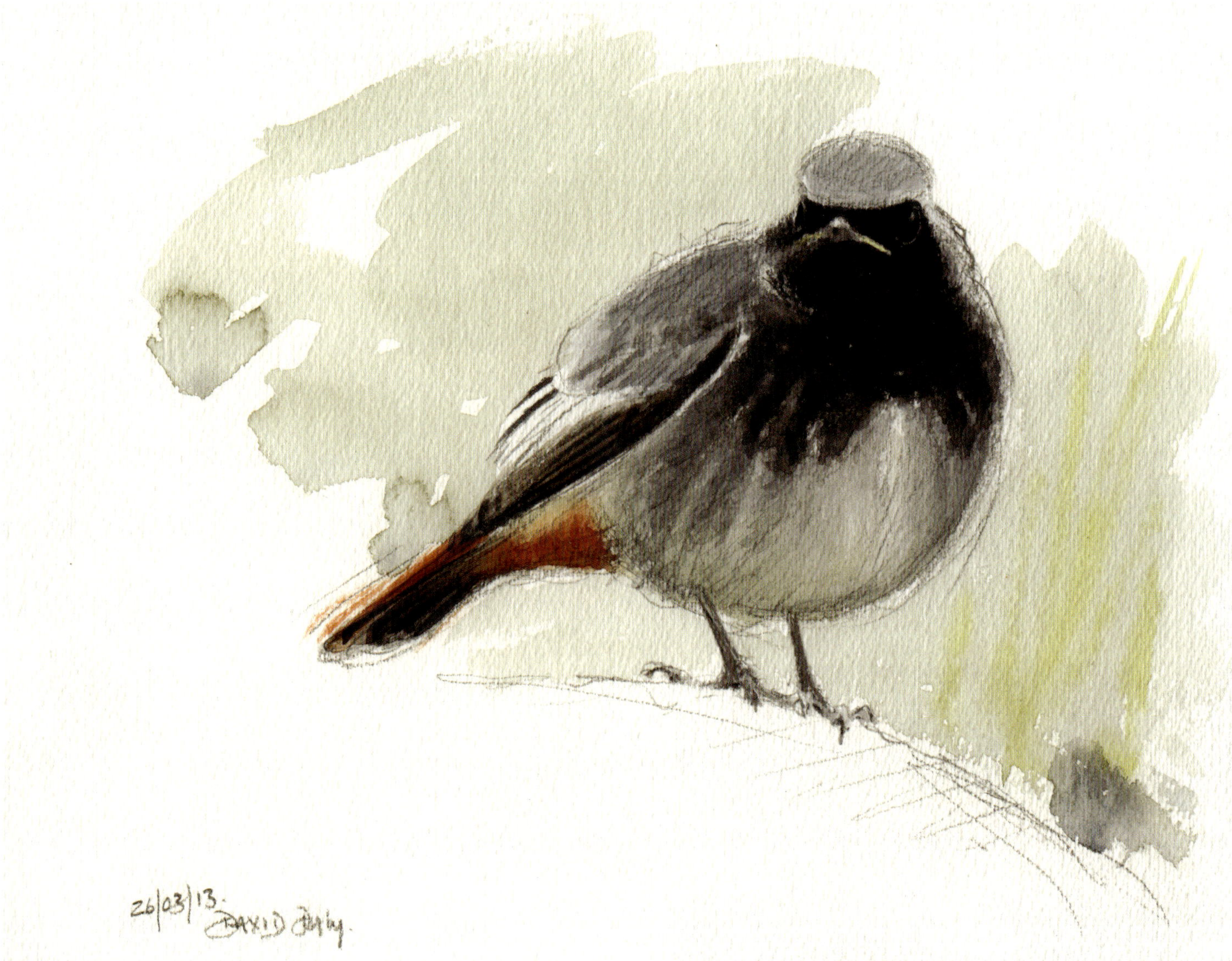


*Black Redstart,* watercolour

# Dave Daly

This beautiful male Black Redstart stayed for several days towards the end of a very cold March. Feeding on tiny worms on a wet footpath, its plumage was puffed out against a bitterly cold east wind. The rich charcoal greys and blacks blending softly into each other made a sweet contrast to the flickering red tail. Sketching and painting a co-operative species is always rewarding.

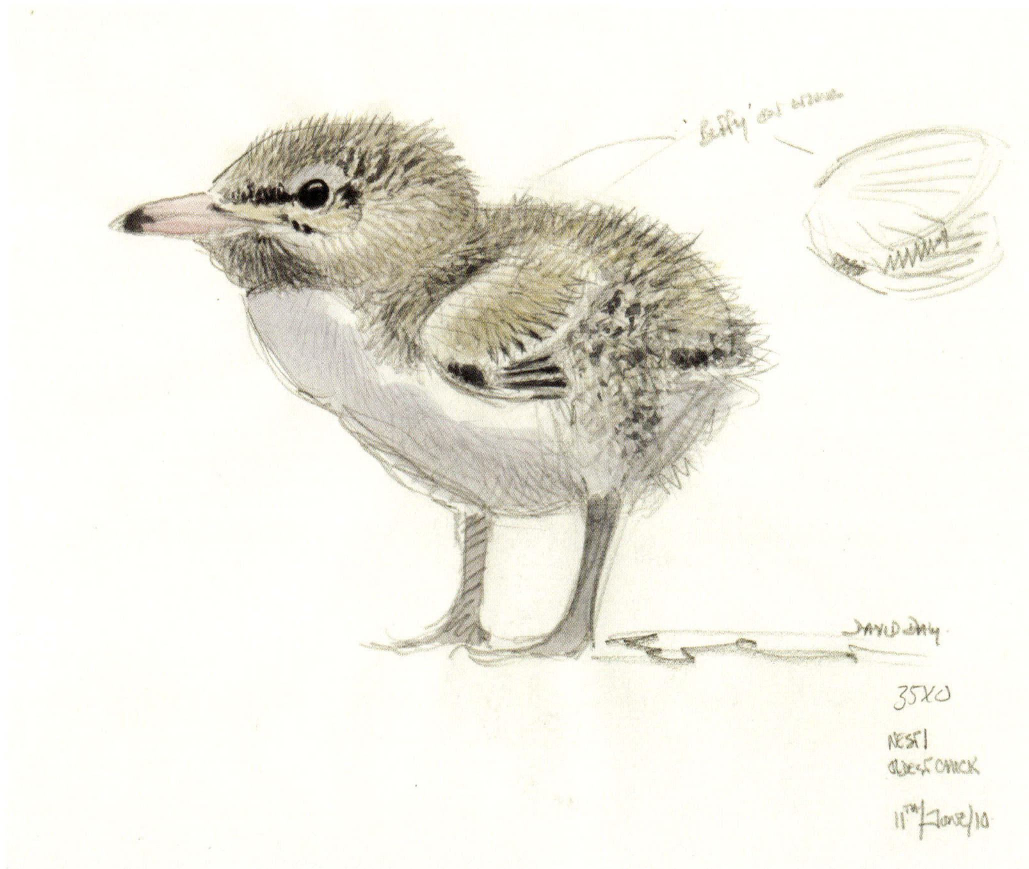

*Roseate Tern Chick,* watercolour and pencil

I'm lucky enough to have studied Roseate Terns at close quarters over the past fifteen years. As the breeding colony progresses, the development of ringed (banded) chicks can be followed closely. With each passing day a chick's appearance will change, yet each individual will retain its own subtle characteristics.
They are a joy to sketch.

# Nick Derry

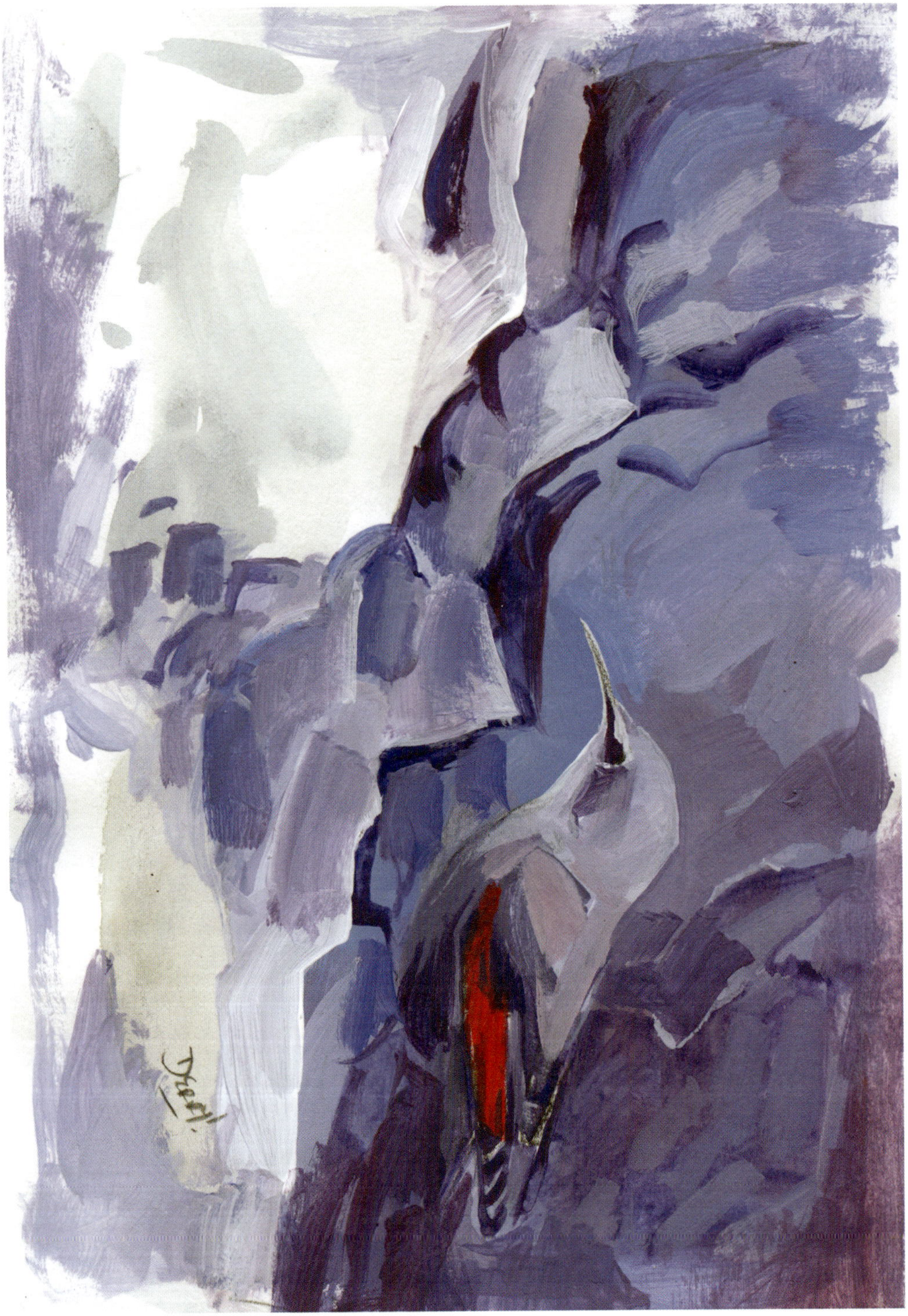

*Wallcreeper,* acrylic on paper

Perhaps my 'signature' bird. Every encounter I've had with this species has been memorable and I even have a Wallcreeper tattooed on me.

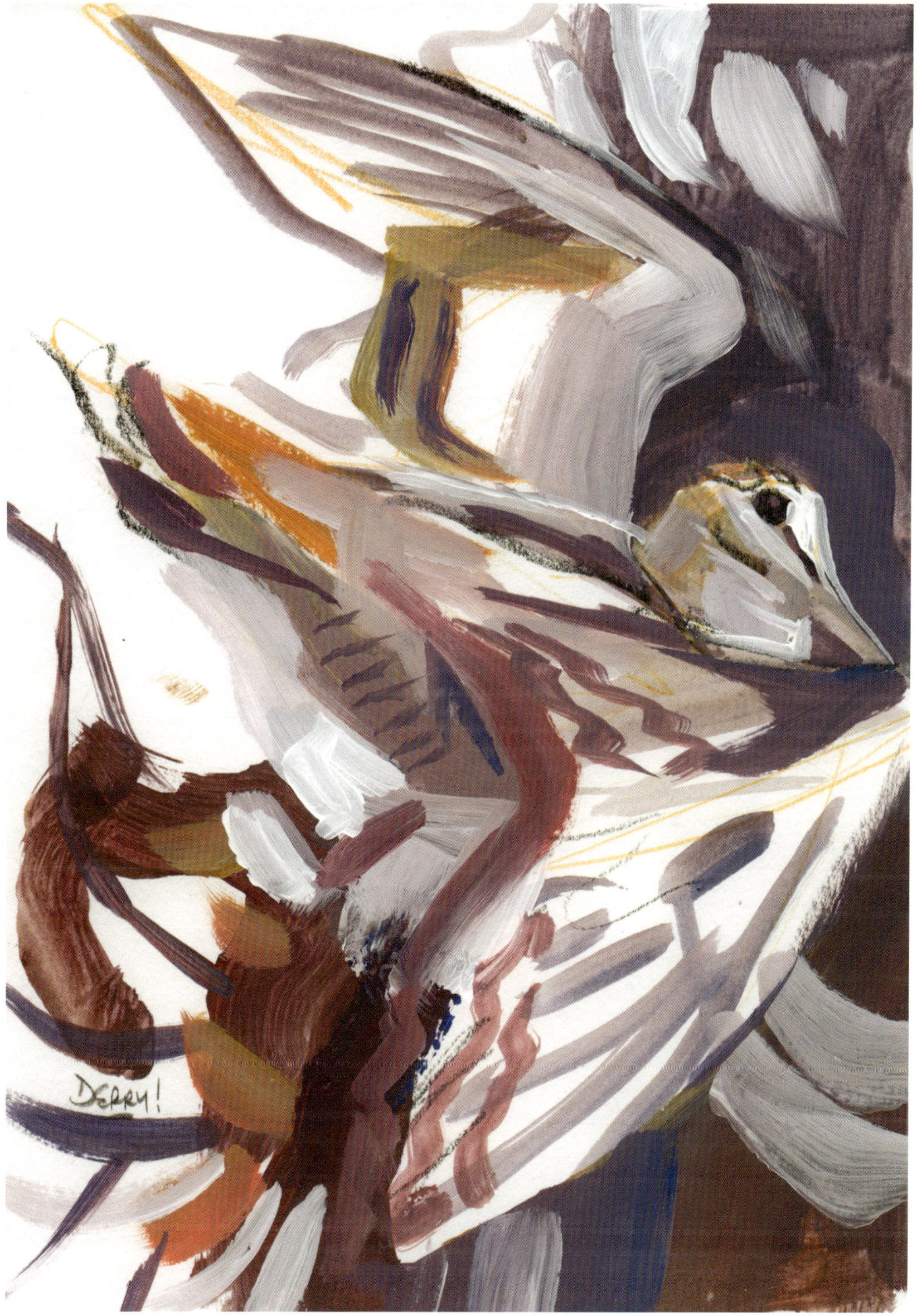


*Woodcock,* acrylic on paper

Hopefully this image is distant enough from the normal 'sporting' image of a perfectly detailed bird lazily flapping into a Constable landscape. Truth is they fly off so quickly that you don't see much of them at all.

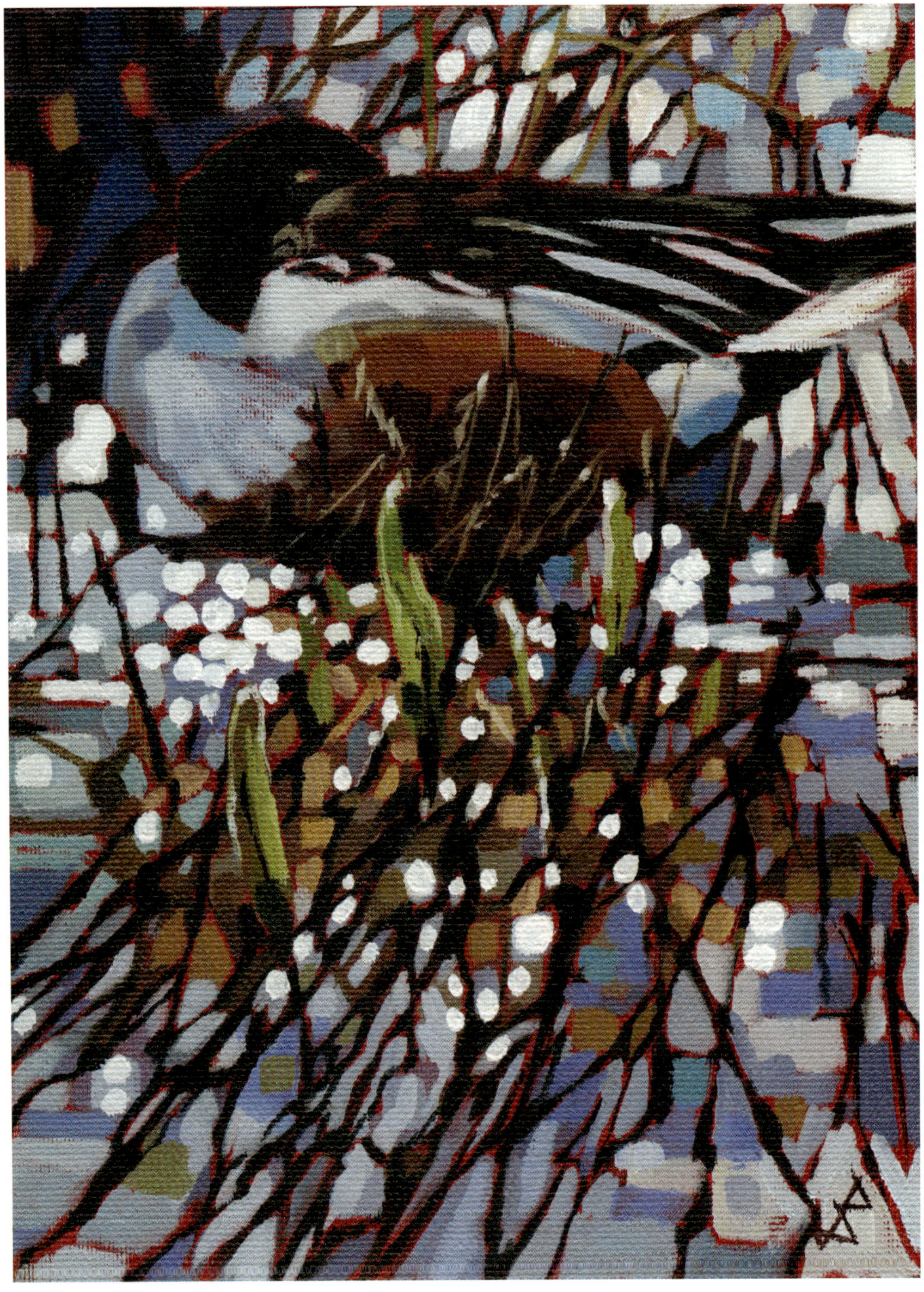

# Brin Edwards

*Sleeping Shoveler,* oils on canvas

I often paint birds against the light. This drake Shoveler settled down in front of a hide at Slimbridge WWT with the evening sunlight sparkling off the water.

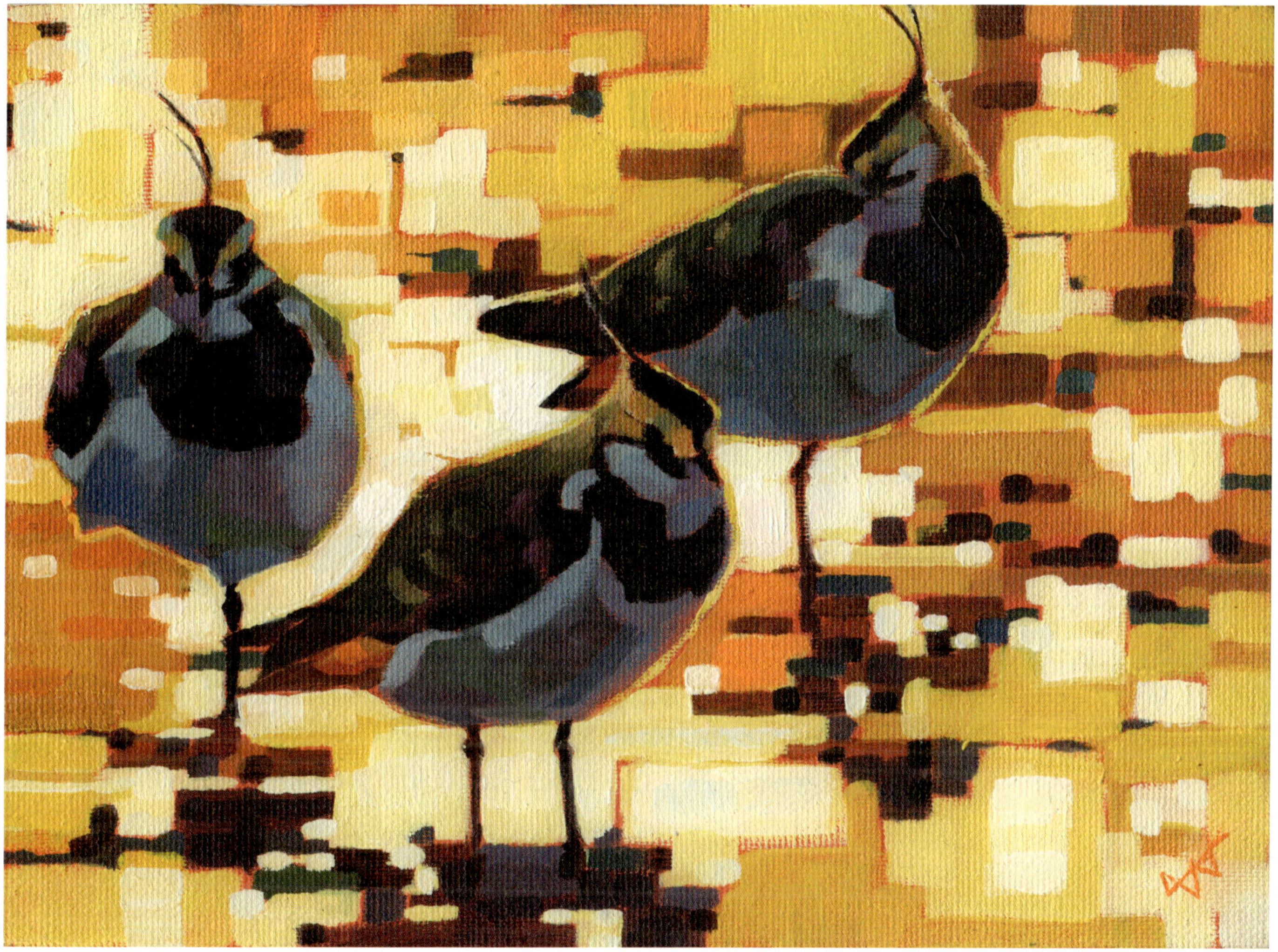

*Lapwings Yellow Light*, oil on canvas

I never tire of painting Lapwings. These three were on the Hayle estuary with the light bouncing off the wet sand and the colours turned up to eleven.

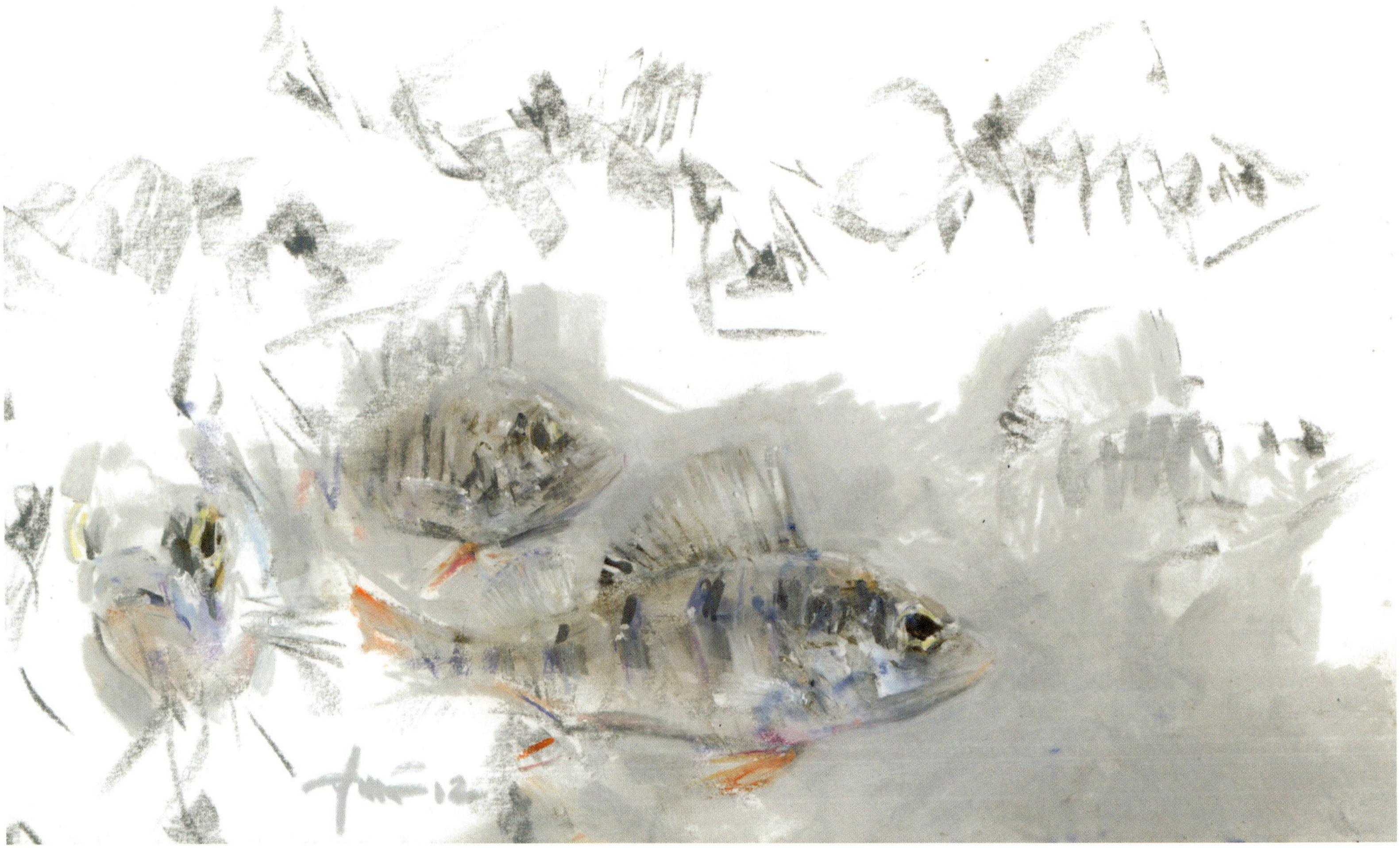

*Perch,* oil pastels

## Carl Ellis

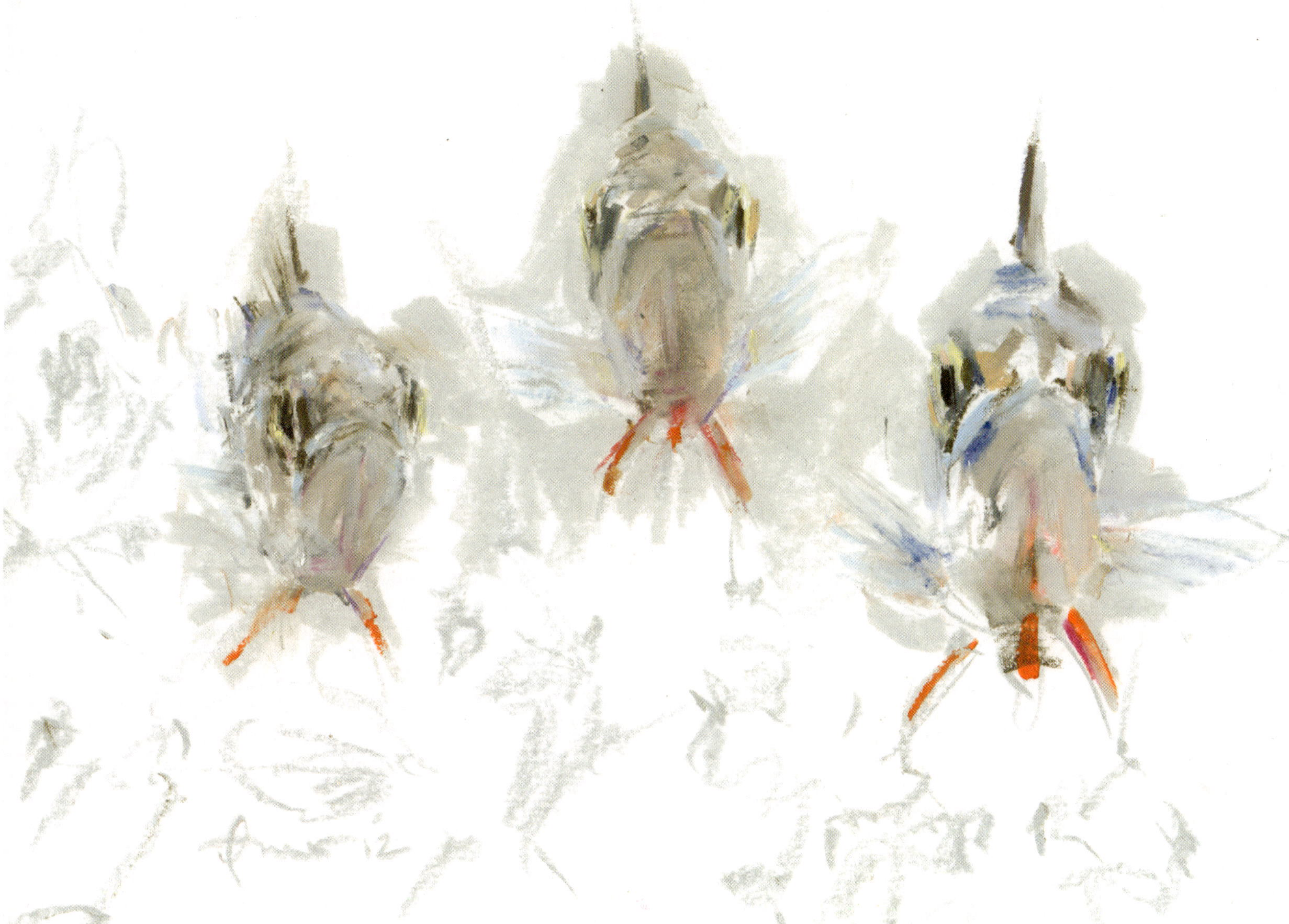

*Perch,* oil pastels

…another tense 'who's watching who' encounter begins to play out…

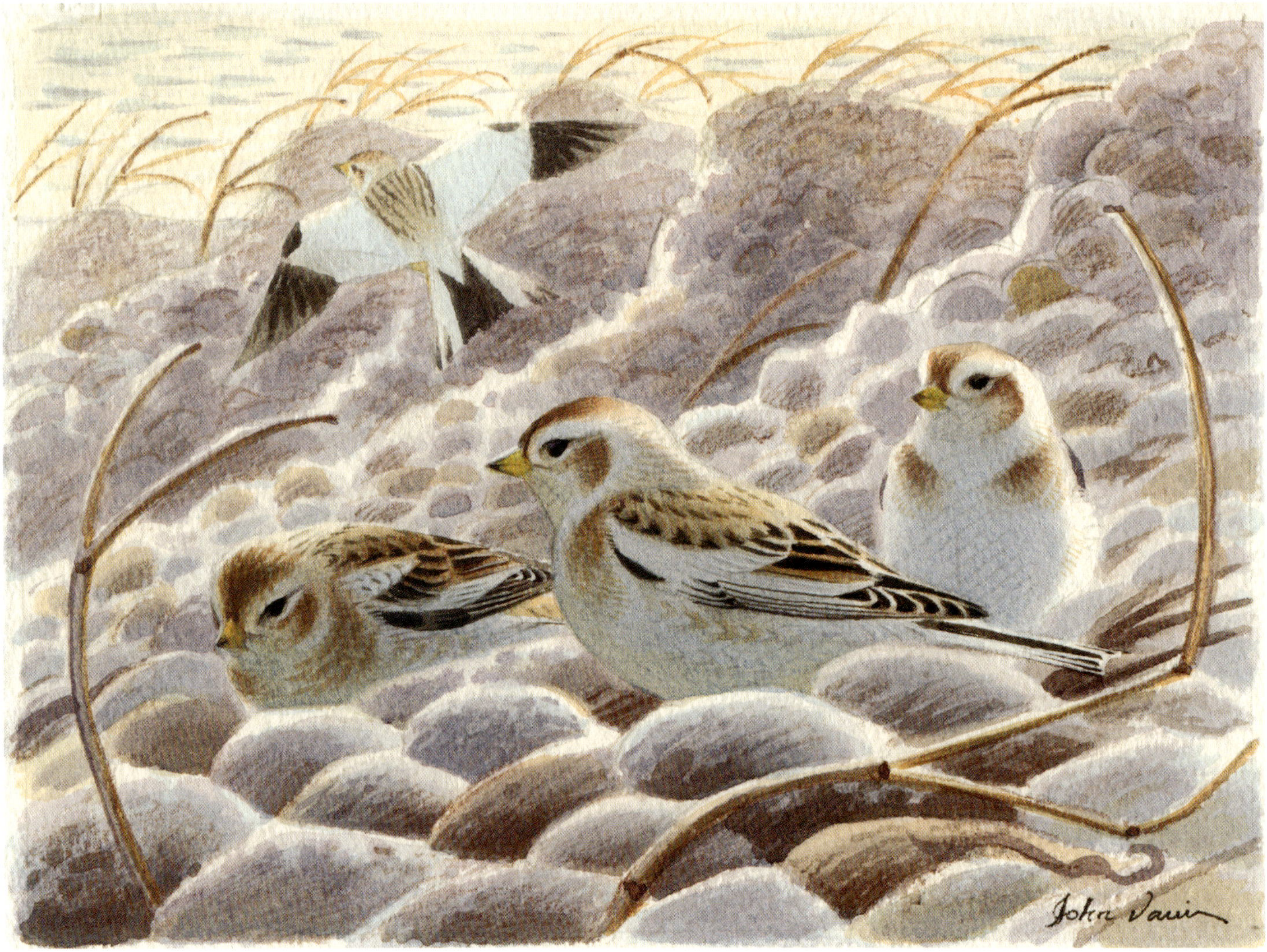

*Snow Buntings At Blakeney Point,* watercolour

# John Davis

I bumped into this group on a recent visit to North Norfolk on a cold winter's day. Very confiding, allowing me to sit and sketch close-by. They would suddenly all fly up and land again further along the beach. Very beautiful against the dark pebbles and dead stalks of Yellow Horned Poppies.

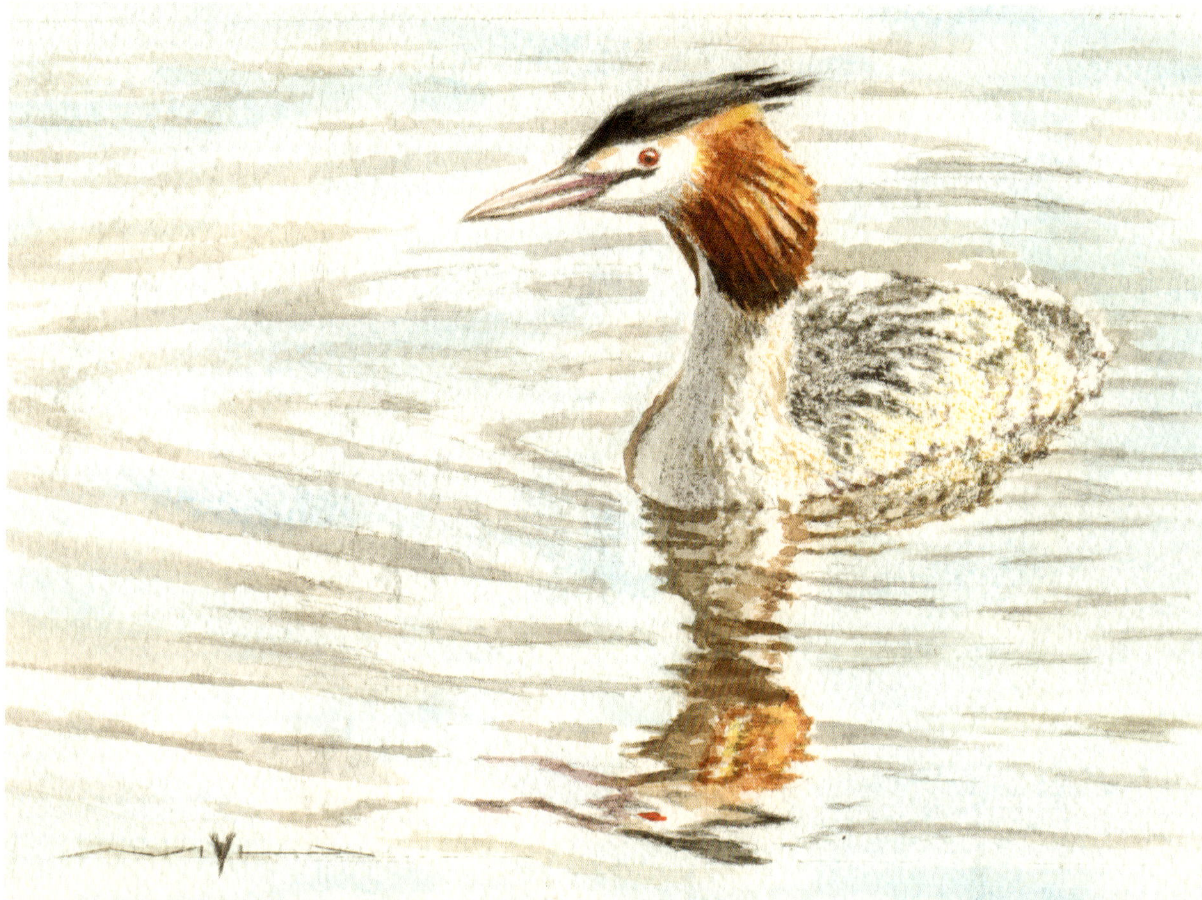

# Michael Hampton

*Great Crested Grebe*, watercolour

Watching the Norwood grebes restarted me bird painting, with their fascinating displays and striking plumage. A grebe head is my logo. South Norwood lake was a reservoir for the Croydon Canal, one of the last to be built and the first to close.

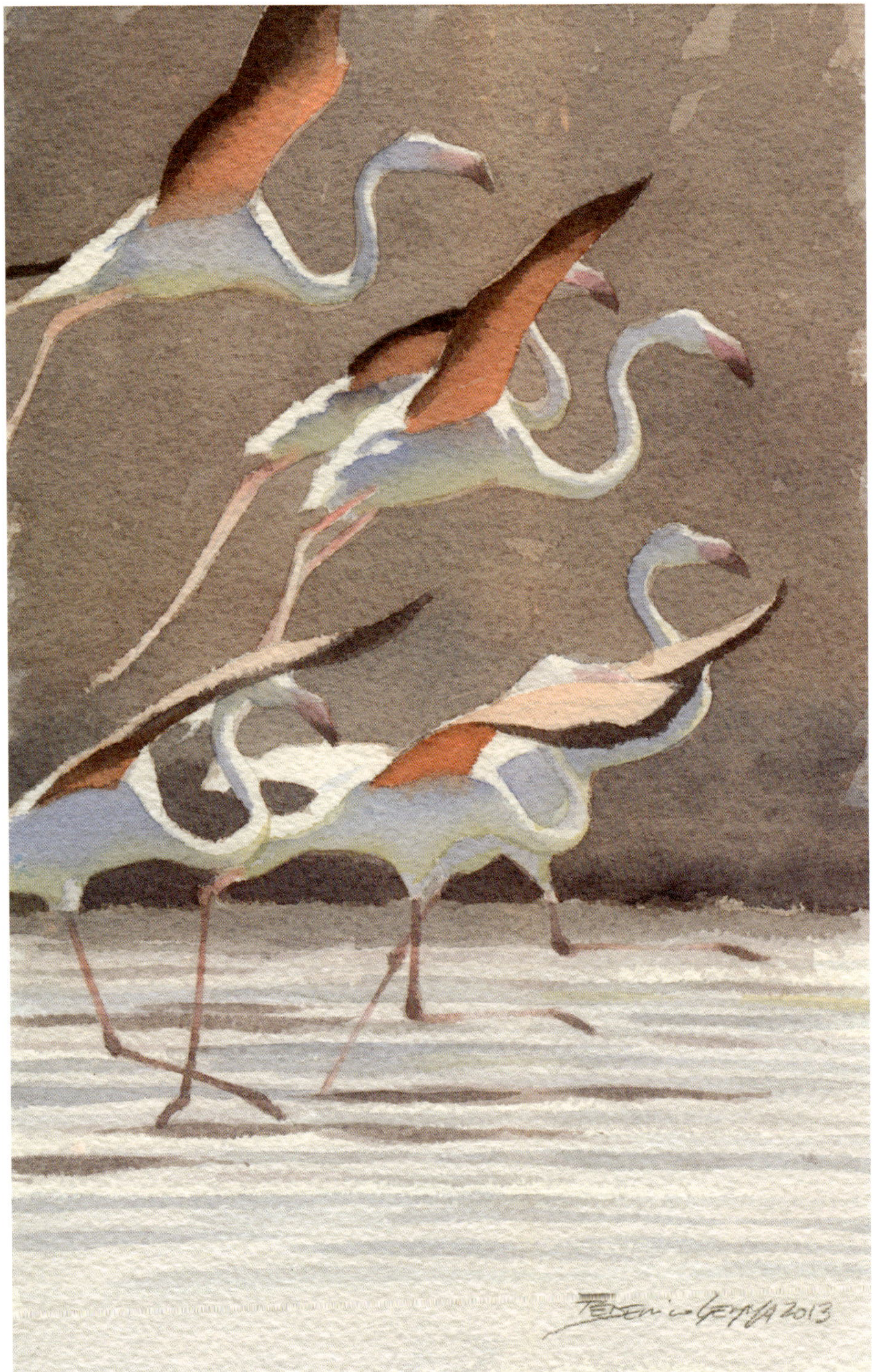

# Federico Gemma

*Greater Flamingos Landing*, watercolour

Saline di Tarquinia, Latium, Italy. These birds are among my favourite subjects and I'm always attracted to how shadows shape the forms of the tiny bodies, enhancing the pale pink of the birds in light and water reflections. However, I'm always astonished when they fly revealing the bright red of the wings with the fine black border.

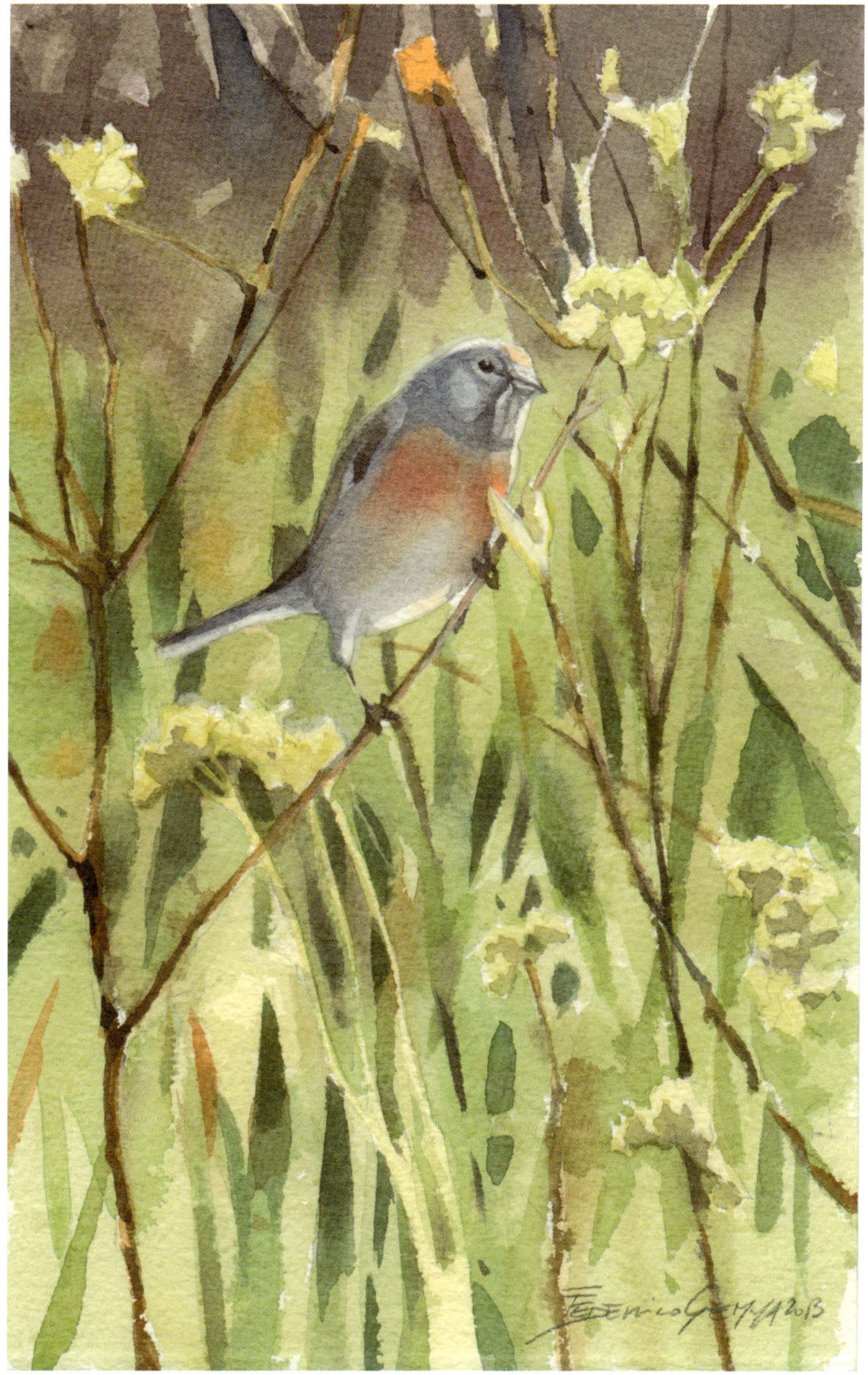

*Linnet,* watercolour

Tolfa Mountains, Latium, Italy. Looking for birds on a sunny afternoon, a flock of colourful finches crossed my path and settled in a field close to me. Looking closer, I discovered a group of Linnets feeding between flowers and grass in a bright, yellow-green light. I painted the male with the distinctive and so attractive red breast.

# Robert Gillmor

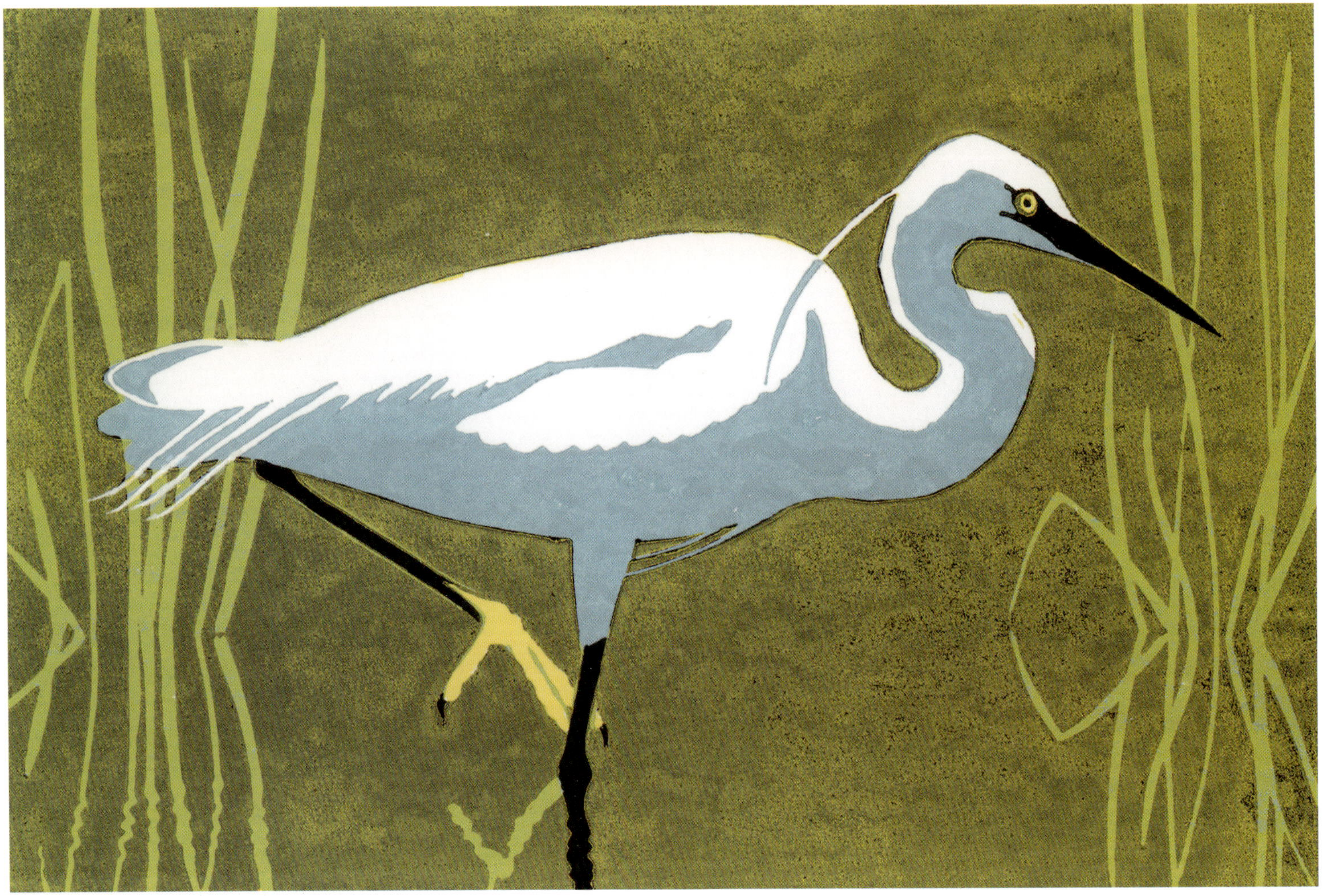

*Little Egret,* linocut

In this small linocut I returned to a subject tackled before – a favourite bird, first encountered in East Africa. But this time I wanted to get more out of less – by overprinting to gain extra colours. There are three basic colours: blue, black and yellow. Yellow printed over blue makes pale green and over black, a darker green.

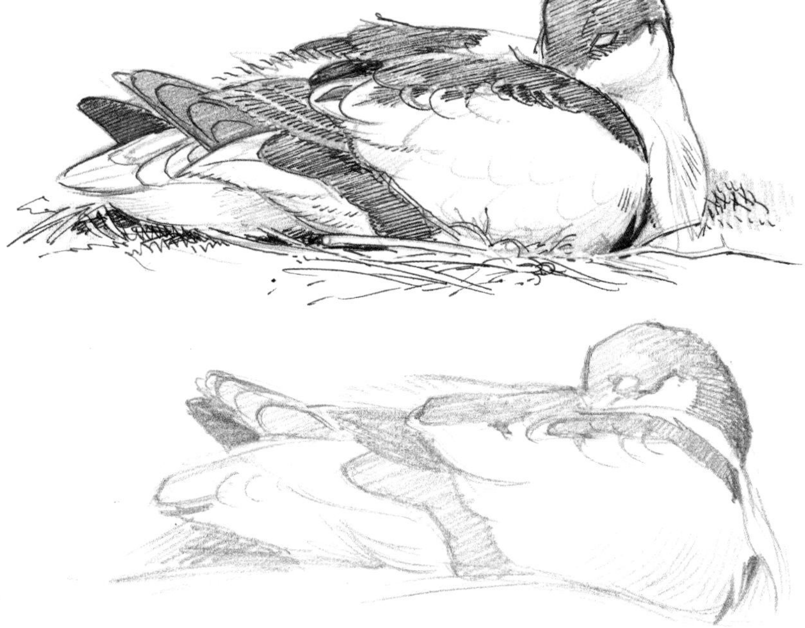

*Sleeping Avocets,*
pencil, pen and ink sketches.

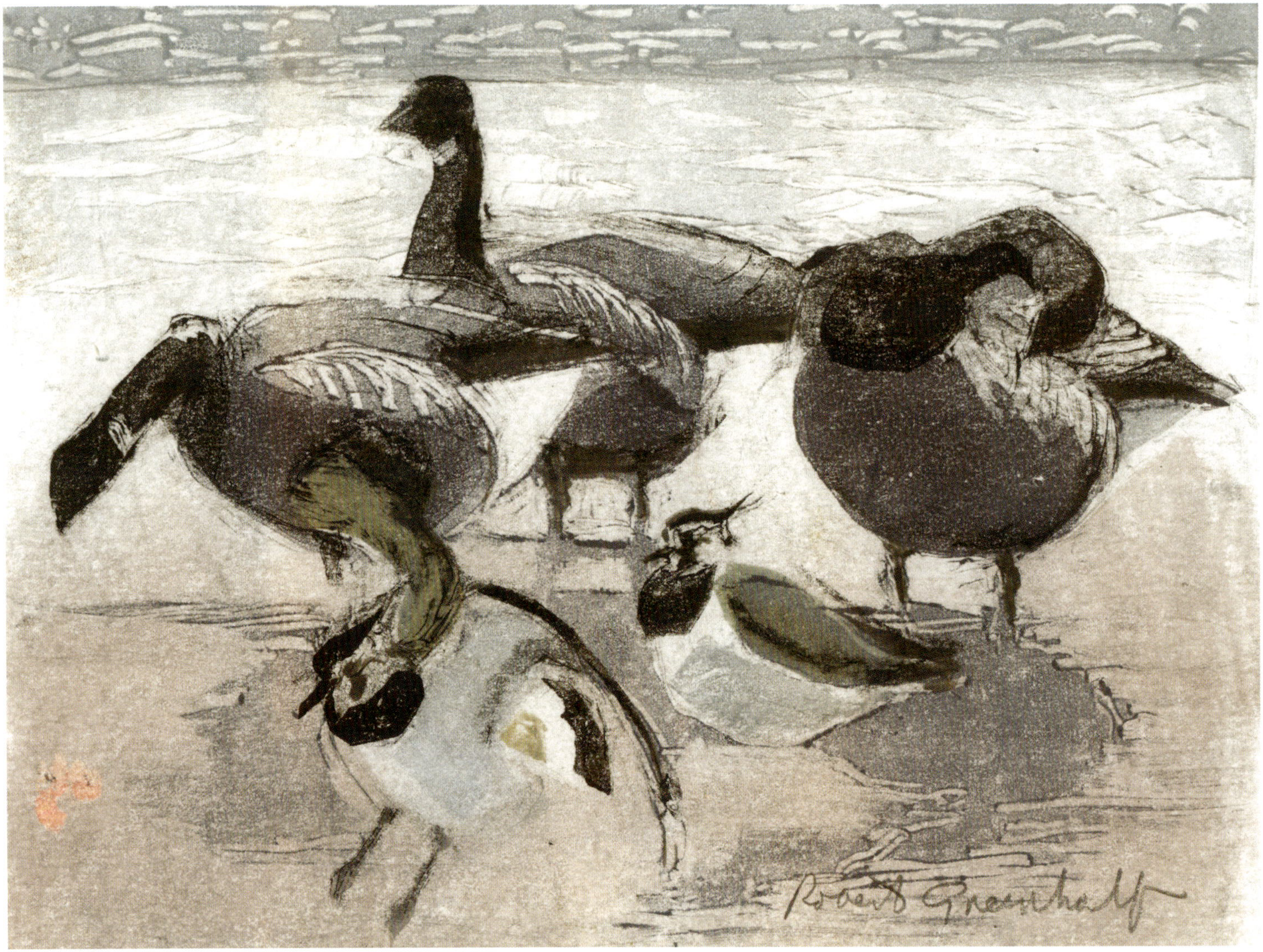

# Robert Greenhalf

*Brents & Lapwings*, monoprint

January, Cley, Norfolk, with artist friends: Harriet Mead and Russ Heselden. After tea and cake with Sarah and Rachel at the Pinkfoot Gallery, we went on to the nature reserve. A small flock of Brents flew in briefly to drink, bathe and preen amongst Lapwings. My frantic sketches were used later as inspiration and reference for this monoprint.

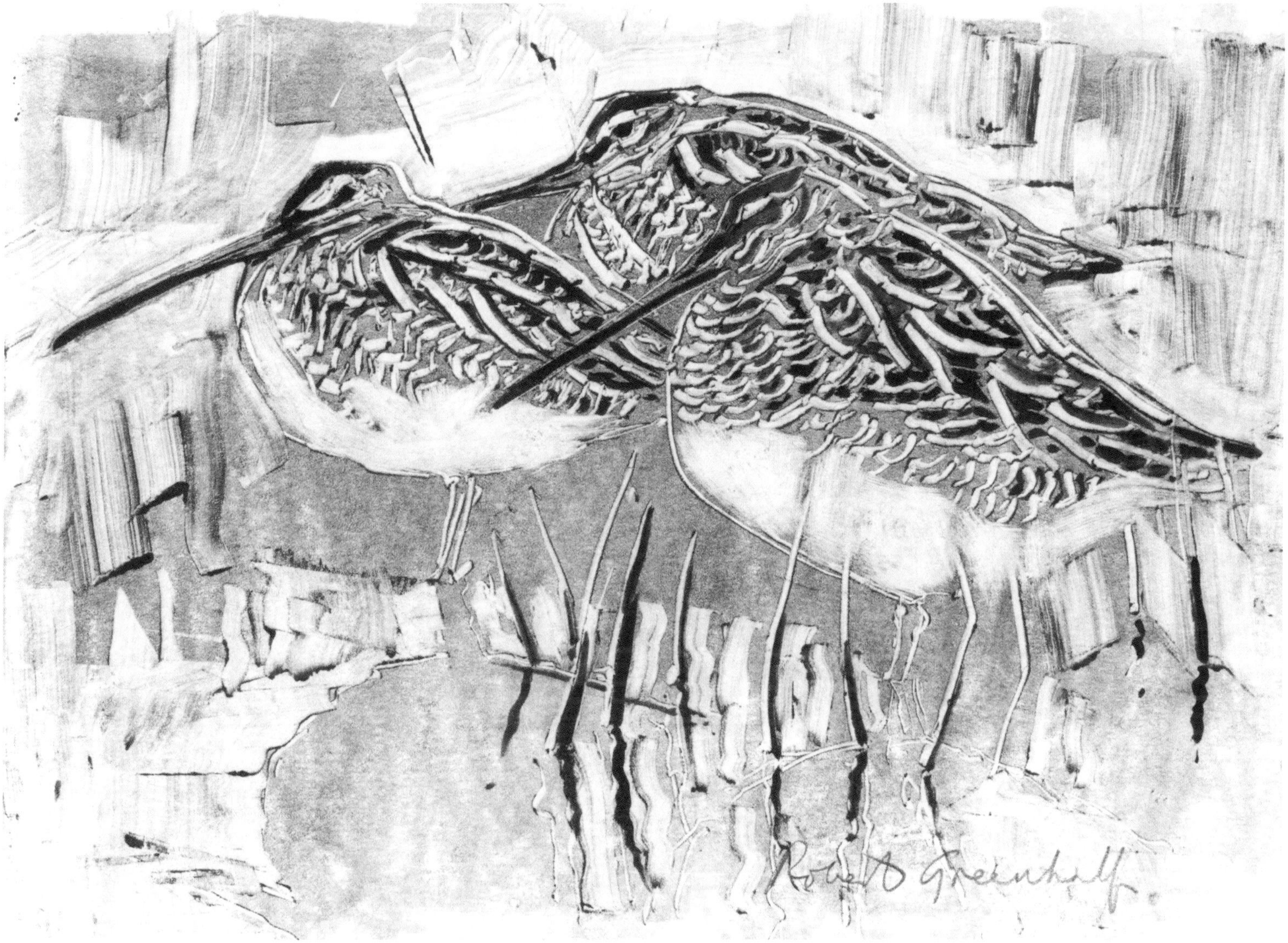

*Snipe*, monoprint

Cold but sunny morning in Janurary at Rye Harbour Nature Reserve in Sussex. Three Snipe were sunning themselves in the lee of a bank. Snipe at rest are the most obliging of models, moving very little, fortunate as their complex patterning takes time to notate. This monoprint was made later in the studio using field sketches as reference.

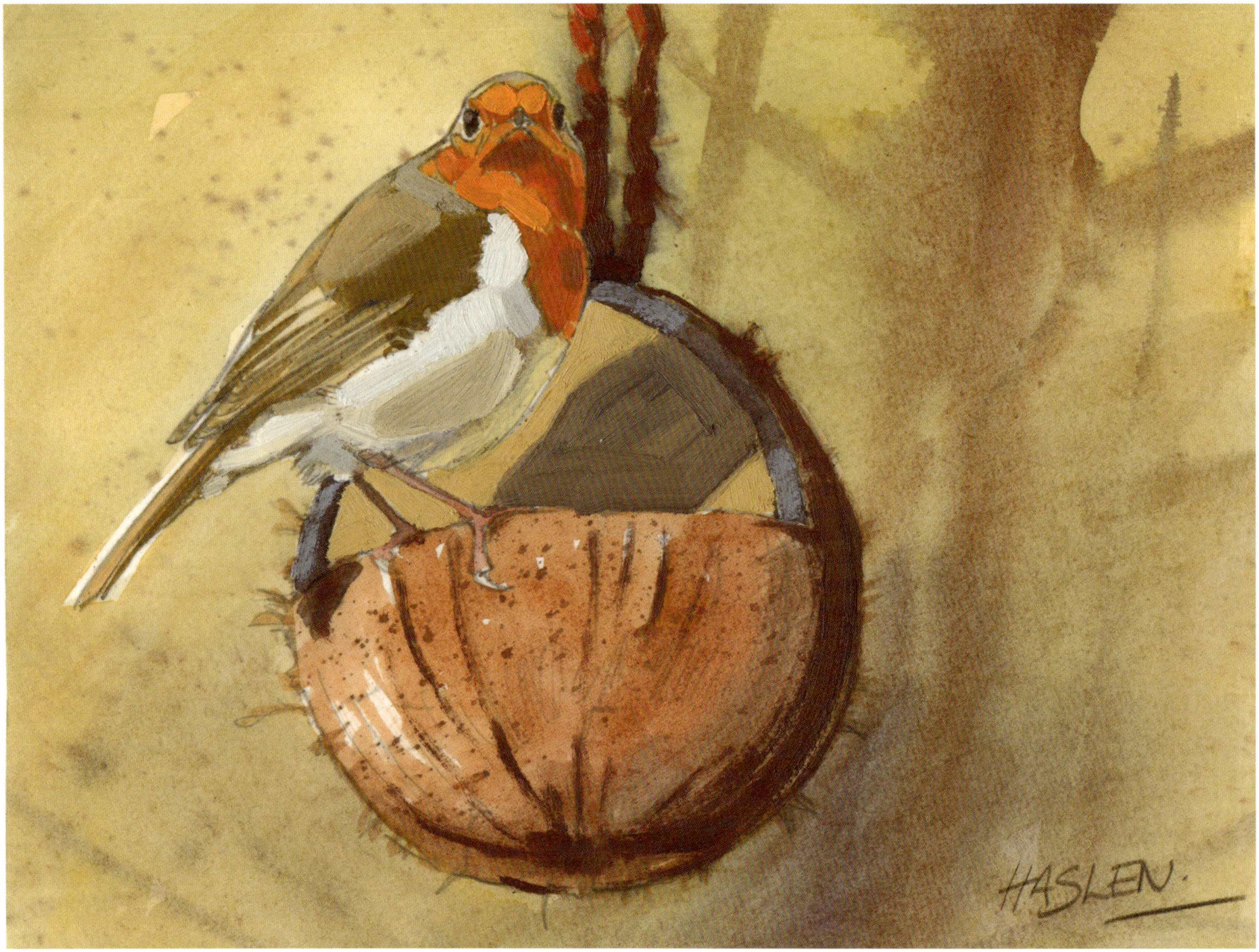


# Andrew Haslen

*Robin,* oil and watercolour

These paintings are the initial studies I made in preparation for a linocut called *Feeding Tree.* I often work in oils and watercolours making a number of small studies before embarking on a larger piece to make the final composition.

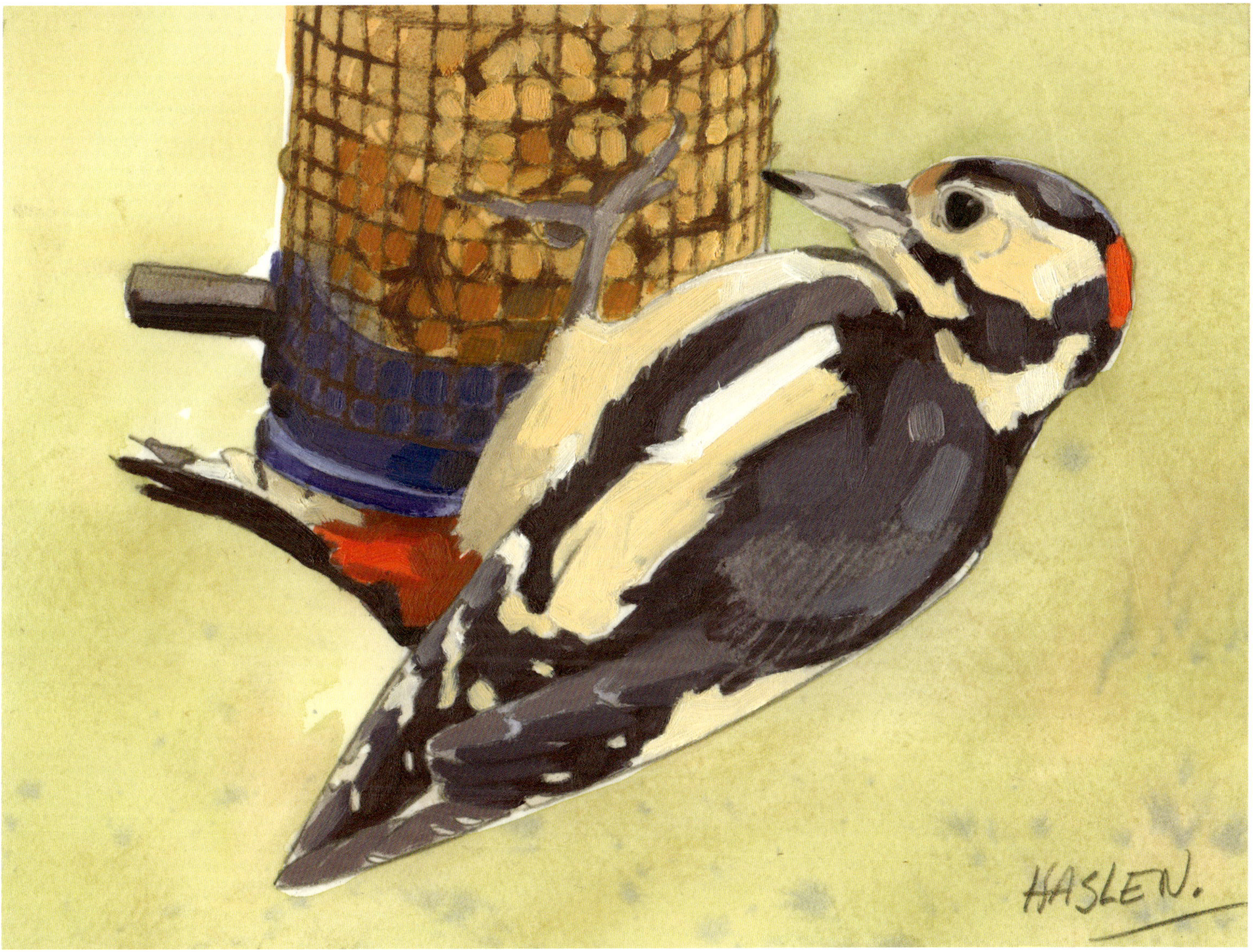


*Great Spotted Woodpecker,* oil and watercolour

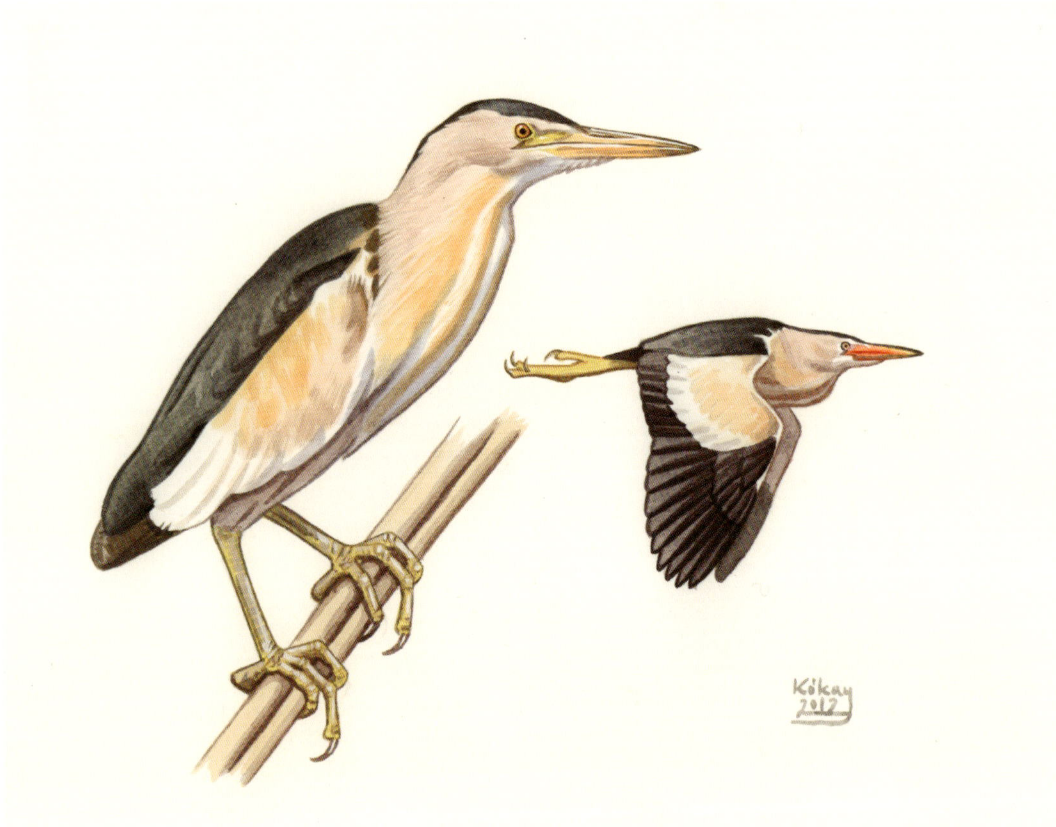

Little Bittern, watercolour illustration painted for BirdLife Hungary

# Szabolcs Kokay

I'm living on an island and my favourite bird on the river is the Little Bittern. I can have very good views of this mostly secretive species near my home.

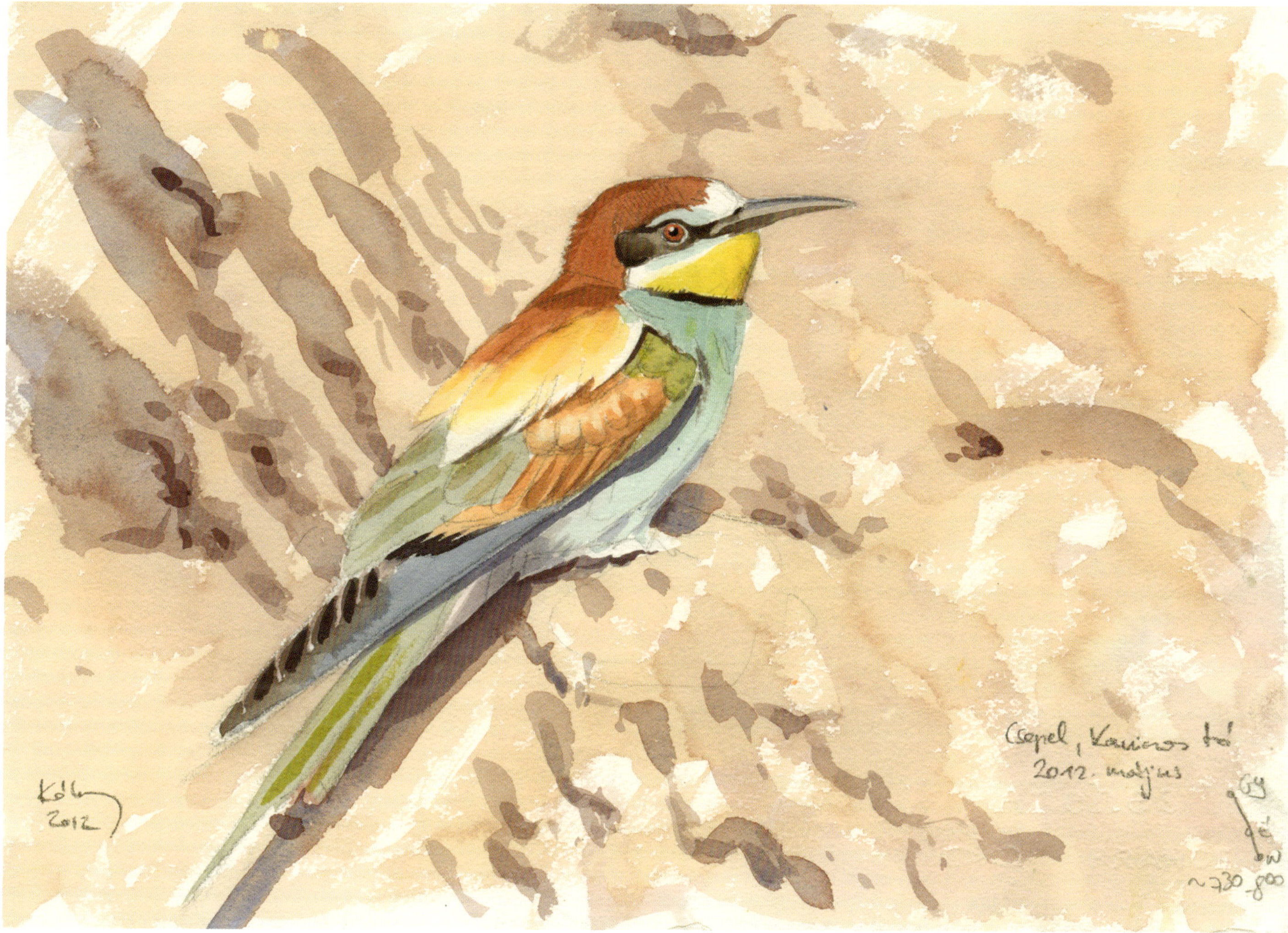


*Bee-eater*, watercolour

While exploring some promising areas near my home in Hungary I was lucky to find a Bee-eater colony of 10-12 pairs. This gave me a good opportunity to study and sketch these colourful birds. I love the challenge of capturing the colours of the Bee-eaters. In fact it was much more difficult to paint the sand-wall of their surroundings.

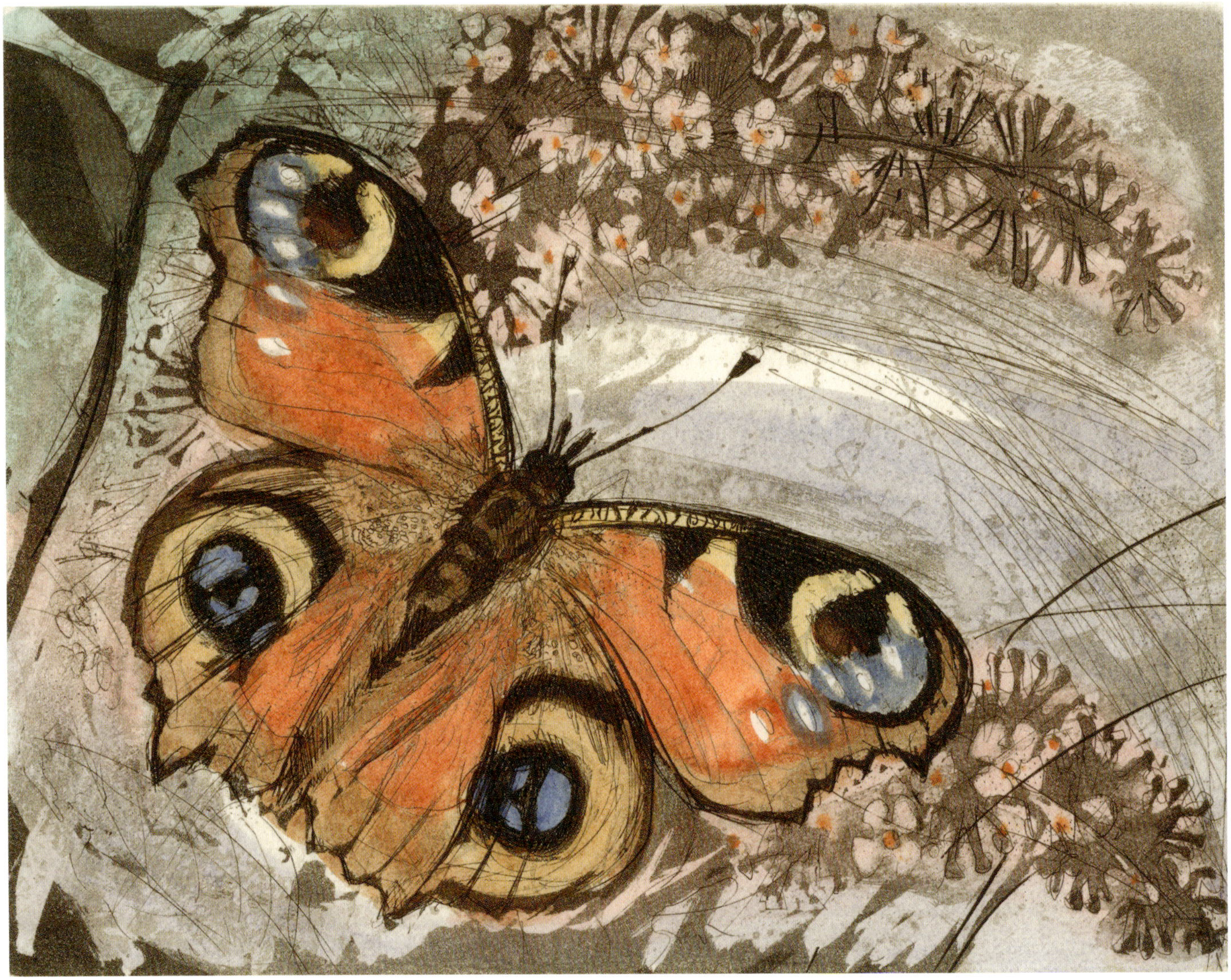

*Peacock on Buddleja*, etching and aquatint with hand-colouring

# David Koster

Some years in Plockton in the north-west Highlands, numerous Peacock butterflies appear when the Dandelions are out and later they feed on the Buddleja. They are tropical and gorgeous-looking in the sunshine. Other years there are few to be seen. They can appear surprisingly late even into November.

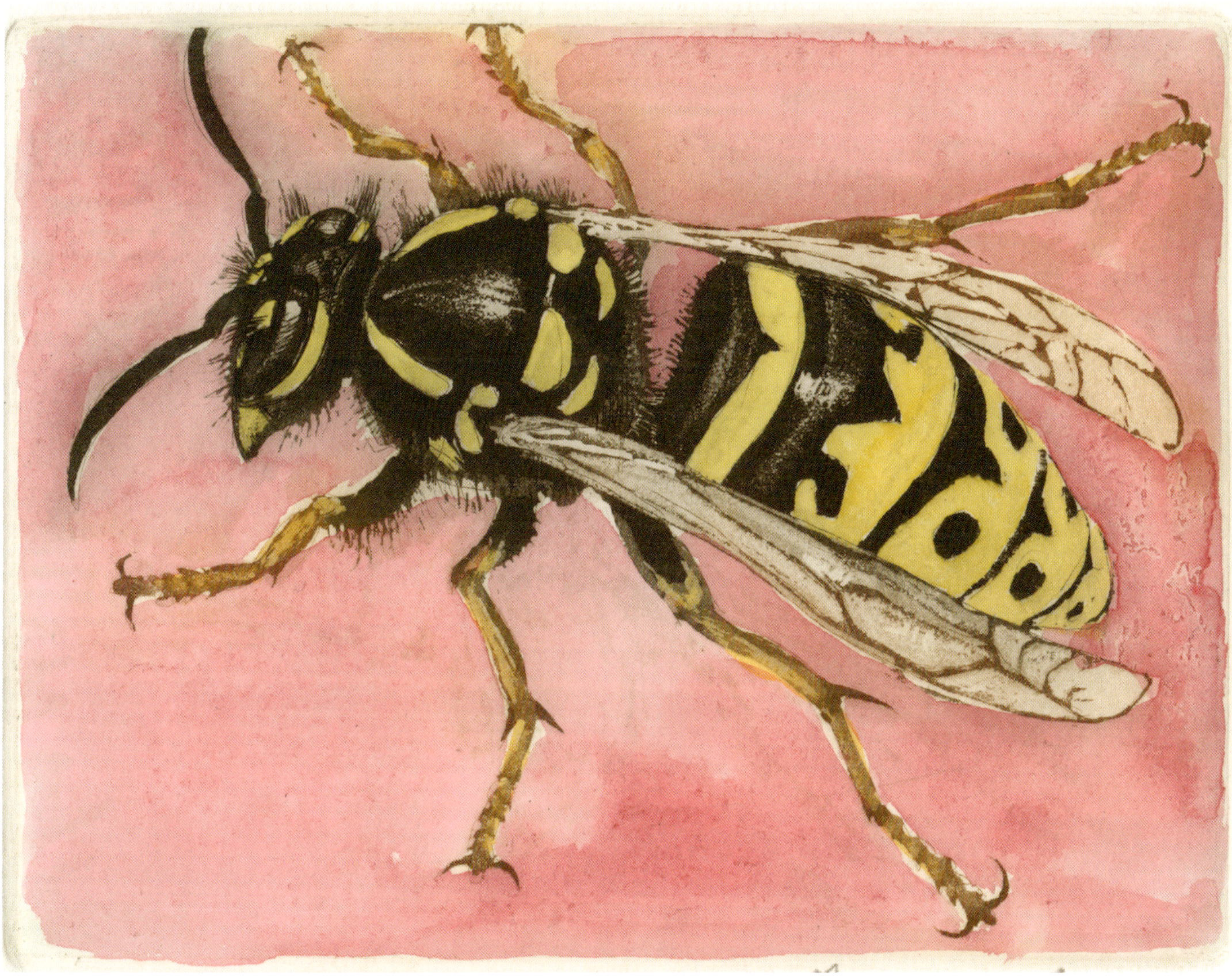

*Queen Wasp,* etching and aquatint with hand-colouring

Queen wasps appear early in the season and can be seen sometimes sunning themselves and as happens on occasions, scraping wood from posts for building their nests.

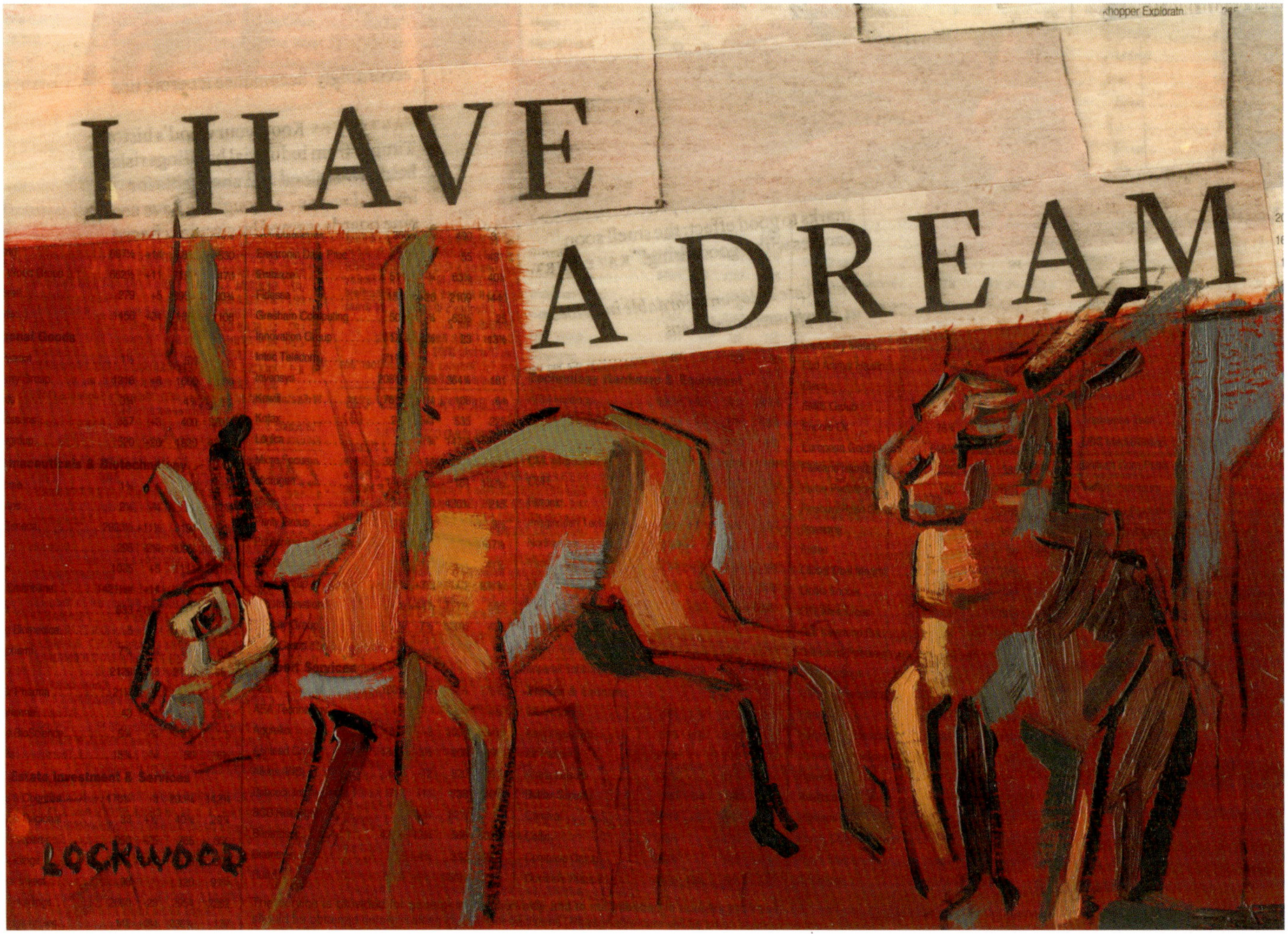


# Rachel Lockwood

*I Have A Dream,* mixed media on board

As I'm driving along, listening to the radio talk of economics, banks and depression, I come across hares in a field. I stop and turn off the engine: silence, then heat rising from the crops. The day is ending and the light changing. Hares run from hedge to hedge and in minutes are gone, absorbed by the flints and dusty earth.

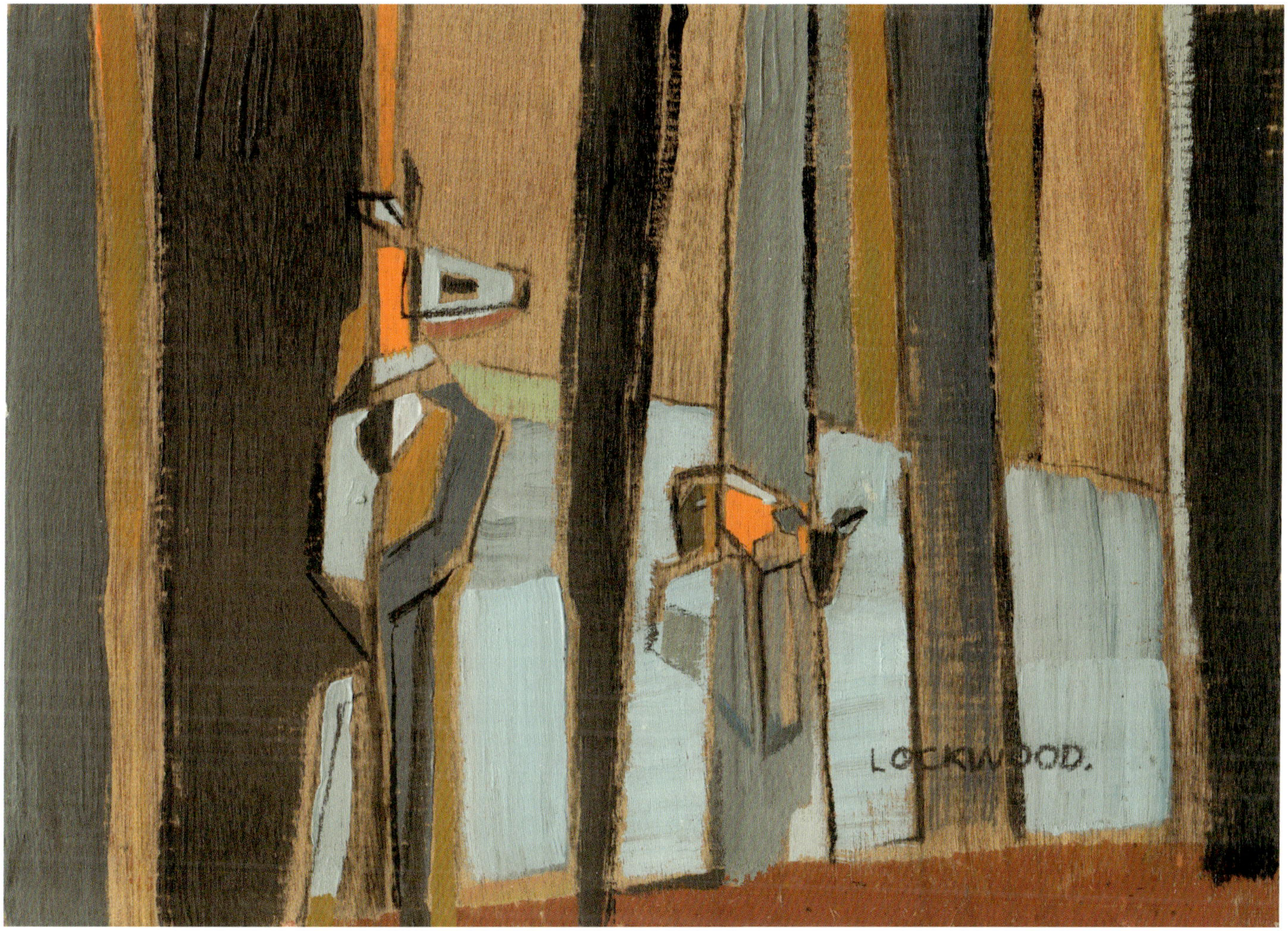


*Mother and Fawn,* oil on board

Swimming the lanes in the local pool, counting down the lengths,
I noticed everyone had stopped and was swimming towards the floor
to ceiling windows. I followed to see and on the other side of the
glass a deer and its week-old fawn were picking their way obliviously
through the hedge. The fawn being protected but given space to learn.

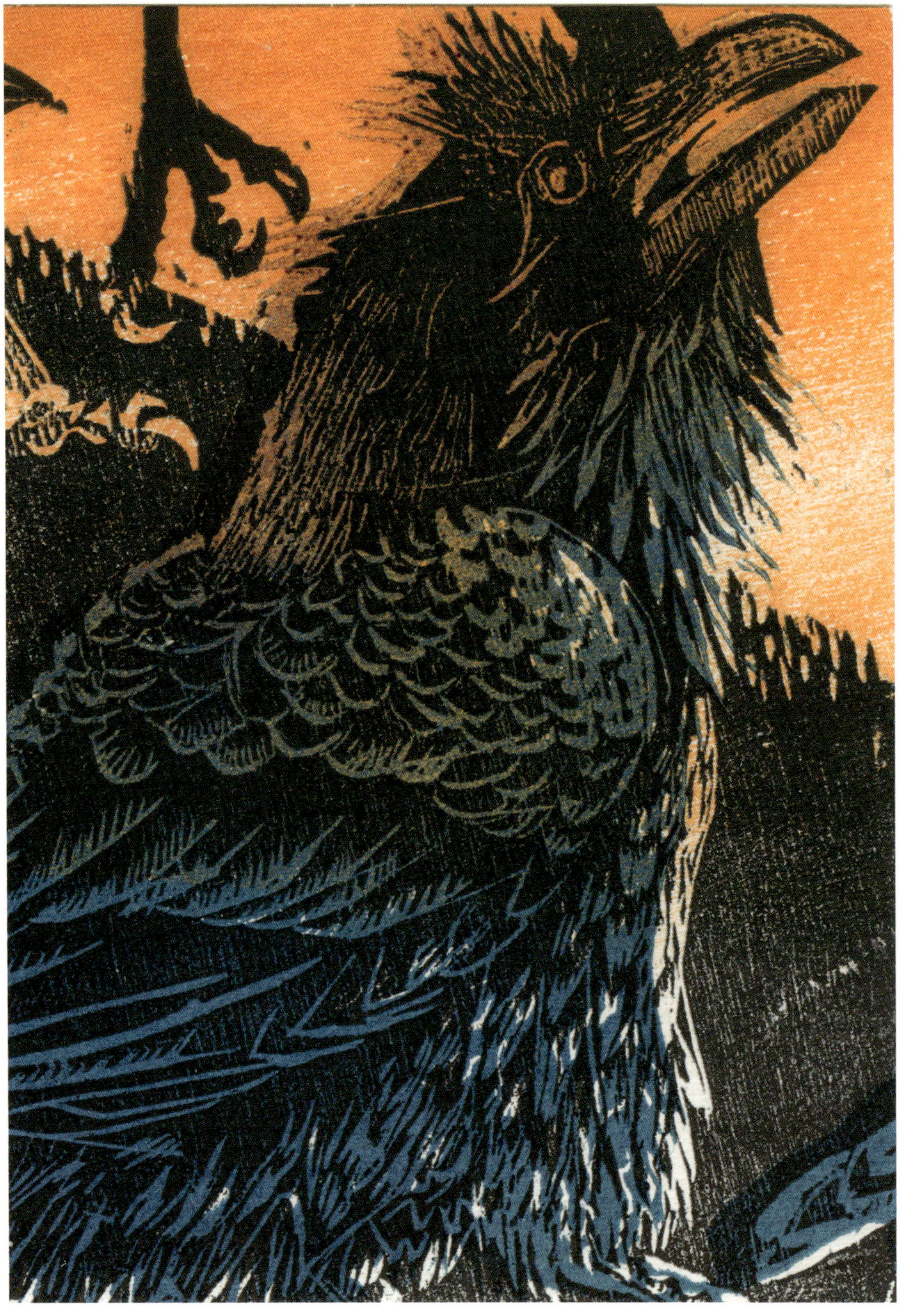

# Julia Manning

*Raven*, woodcut

This is part of a woodcut based on my drawings of Ravens. My obsession with these birds started on Anglesey, where I was lucky enough to see them massing above and roosting in the fir trees of Newborough Forest. I often return to Newborough beach at dusk where there is always a group of Ravens to be seen.

# Nick Mackman

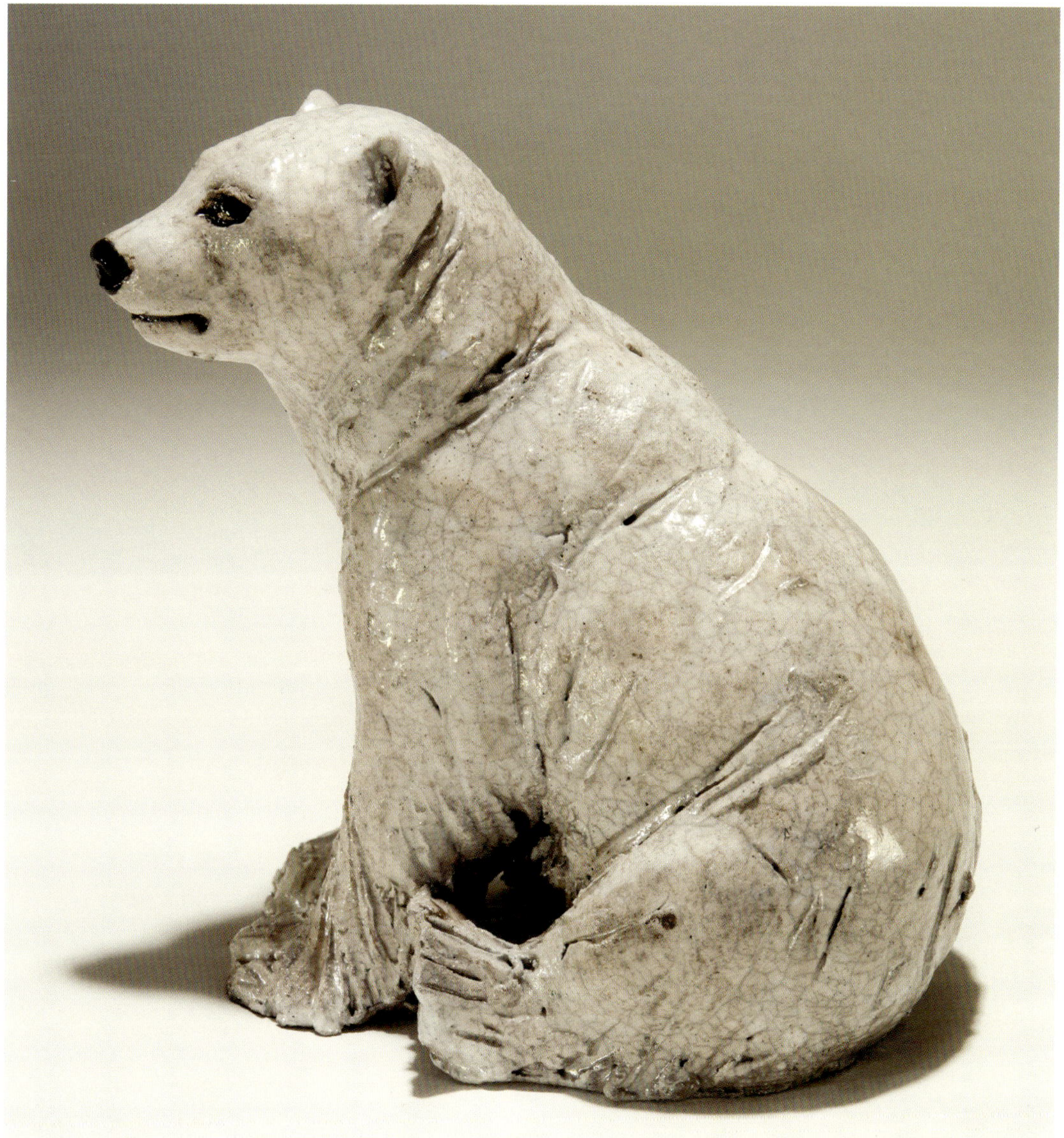

*Polar Bear Cub,* raku-fired ceramic

Polar bears are on everyone's mind. What will the future hold for them? In this piece I wanted to capture the fun in a cub with a bit of hope attached. I aim to tell a story through natural expression. Cubs are cute but their eyes are that of a predator.

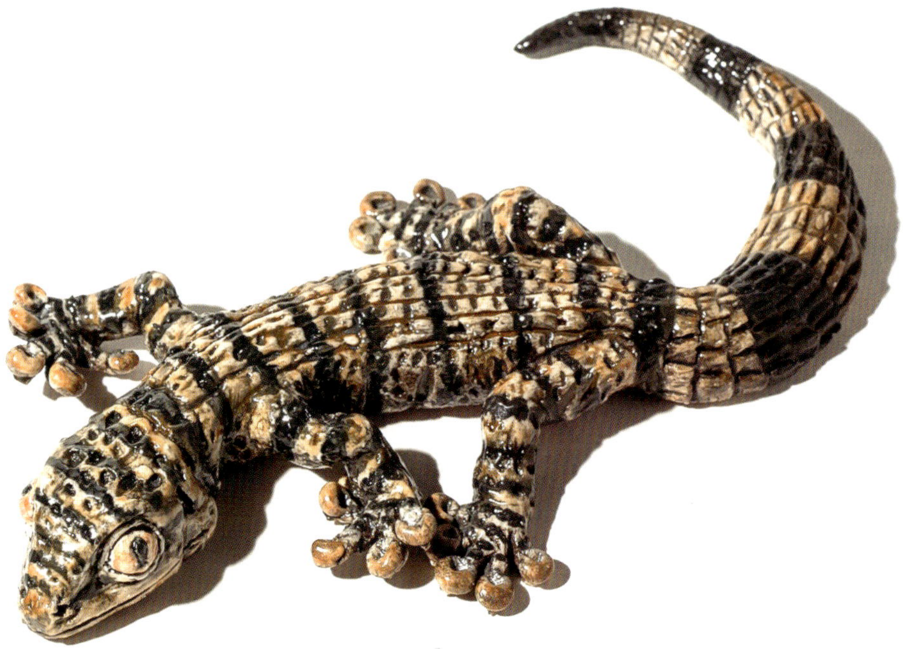

# Jill Moger

*Wall Gecko,* stoneware

The reptile house is being reorganized and not all of the brightly lit and well-furnished vivaria yet have labels bearing the names and origins of their occupants. I catch a brief glimpse of a little brown gecko with knobbly skin as it darts behind the foliage. This sighting doesn't give me enough visual information to formerly identify it, so I'm naming it simply Wall Gecko.

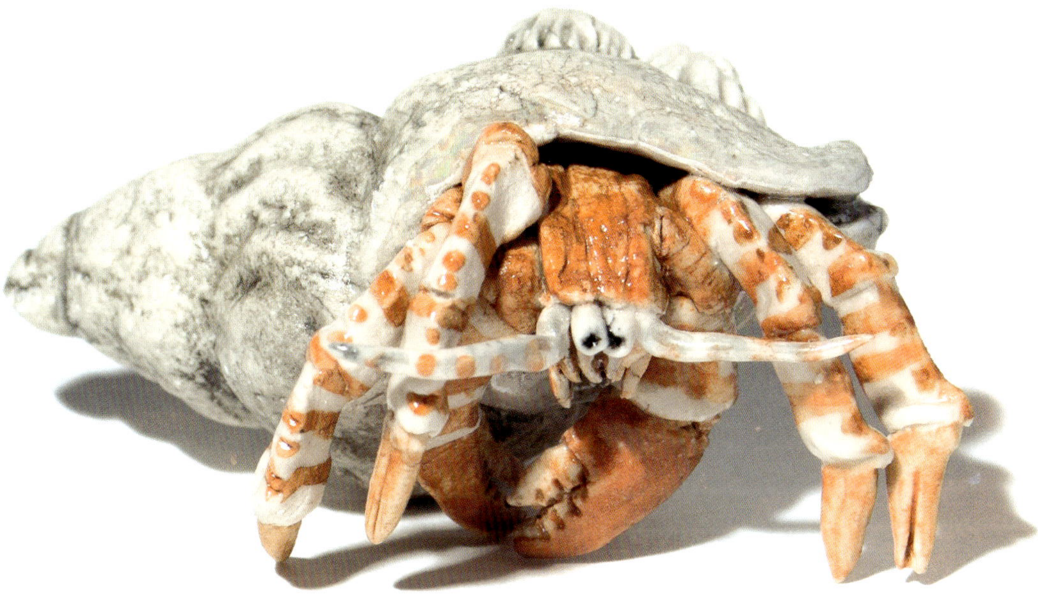

*Hermit Crab*, porcelain

Stepping carefully between rockpools I bend down to pick up a shell and find to my surprise that it is occupied! This little Hermit Crab is surprised too and rapidly retreats back inside its chosen shell. I replace it among the pebbles and wait for it to re-emerge. I smile as it struggles to lift its home awkwardly to go about its business.

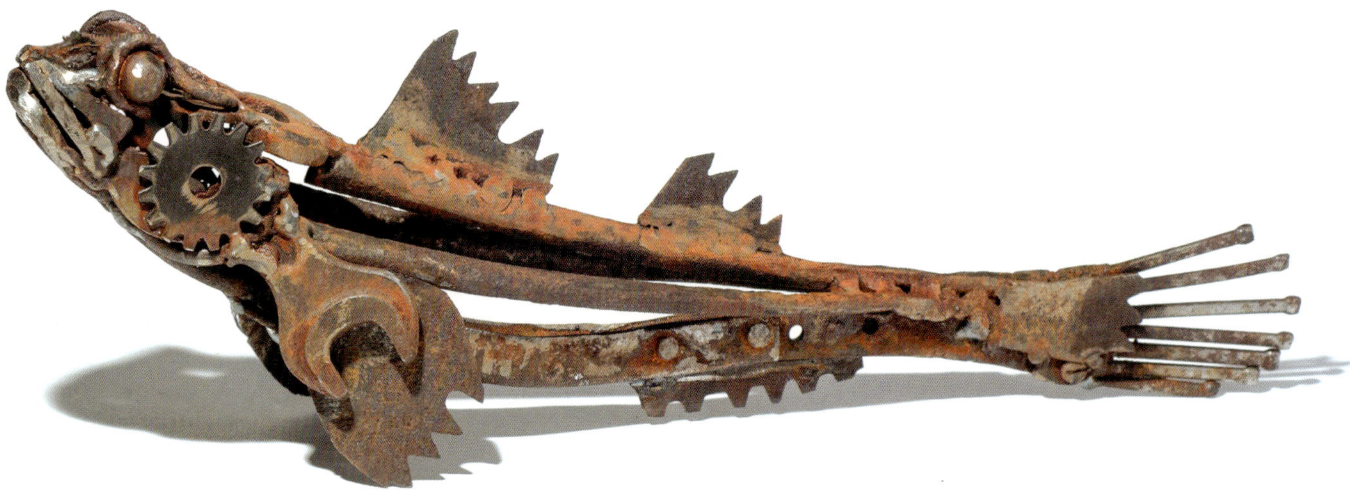

# Harriet Mead

*Sawblade Goby,* welded found objects

My first scuba dive in the sea. Poor visibility and a step into the unknown but within moments I'm entranced. Gobies hug the sand and I attempt to draw them using graphite sticks on the thick watercolour paper. Back in the studio, eyes are depicted with ring spanners and ball bearings while sawblades make the fins.

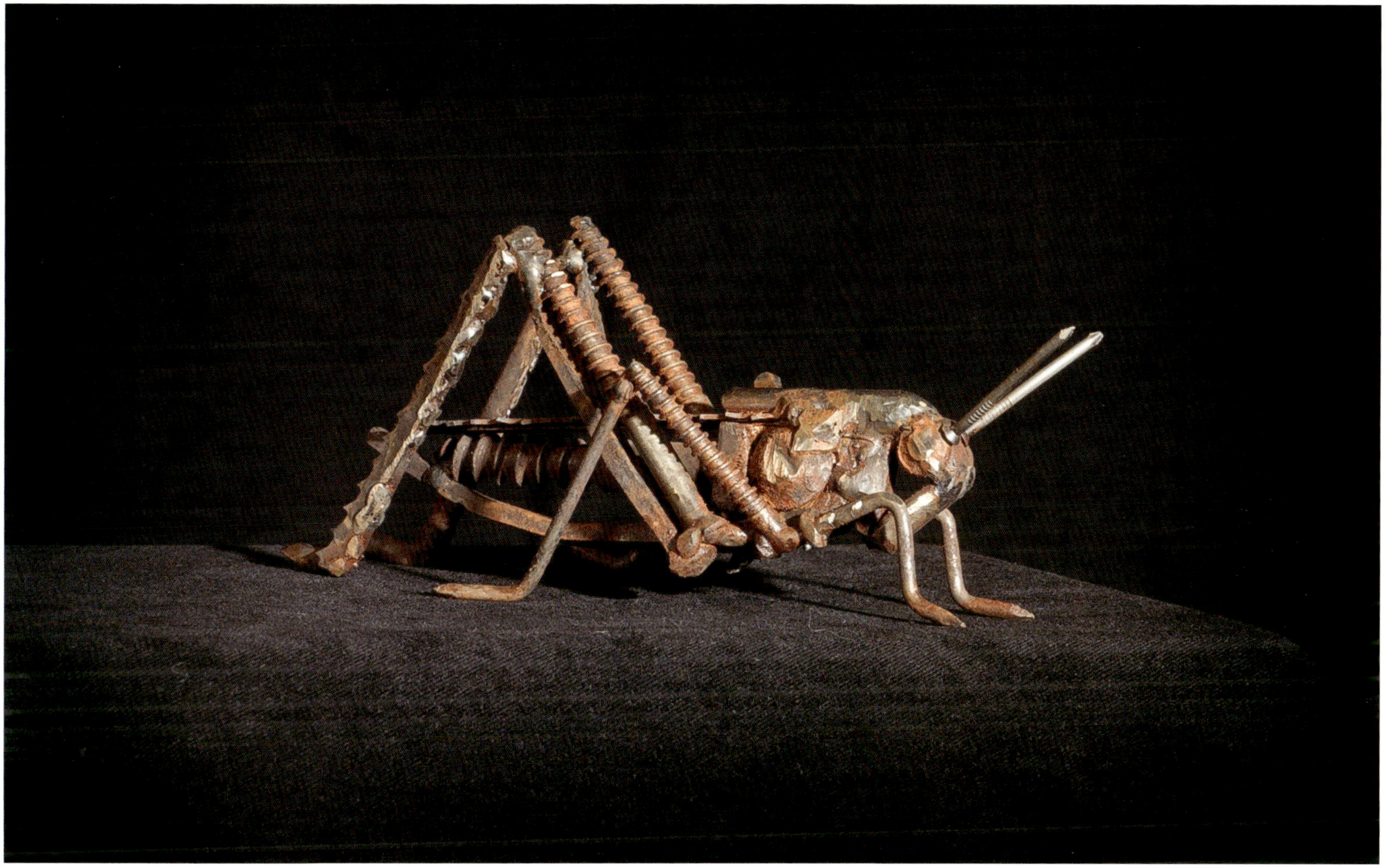

*Grasshopper,* welded found objects

One of those late summer blooms of grasshoppers hiss and sing in my meadow. Armed with a coffee jar I scoop and pounce to catch them. Drawing them, I find Long Winged Conehead and Roesel's Bush Cricket among the Mottled, Field and Meadow Grasshoppers. Back at the studio a quick sketch in steel with band saw blade for the spiked legs.

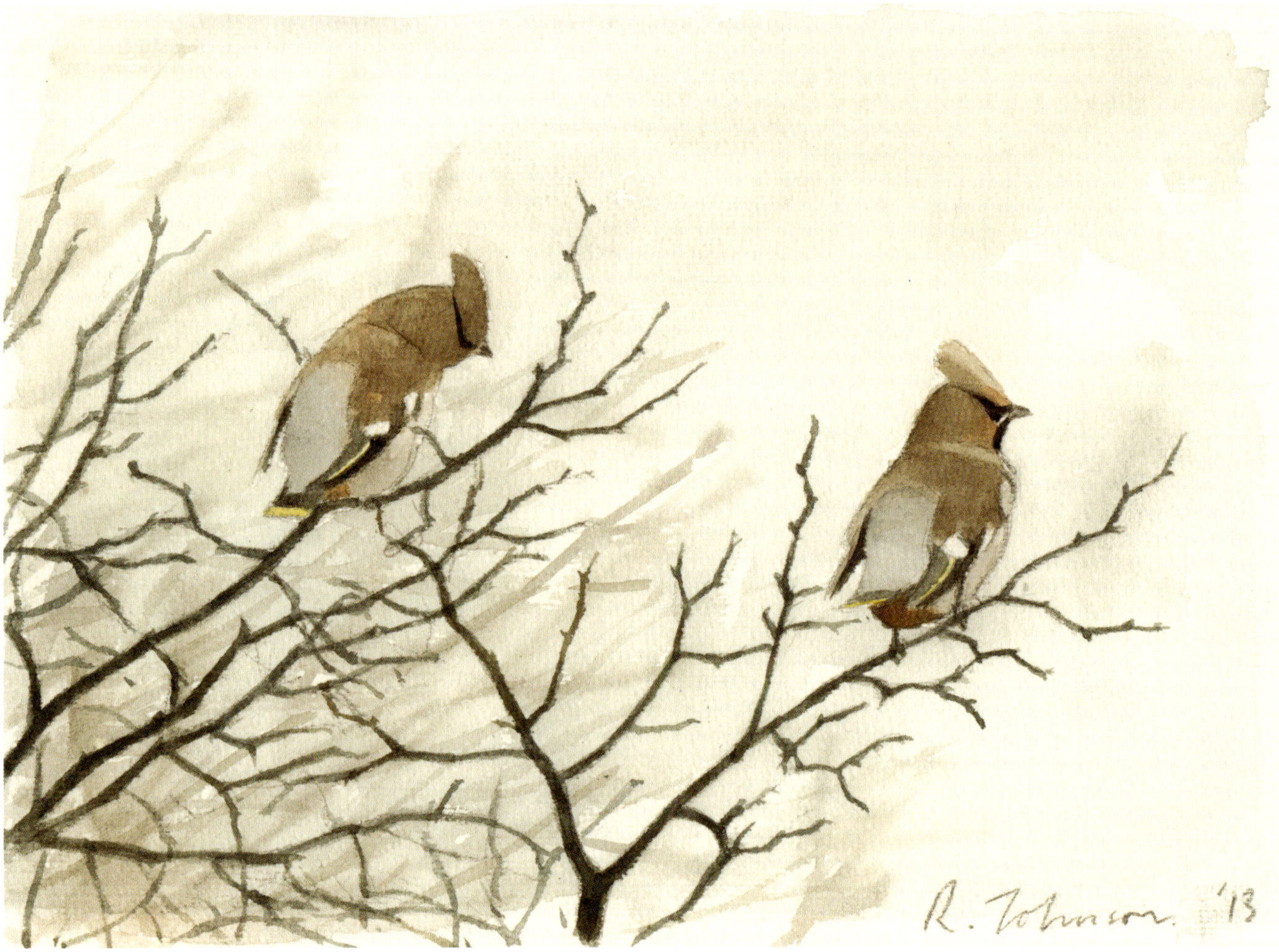

# Richard Johnson

*Waxwings,* watercolour

Two of a flock of about 20 birds which brightened up a grey March day.

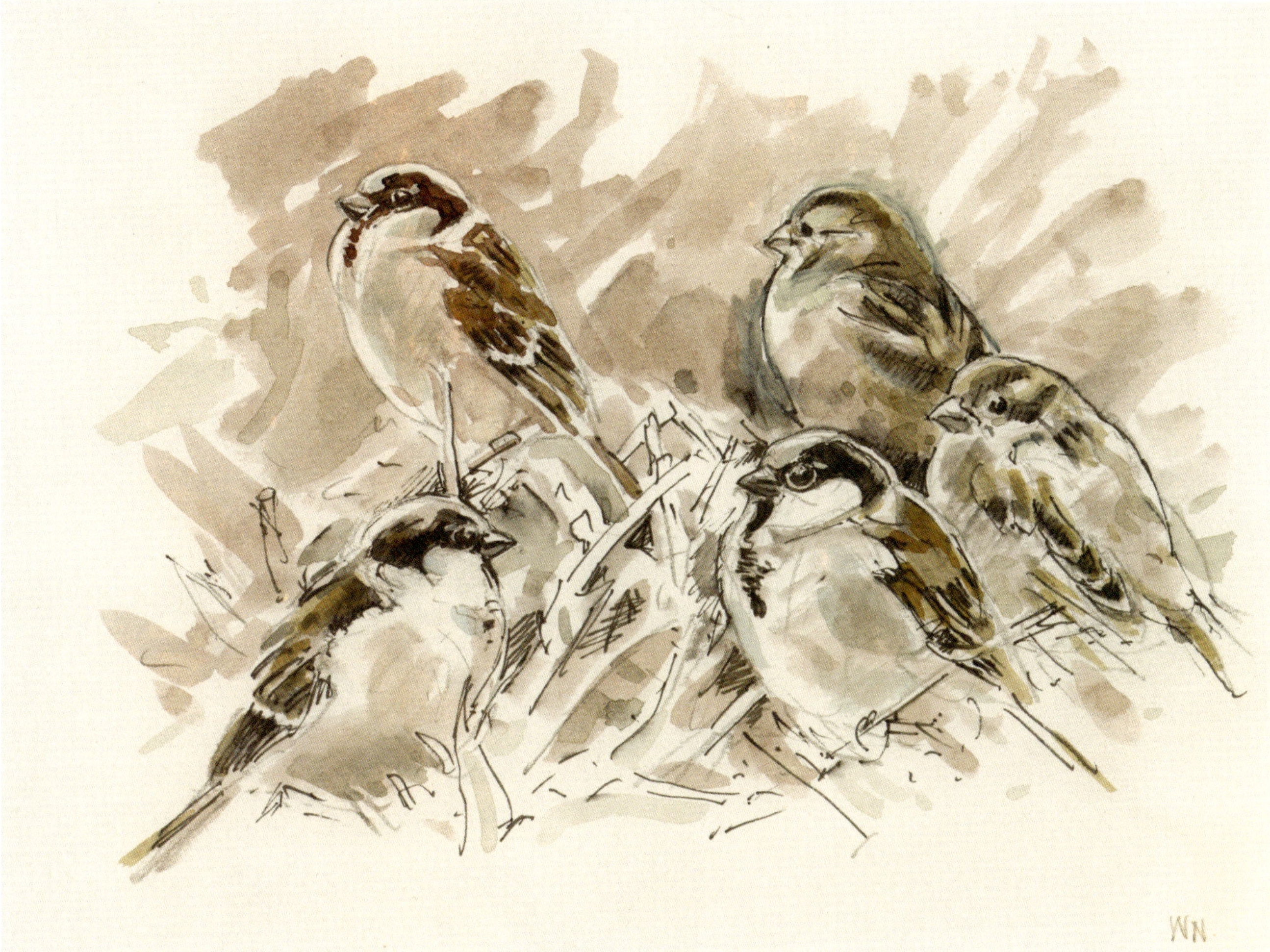

# Willam Neill

*House Sparrows*, pen, ink & wash

My neighbours are BTO ringers so all my House Sparrows have numbered rings. They are doing a study at the moment. Good fun to check who's there, but you do get concerned when one disappears! They sit just outside my studio window.

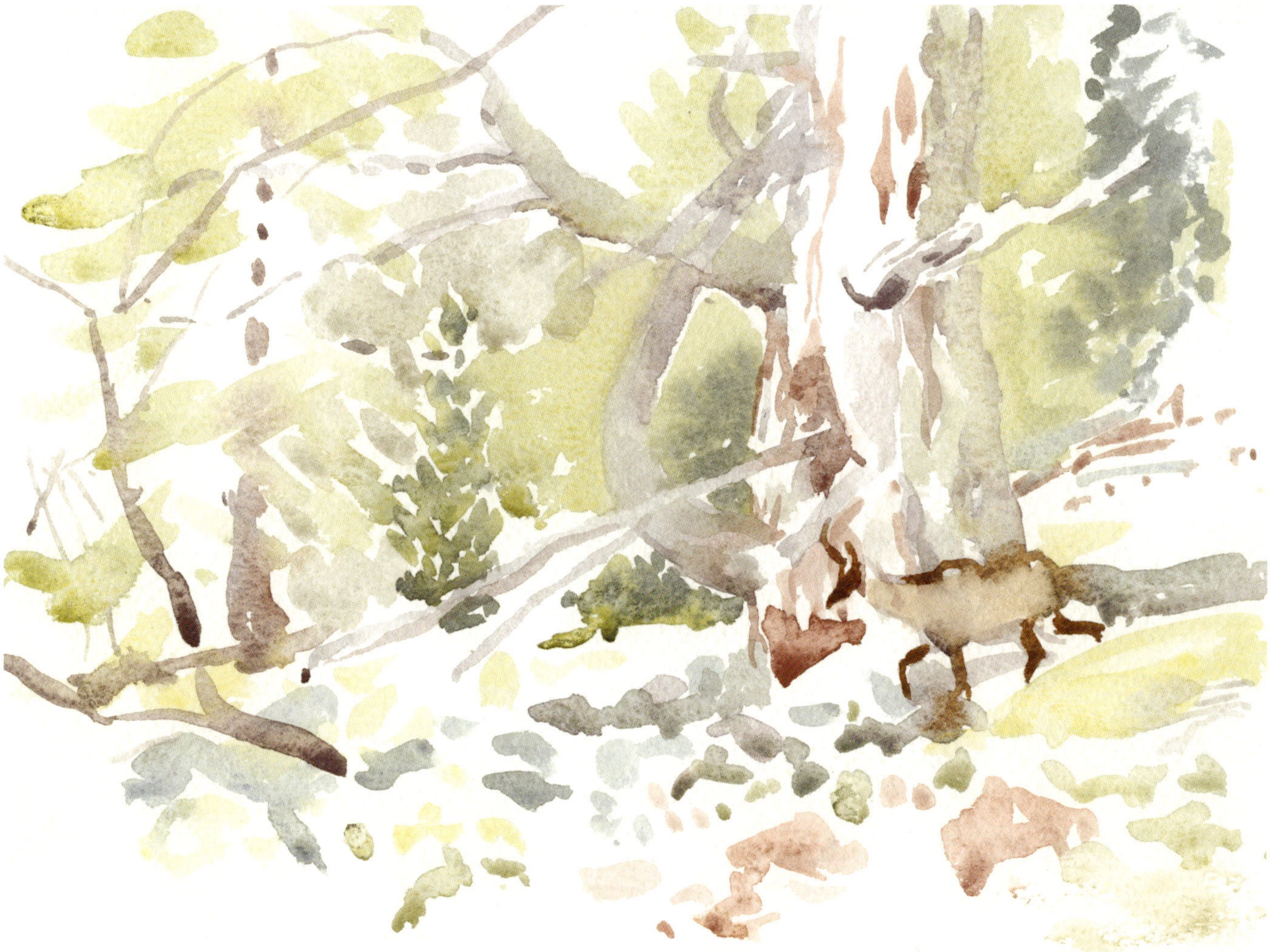

# John Paige

*Chamois*, watercolour

June in the Alps-Maritimes. A period of fine mornings that turned into rain, thunder and snow. Chamois were grazing out on the open hillside. I was painting under a low-spreading fir tree at the edge of the wood. Suddenly this Chamois came down into the wood. Perhaps she was looking for a sheltered place to give birth.

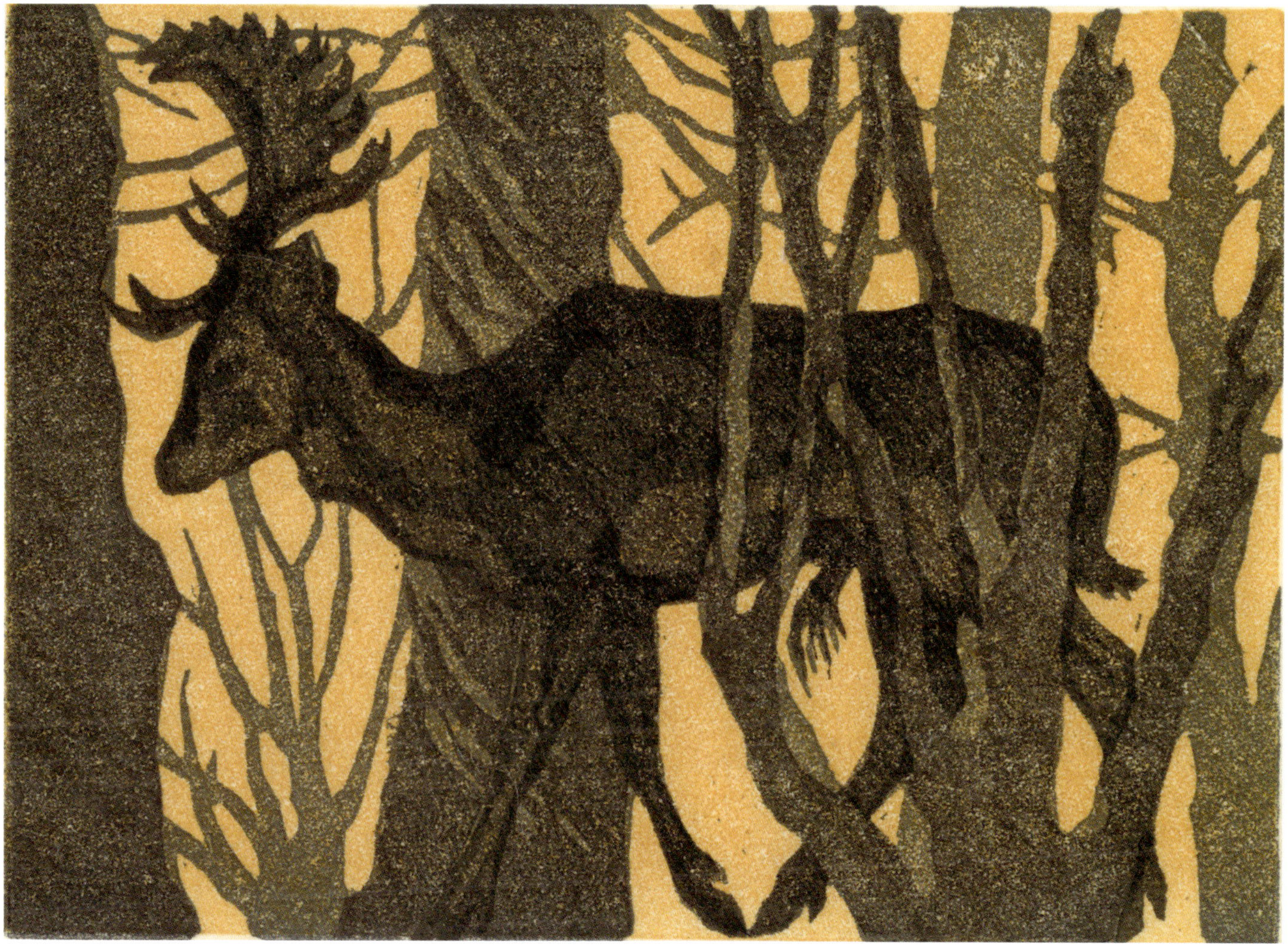

*Horizontal Shadow,* linocut

I like to walk in woodland looking for deer. The surroundings consist of dark, vertical shapes and the light is not very bright. A horizontal shadow materializing amongst the dark verticals is often my first realization that deer are there.

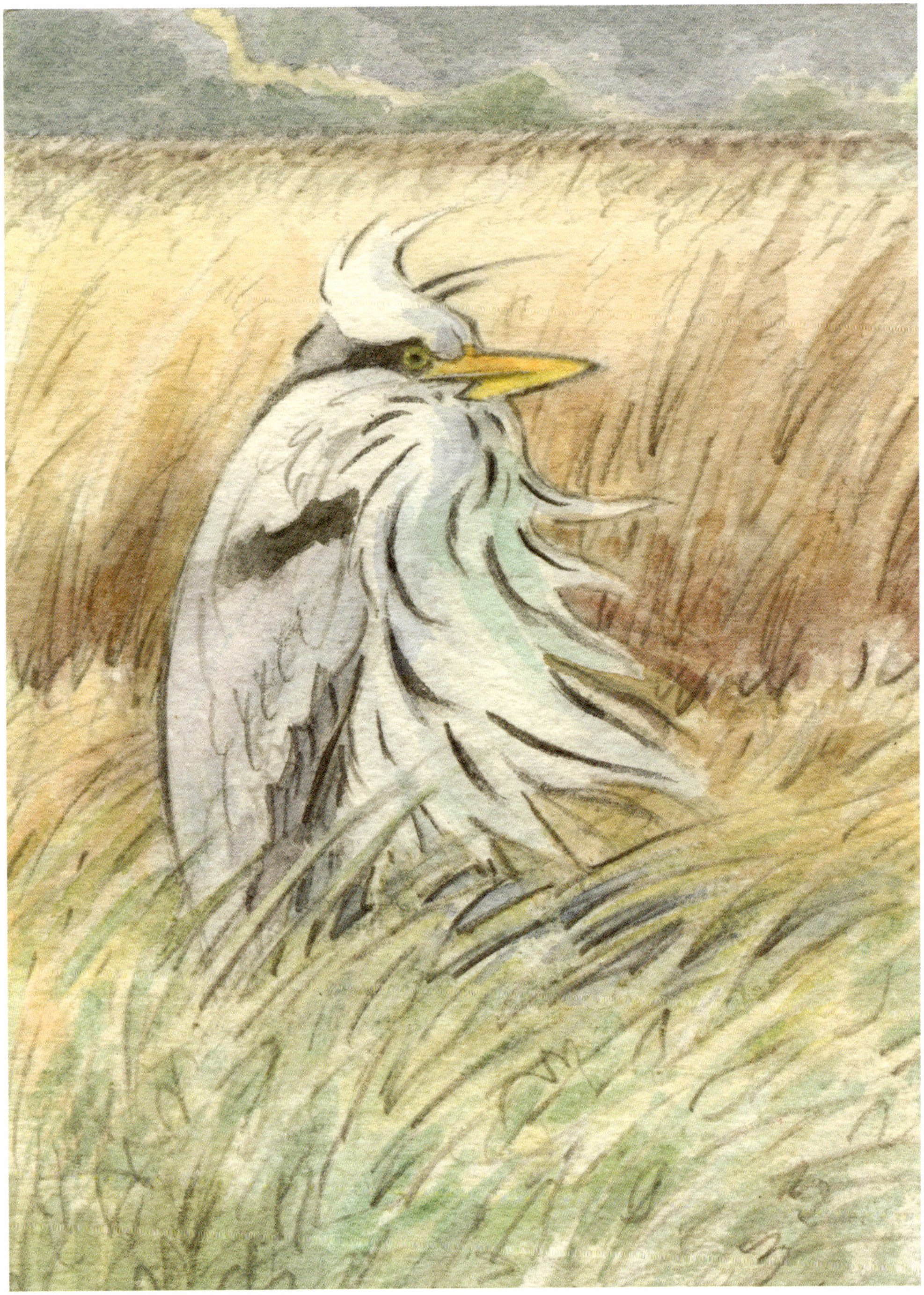

# Peter Partington

*Heron,* pencil and watercolour

I saw this Heron at Minsmere, hunkering down against the east wind from the North Sea. Its long plumes, the reeds and grasses in the foreground flowing in the breeze provided an unusual aspect to the normally angular and elegant bird.

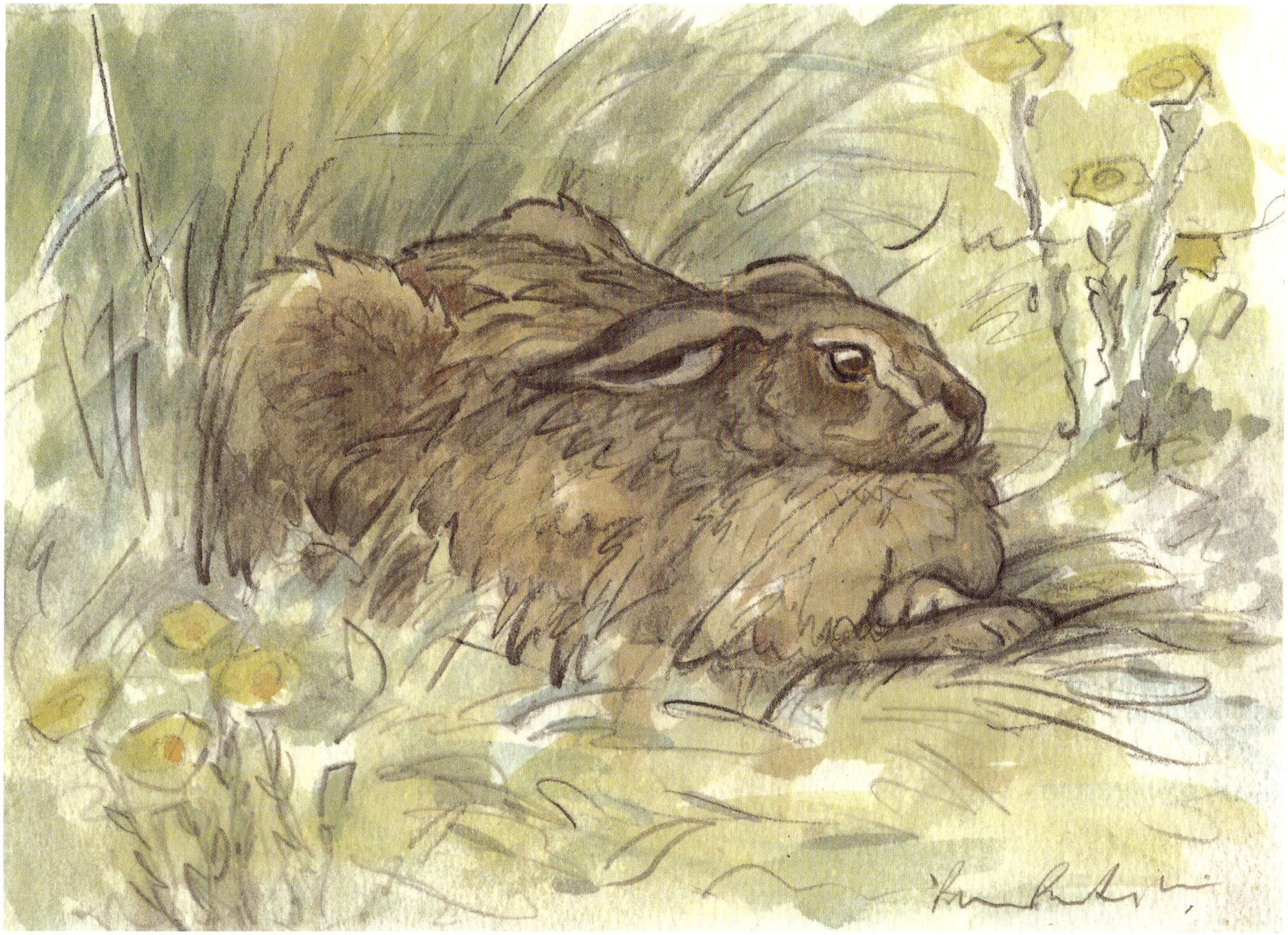

*Hare,* pencil and watercolour

I saw this hare recently at the mere behind Monks House on the Northumberland coast where Dr. Eric Ennion directed his field study centre for many years. It paused for a while in the grasses out of the gale, until it was joined by another and then galloped off. I stayed at the centre when young; I was too shy to mention to Dr. Ennion my interest in art and how much I admired his work.

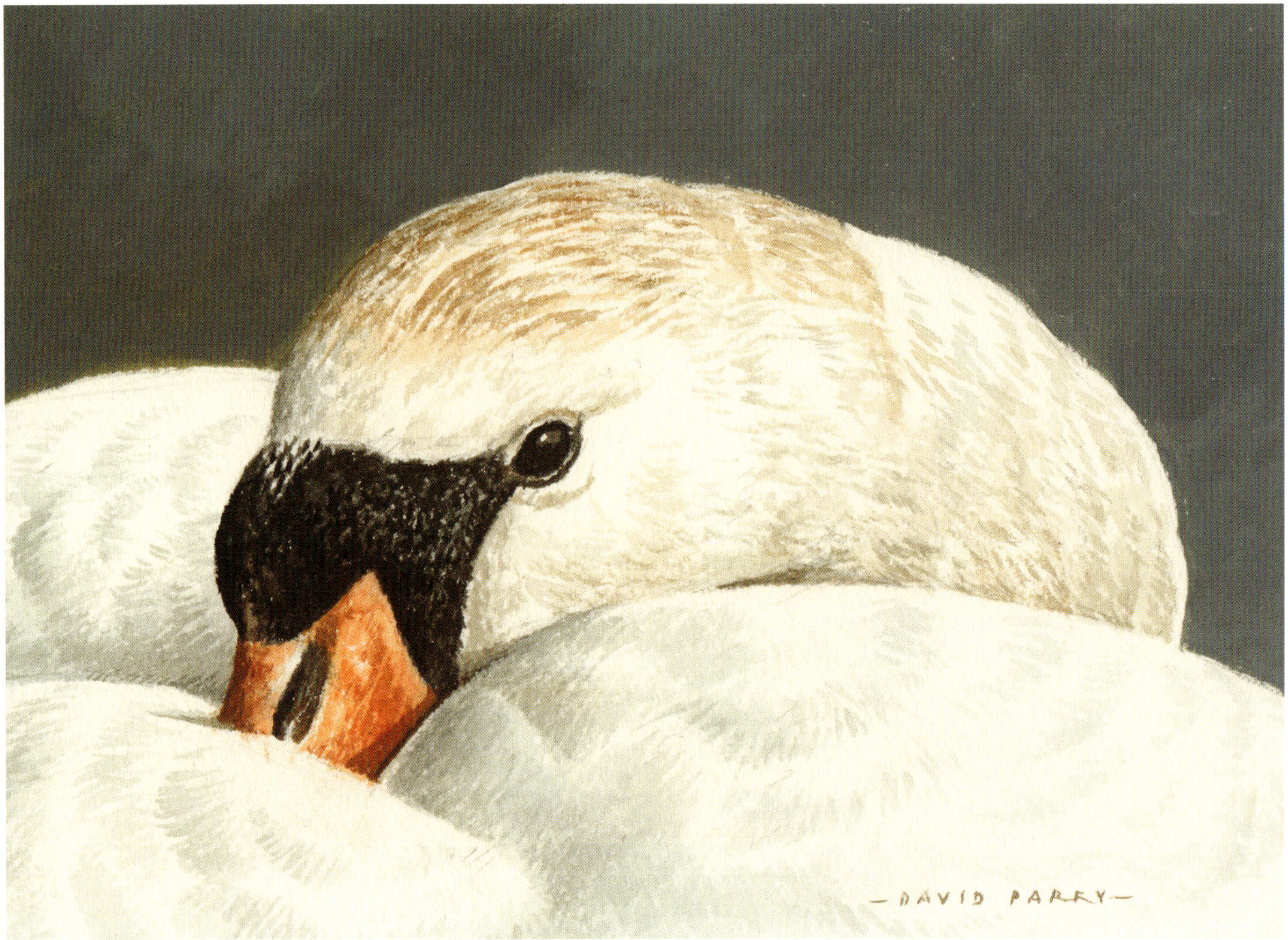


# David Parry

*Mute Swan,* watercolour and gouache on board

This cob Mute Swan is from studies made at the Swannery at Abbotsbury in Dorset. Anyone with a love of swans should visit and be surrounded by hundreds of them in all stages of life.

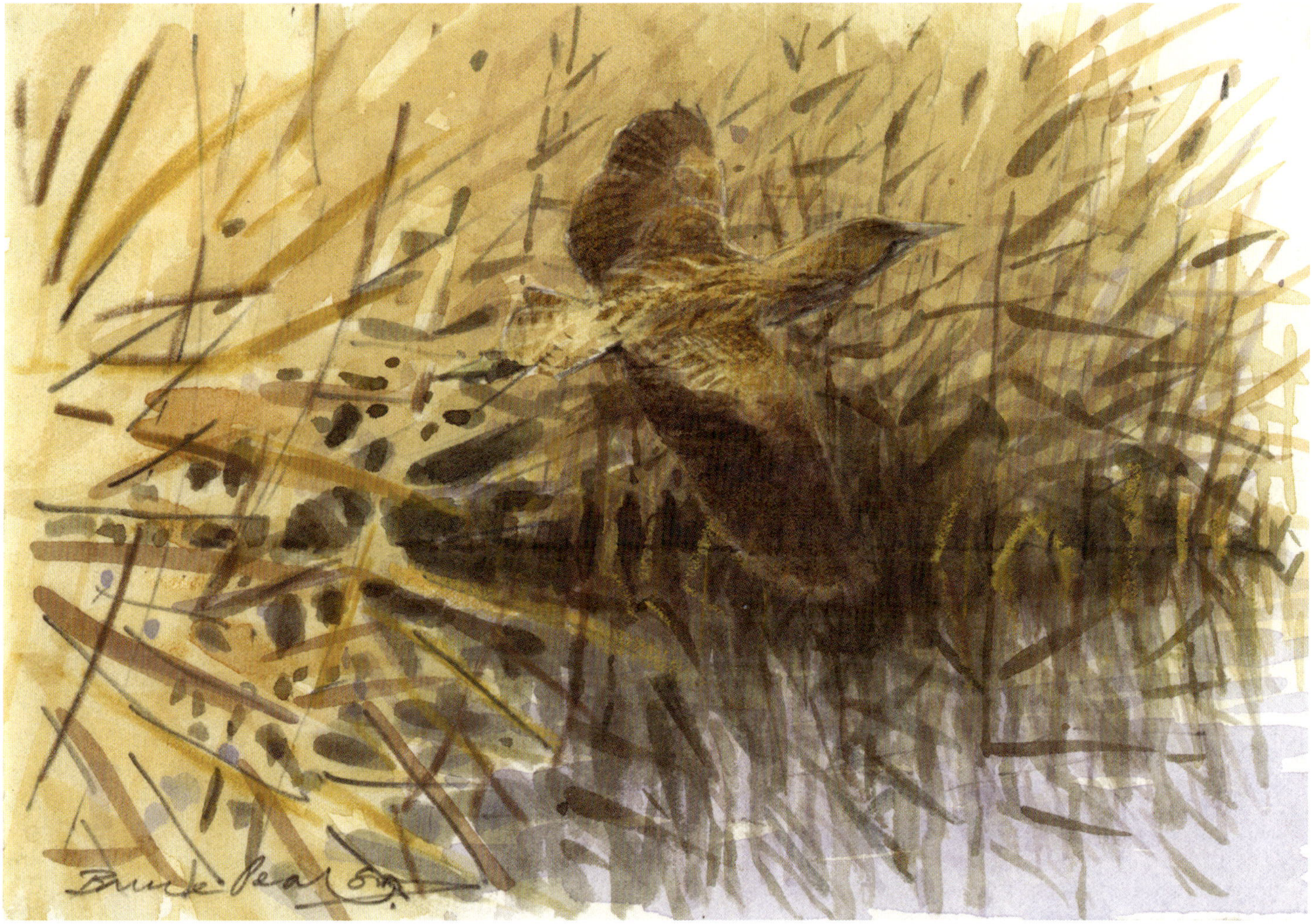

# Bruce Pearson

*Bittern,* watercolour

In flight Bitterns have an almost reptilian look - and gliding low over the reeds about to drop down and vanish in a moment, that sense is heightened (to my eye, at least).

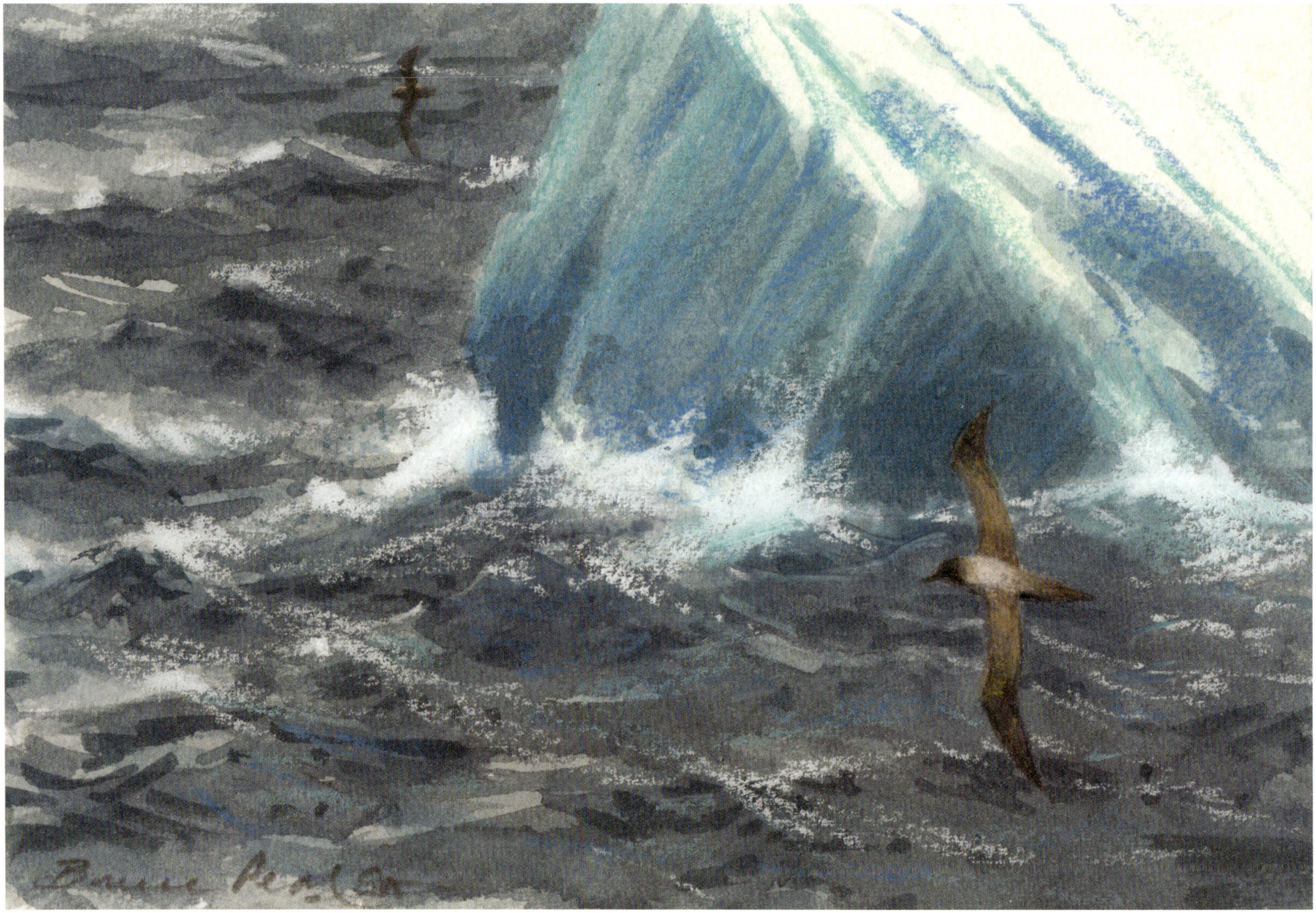

*Light-mantled Albatross,* mixed media on paper

# Bruce Pearson

Piercing turquoise blues and deep indigo dominate the icy colours of the Southern Ocean, its stormy seascape flecked with powdery blues, greys and charcoal blacks, and the chequerboard patterns of passing seabirds flashing brilliant white as they sheer and turn above the waves. The unmistakeable warm brown tones and sharply pointed form of Light-mantled albatross, is always particularly striking.

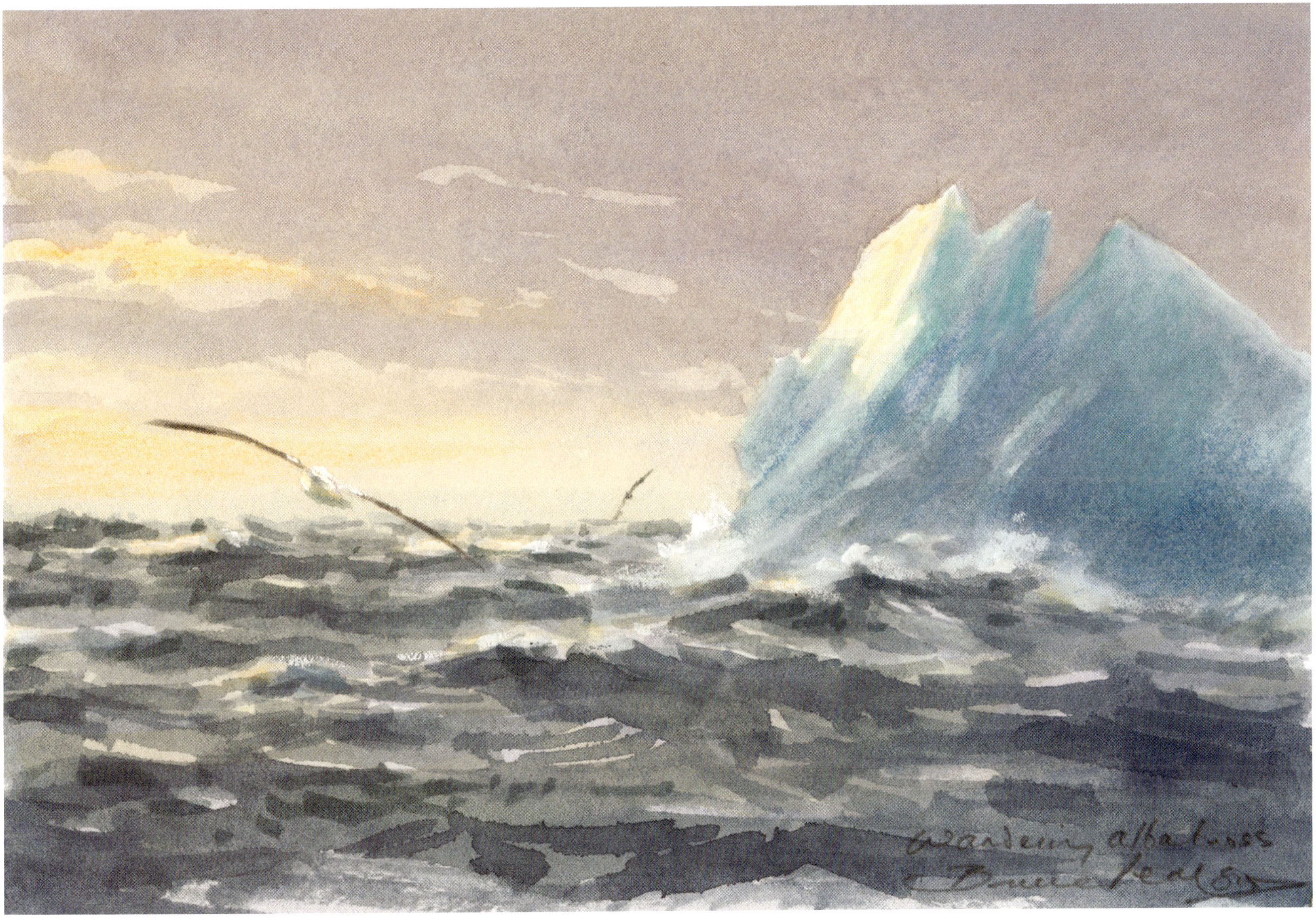


*Wandering Albatross*, mixed media on paper

With huge wings slightly drooped, Wandering Albatrosses sweep downwind across rolling wave fronts gaining speed then arcing high into the wind before dropping down the following wave. In this way they are able to cover huge distances with barely a flap of their wings. Their effortless pattern of flight gives an impression of slow-motion and implies their relative enormity.

# Antonia Phillips

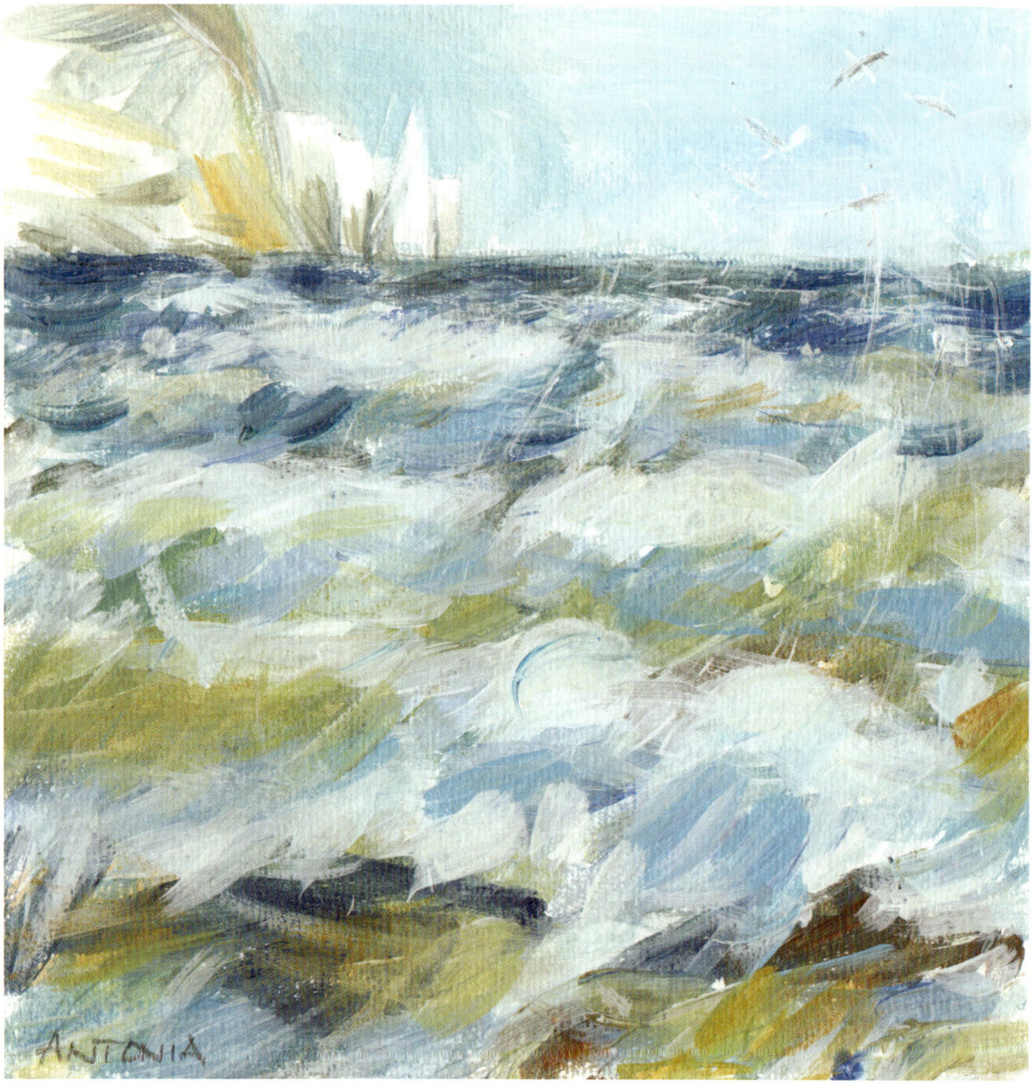

*January 17th, Swanage,* acrylic on paper

The view from my studio in Swanage with chilly winds and colourful seas. Seagulls wheel and demonstrate their part in the landscape.

*Snaefelsjøkull, Iceland,* acrylic on paper
*right*
This image represents my other favourite place to sketch. From a bus out of Reykjavik, this glacier was inspirational in the novel *Journey to the Centre of the Earth*. Fulmars fly with stiff wing over the lava.

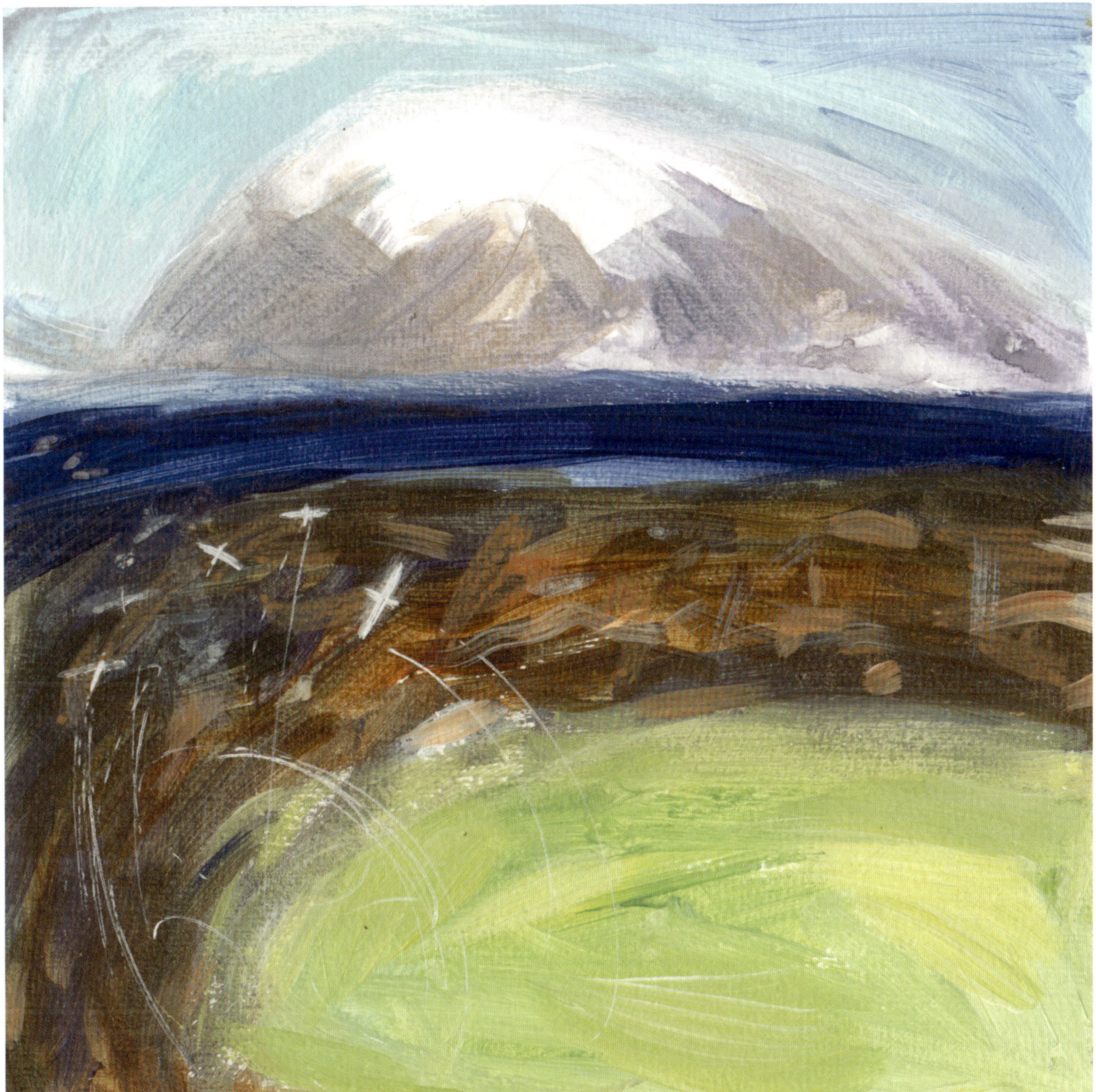
ANTONIA

# Nik Pollard

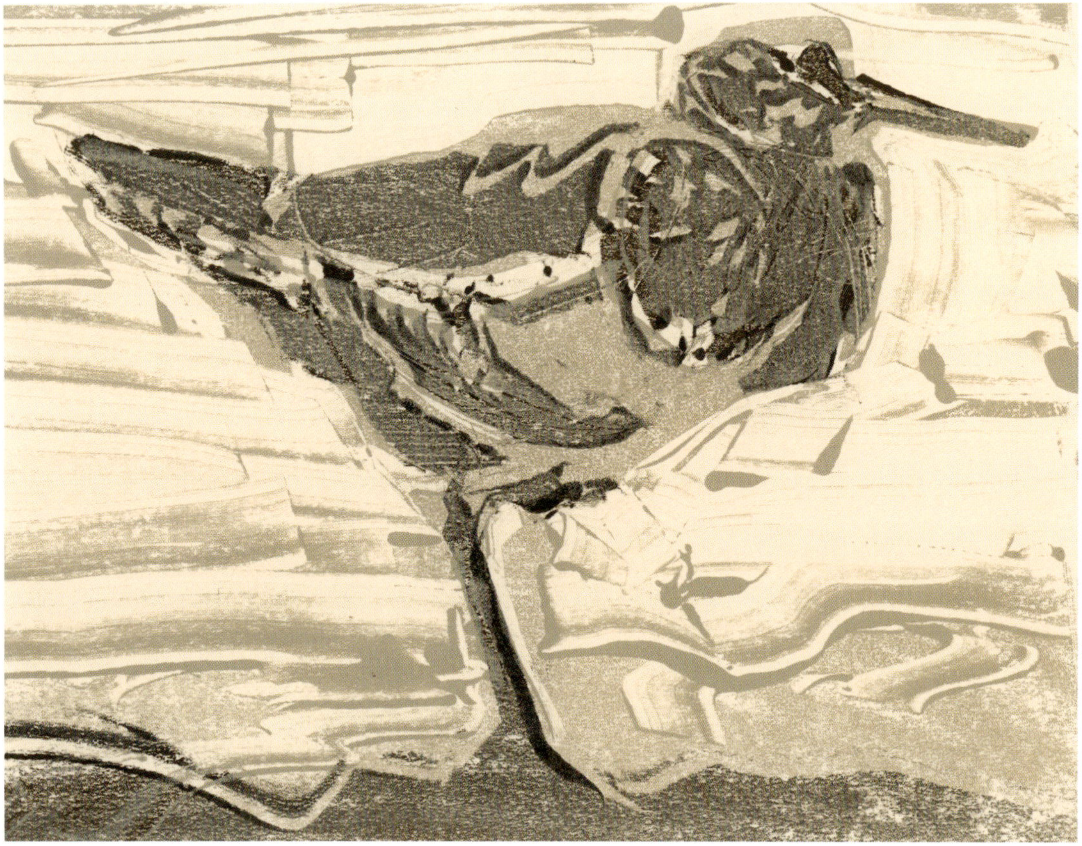

*Redshank,* monotype

Taken from my studio workbook, these images were made in preparation for a more complex composition. It is from a series of paintings and prints based on the Severn Estuary.

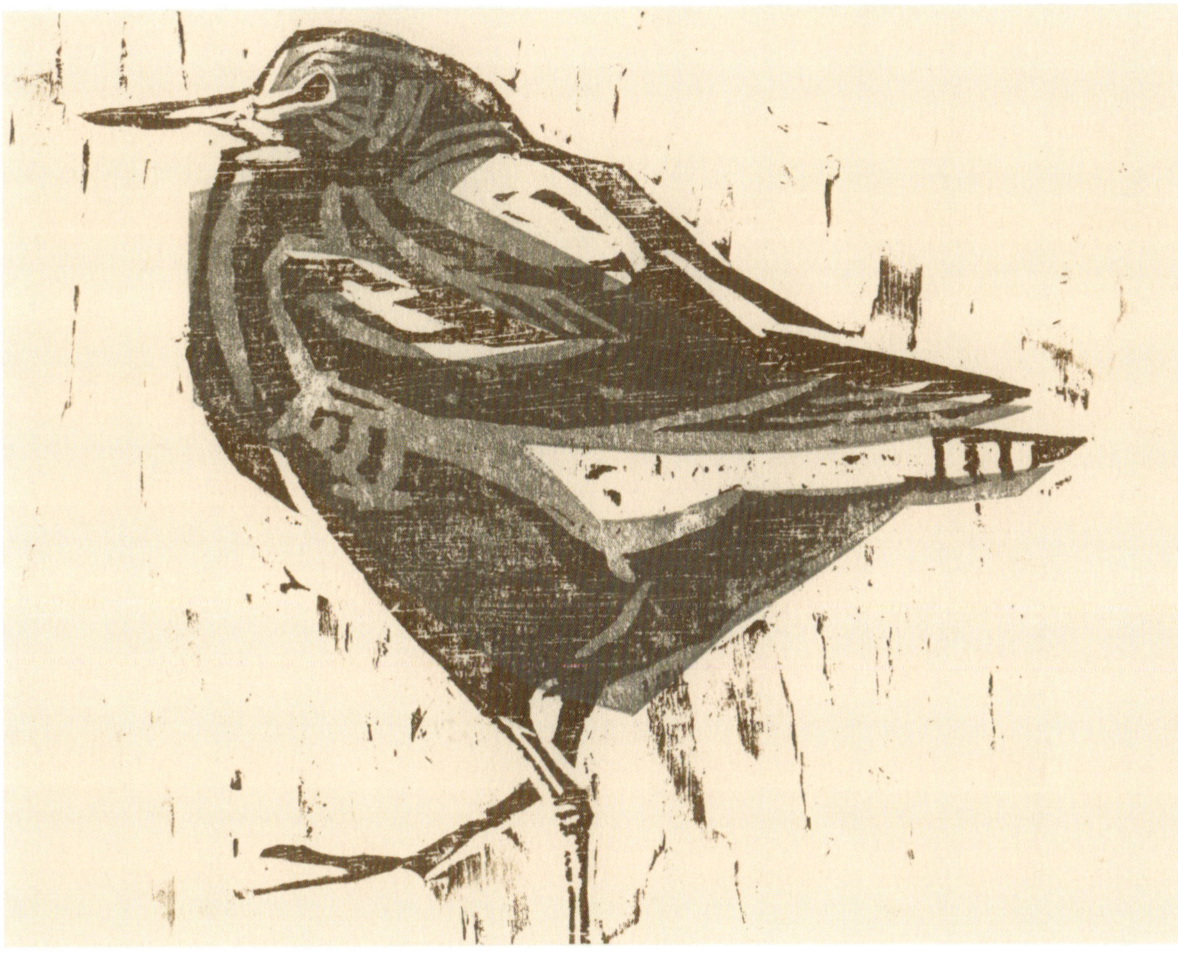

*Redshank*,
relief print, wood card

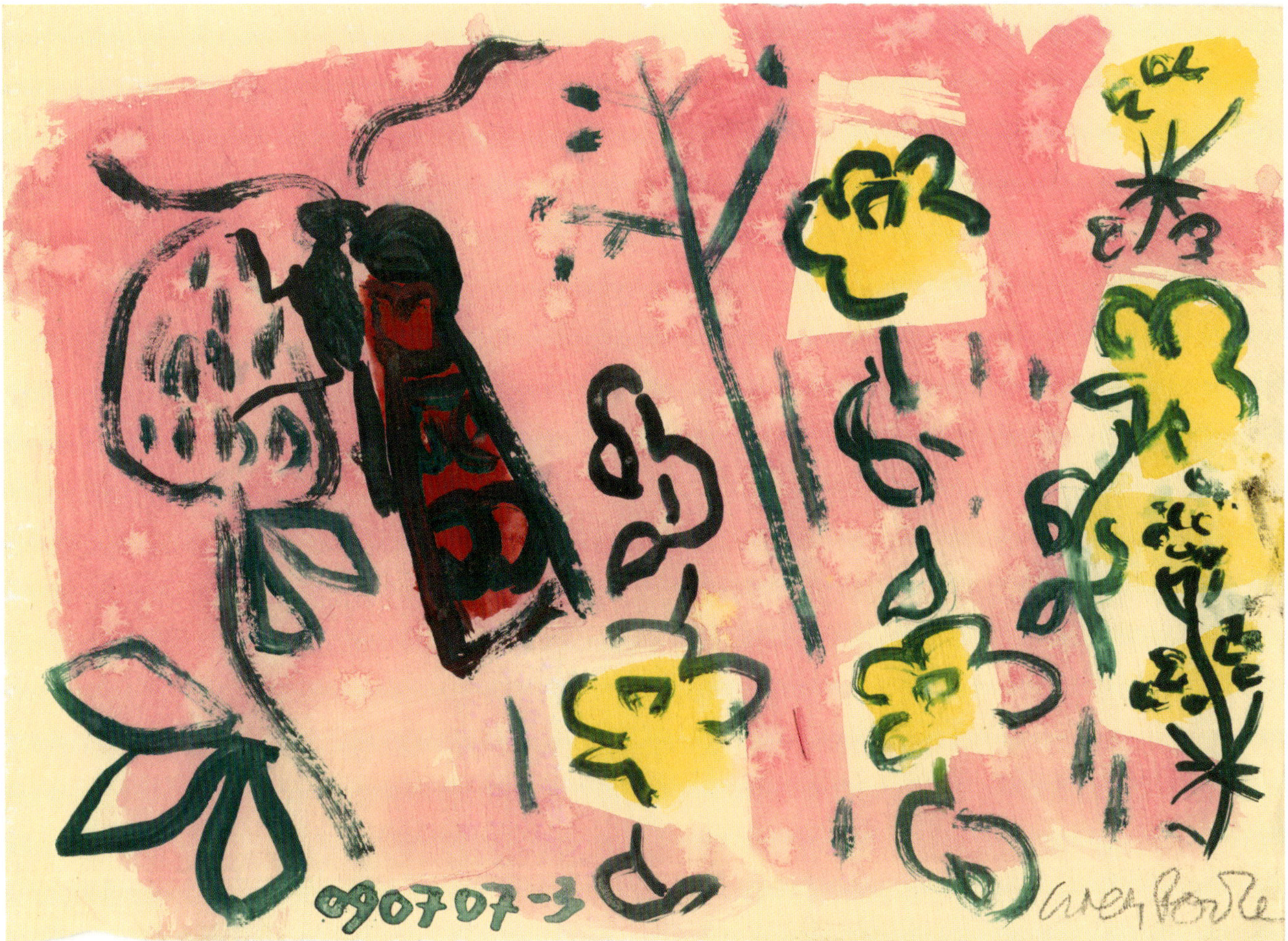


# Greg Poole

*Burnet and Yellow Flowers*, gouache on paper

There was a profuse flowering of Rock Roses on the Mendip hillsides in 2007. I made this rain-pocked gouache sketch of a Burnet moth in early July.

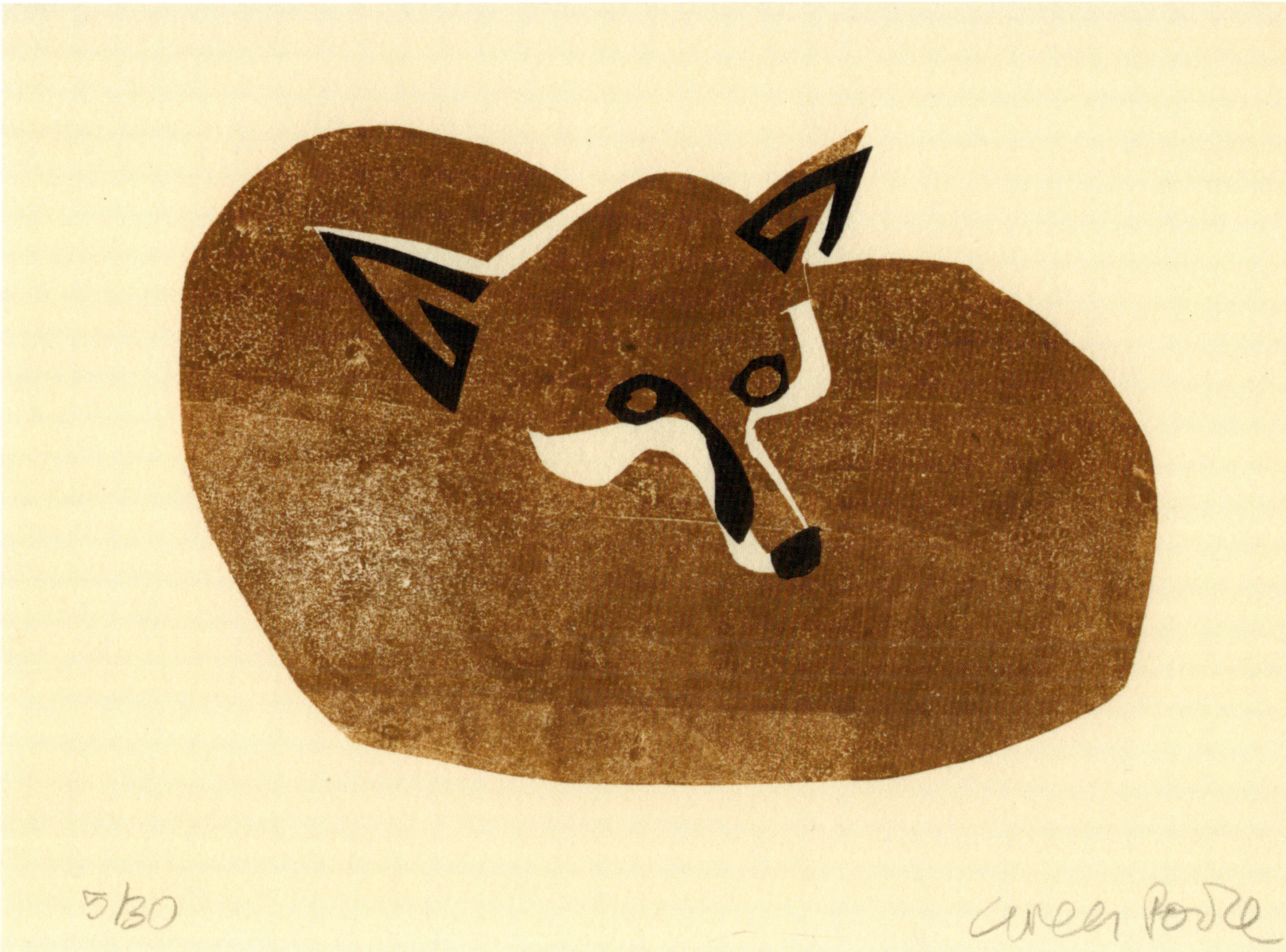


*Fox*, screen print

My telescope was filled with a sleeping Fox in prime condition. Unwilling to move it twitched ears and looked suspiciously in my direction, but carried on dozing. Something special to share time with this animal laid out asleep on the woodland floor…quite different to seeing a Fox on the allotments at home.

# John Reaney

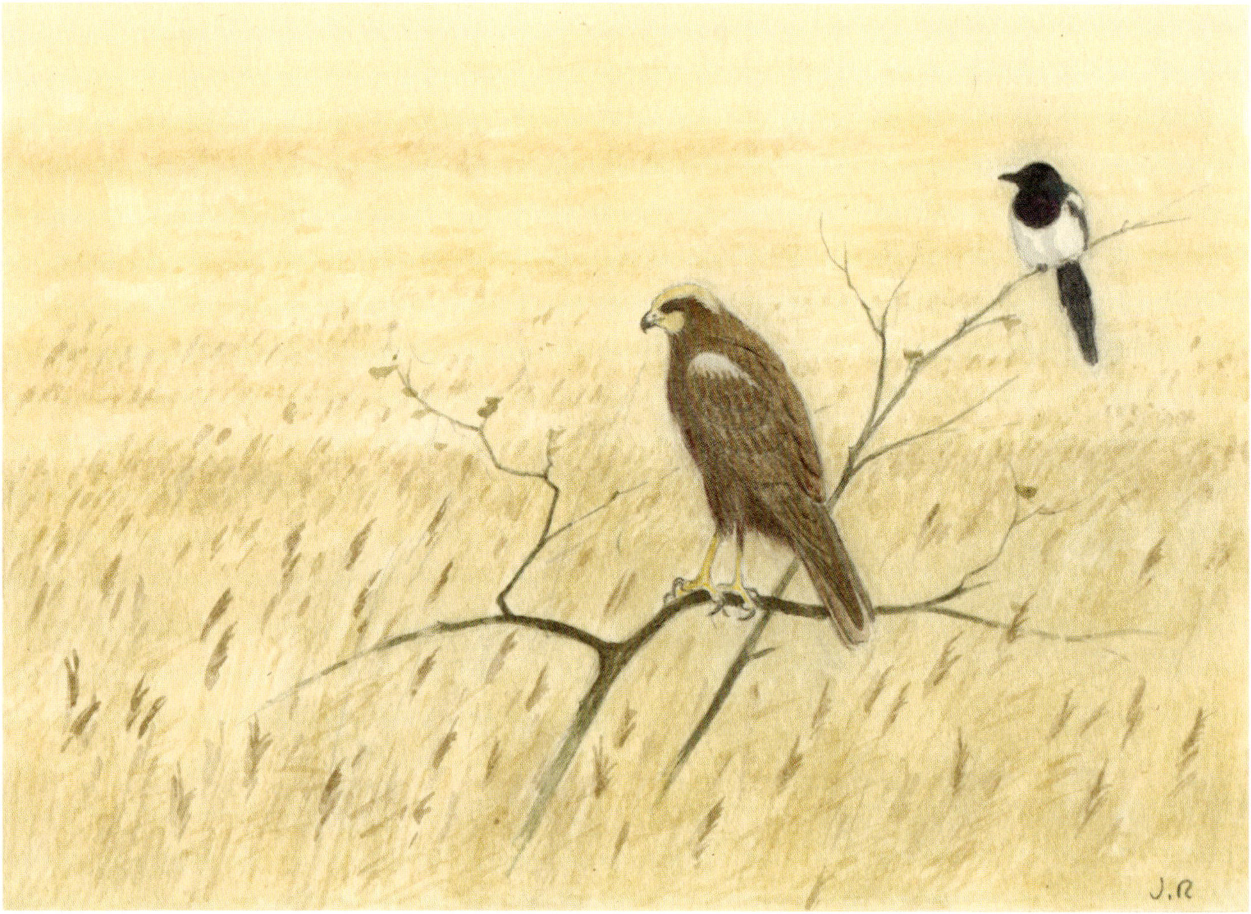


*Marsh Harrier with Magpie*, watercolour

Pity the poor harrier! Wherever it goes there will always be a pest like this Magpie, which would just not leave this harrier alone. Wherever she went the Magpie followed, chattering. Eventually she tired of its pestering and turned on it. It fled protesting, no doubt looking for a softer touch to bother.

# Alastair Proud

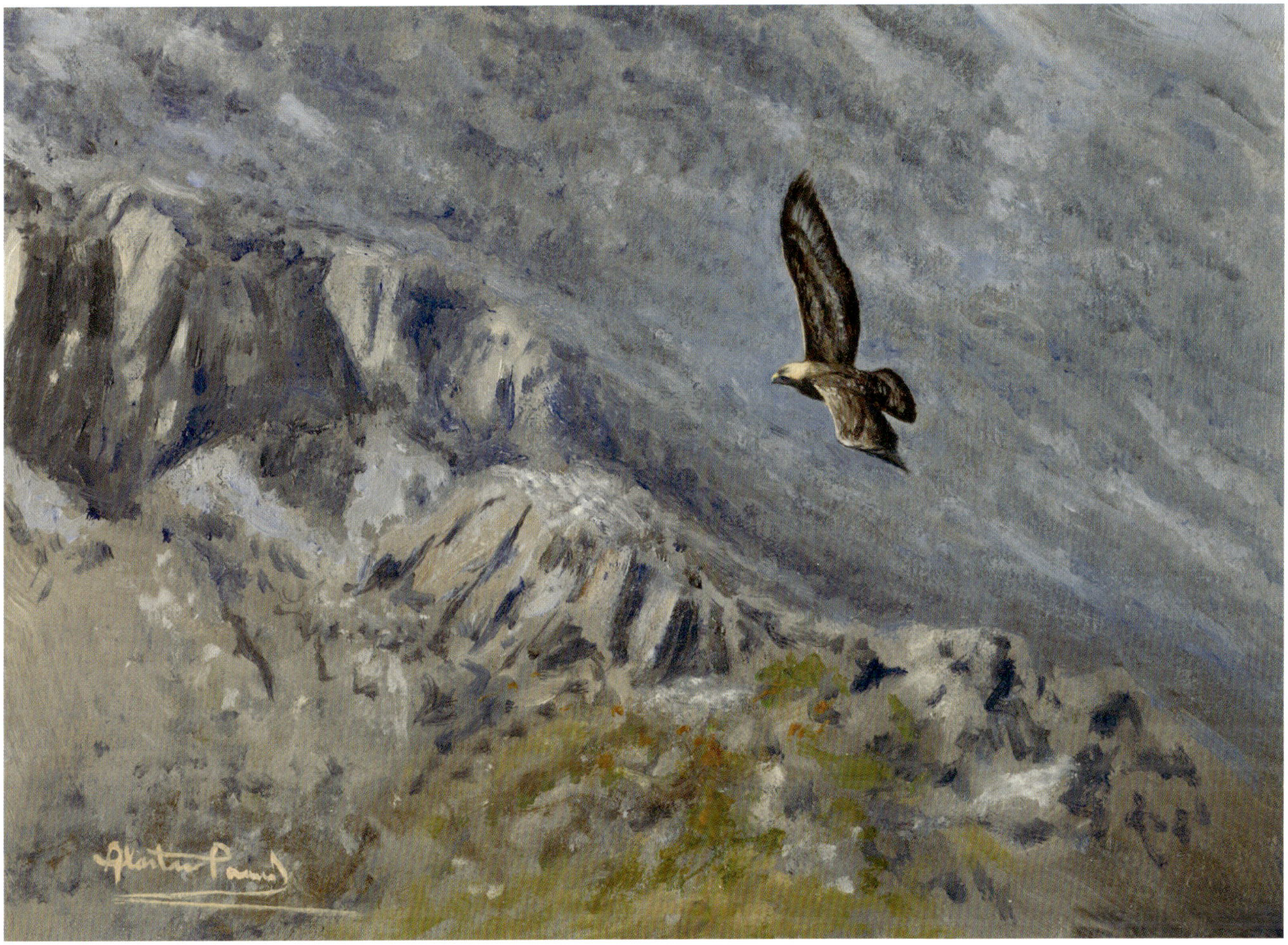

*Golden Eagle*, oil on board

To start with you're in a special place; physically challenging, spiritually uplifting and scenically superb. I am talking of Ptarmigan grounds in the Scottish Highlands. Although the eagle will not linger after making its appearance, its presence will remain with you. This, my first close encounter with this magnificent bird is relived with every subsequent sighting.

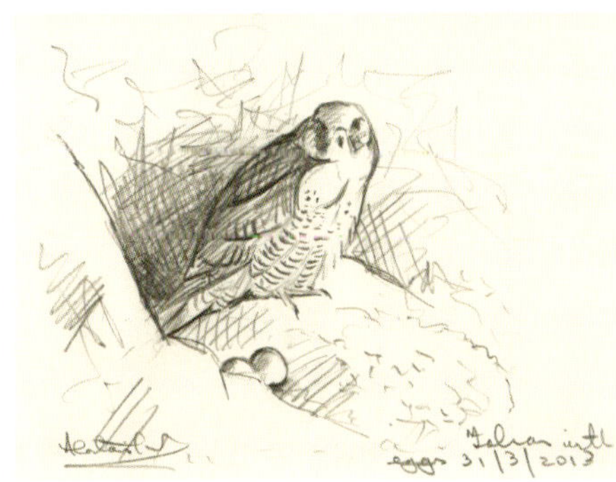

*Peregrine with Eggs*, pencil

# Darren Rees

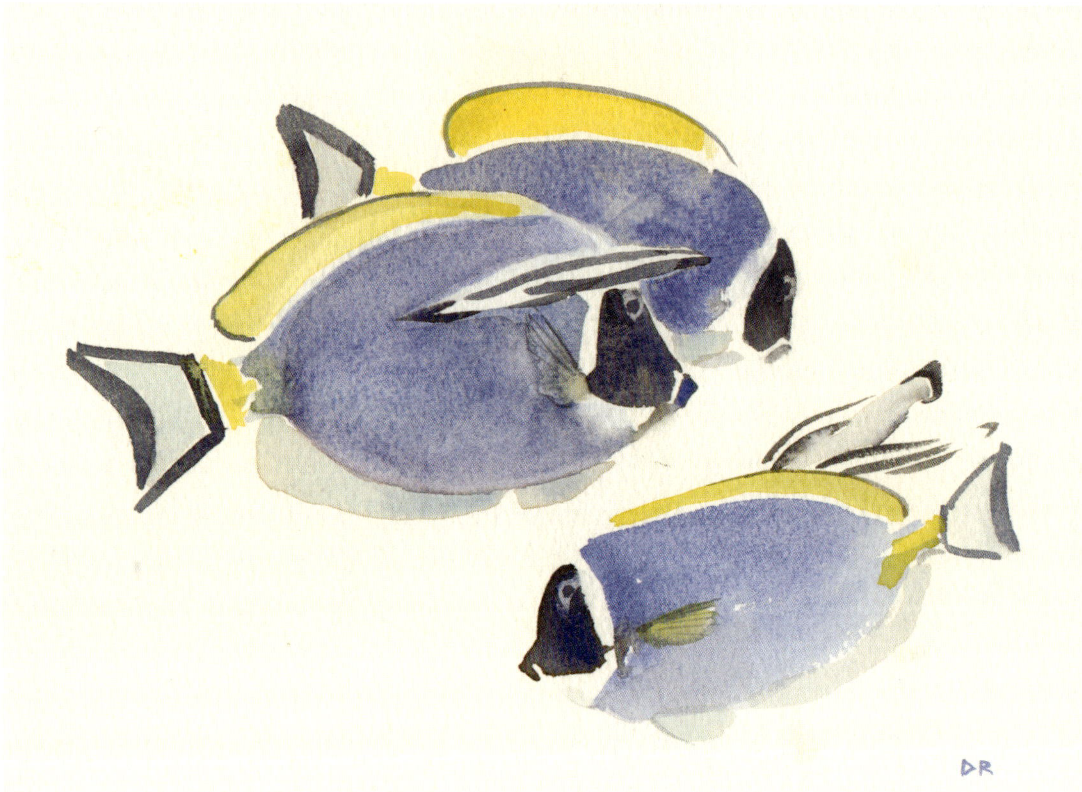

*Powder-blue Surgeonfish*, watercolour

Fresh impressions on board the boat Ari Queen after one of the many magical snorkeling sessions in the Maldives, March 2011. A very special trip to celebrate my 50th birthday.

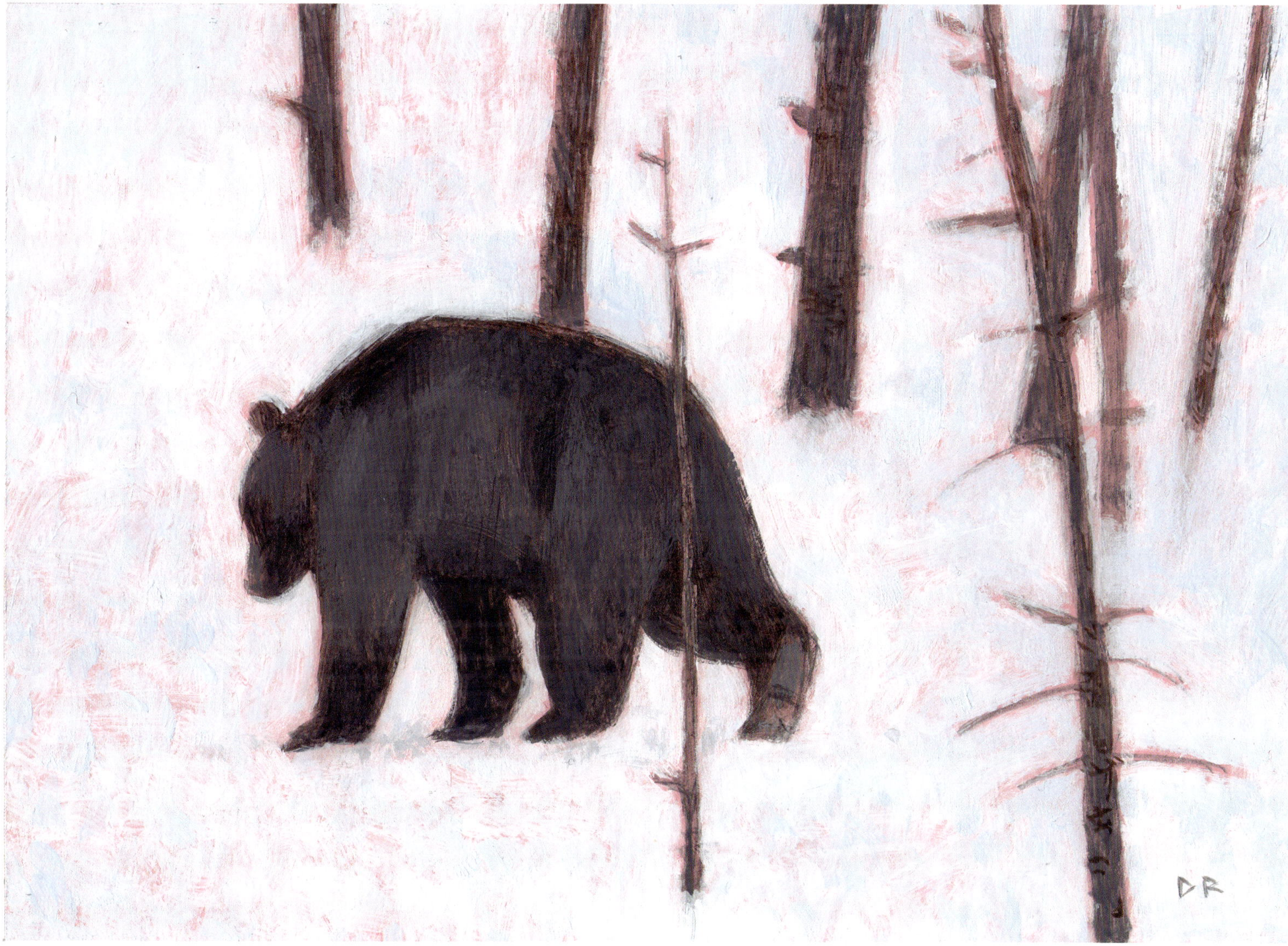


*Black and White*, acrylic on board

The locals in Yellowstone often remind me that in their part of the world there are three seasons; July, August and winter. You really can experience snow at any time of the year and it brings an elegant simplification to the landscape. When bears are out and about there are endless possibilities for compositions – as long as I don't run out of white paint.

# Andrea Rich

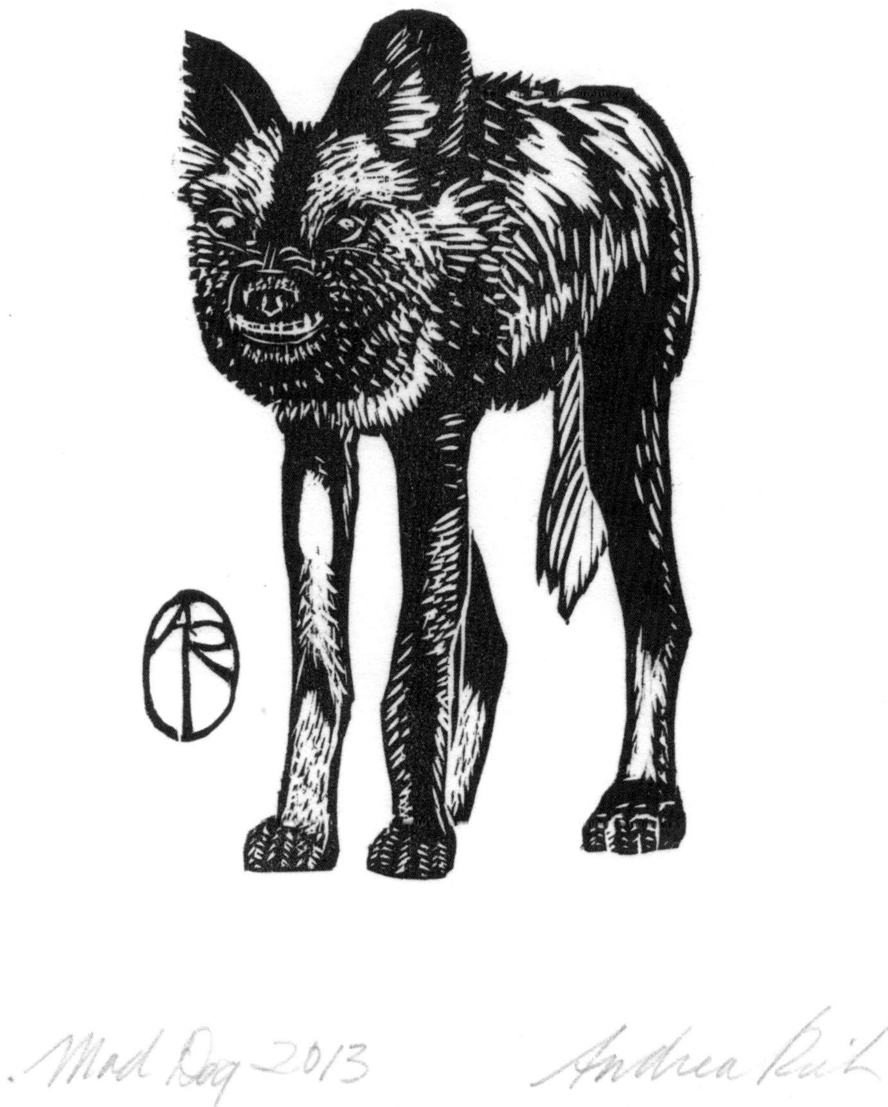

*Mad Dog*, woodcut

I did this print of a Wild Dog as a demonstration of print making I gave at the Leigh Yawkey Woodson Art Museum, Wisconsin. My husband was particularly fond of it and called it Mad Dog.

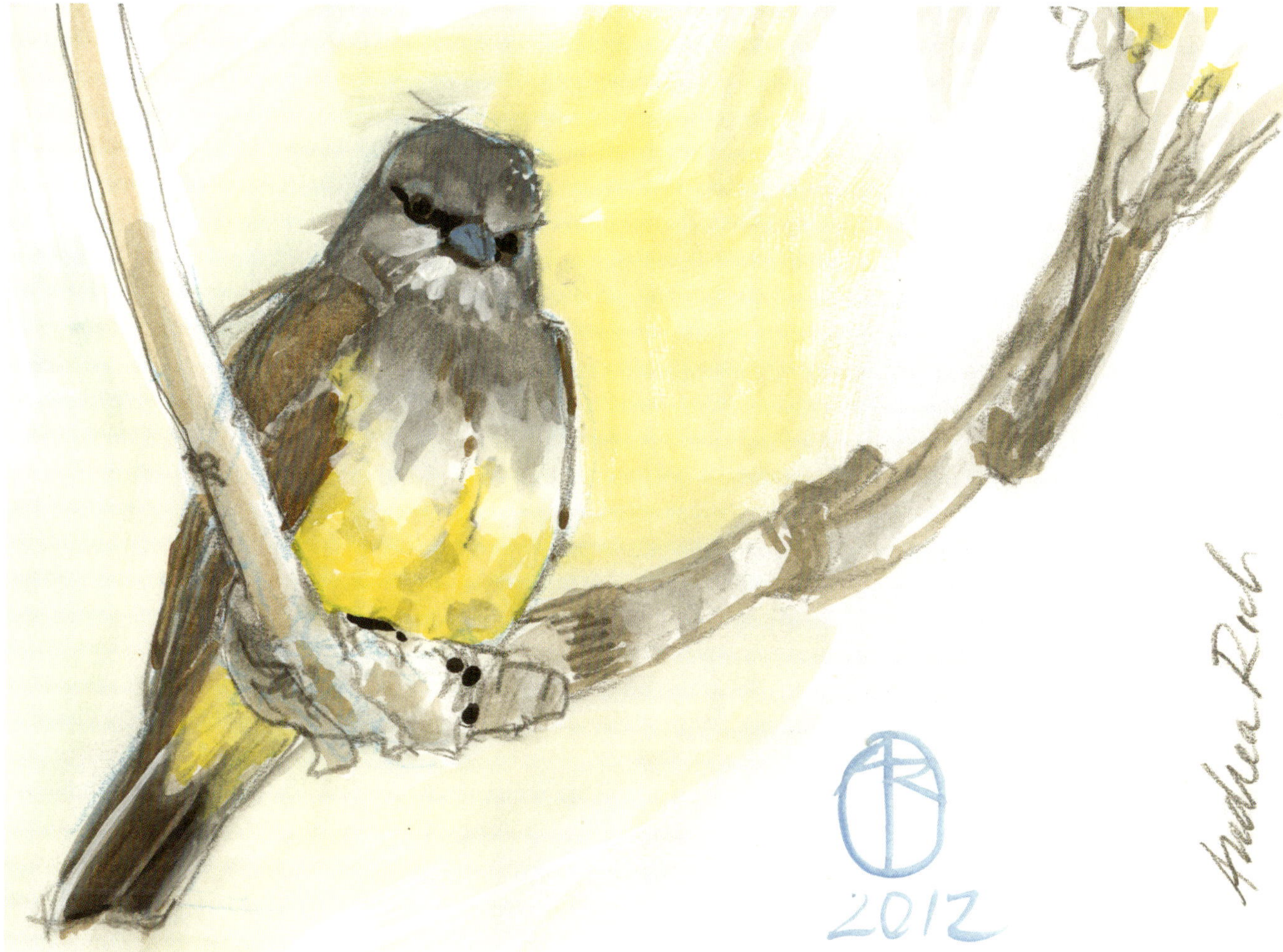


*Kingbird,* watcrcolour

Sometimes it's the attitude that attracts the eye. That was the case with this Kingbird I spotted in central California. The blue bill is just artistic license.

# Dafila Scott

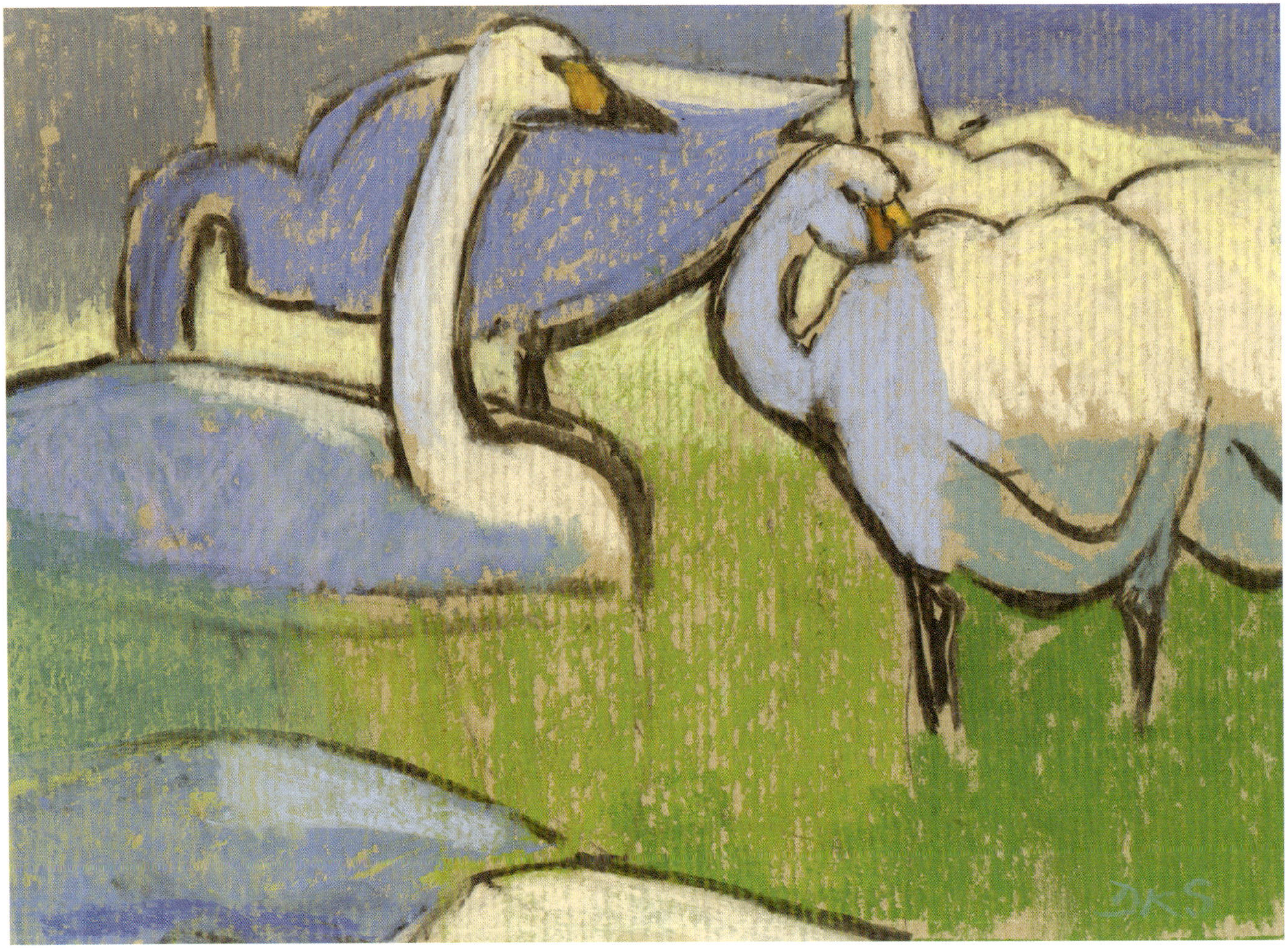

*Bewick's Swans on the Fen*, pastel

On a late winter afternoon, when the sun was low, I saw these Bewick's Swans, some feeding, some resting on the fen near Welney.

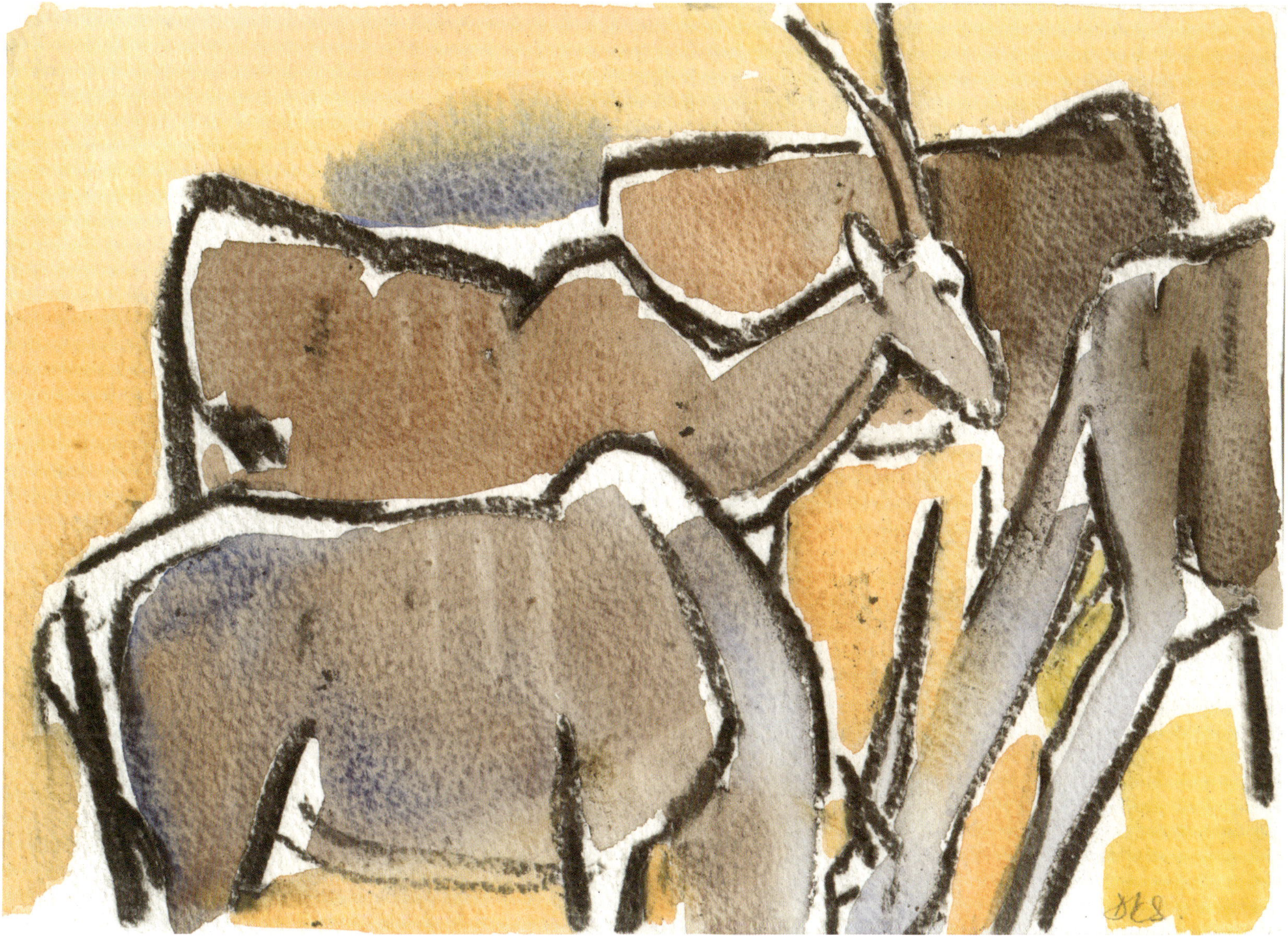

*Eland in the Kalahari,* charcoal and watercolour

These animals were coming to the waterhole to drink. One female has distinctive asymmetric horns. The rains had not begun at this point and everything was very dry and the animals thin.

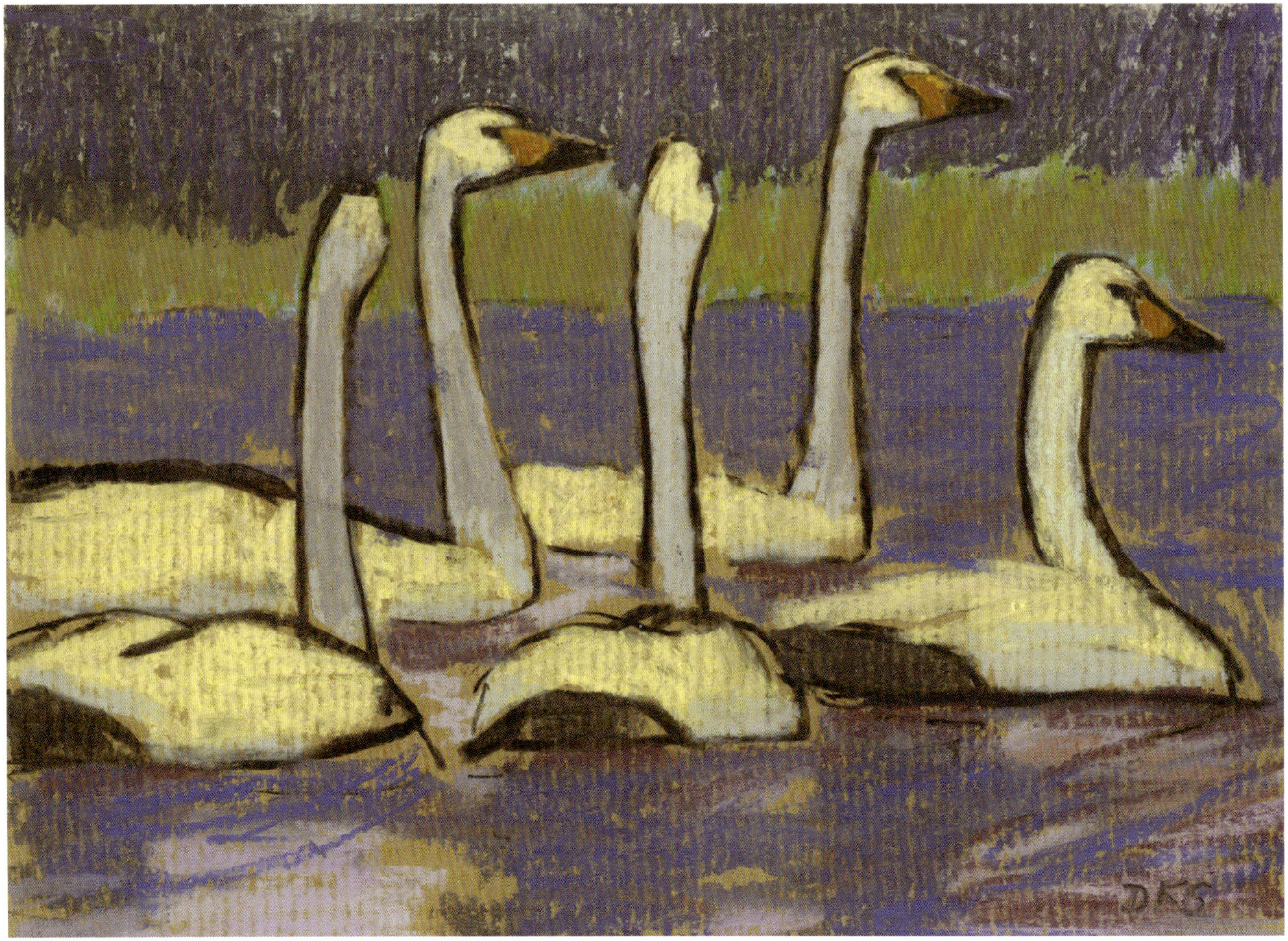

*Bewick's Swans About to Take Off*, charcoal

# Dafila Scott

These birds were bobbing their heads, calling and flattening their bodies in anticipation of take-off. Sometimes they take a long time doing this before they fly. On this occasion it took about fifteen minutes.

# Jane Smith

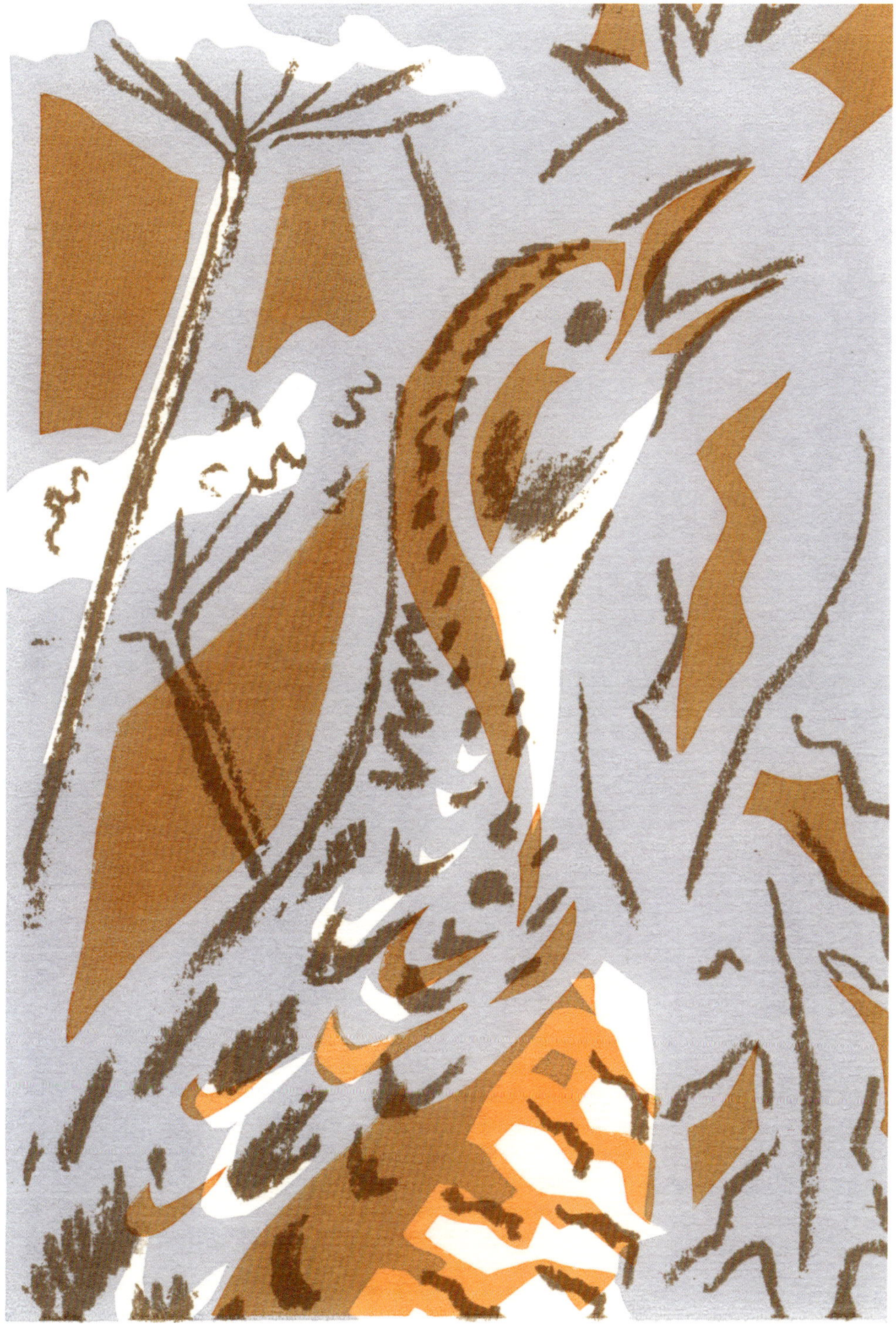

*Calling Corncrake*, screen print

Sitting at the field corner on Oronsay, I could hear the Corncrakes rasping nearby. I started by sketching the thick vegetation: Cow Parsley, nettles and Hogweed. A multistorey jungle. I often find when I'm drawing outdoors that I become part of the landscape. That's when I get my best sightings. This time a brief glimpse of a calling male.

# Chris Rose

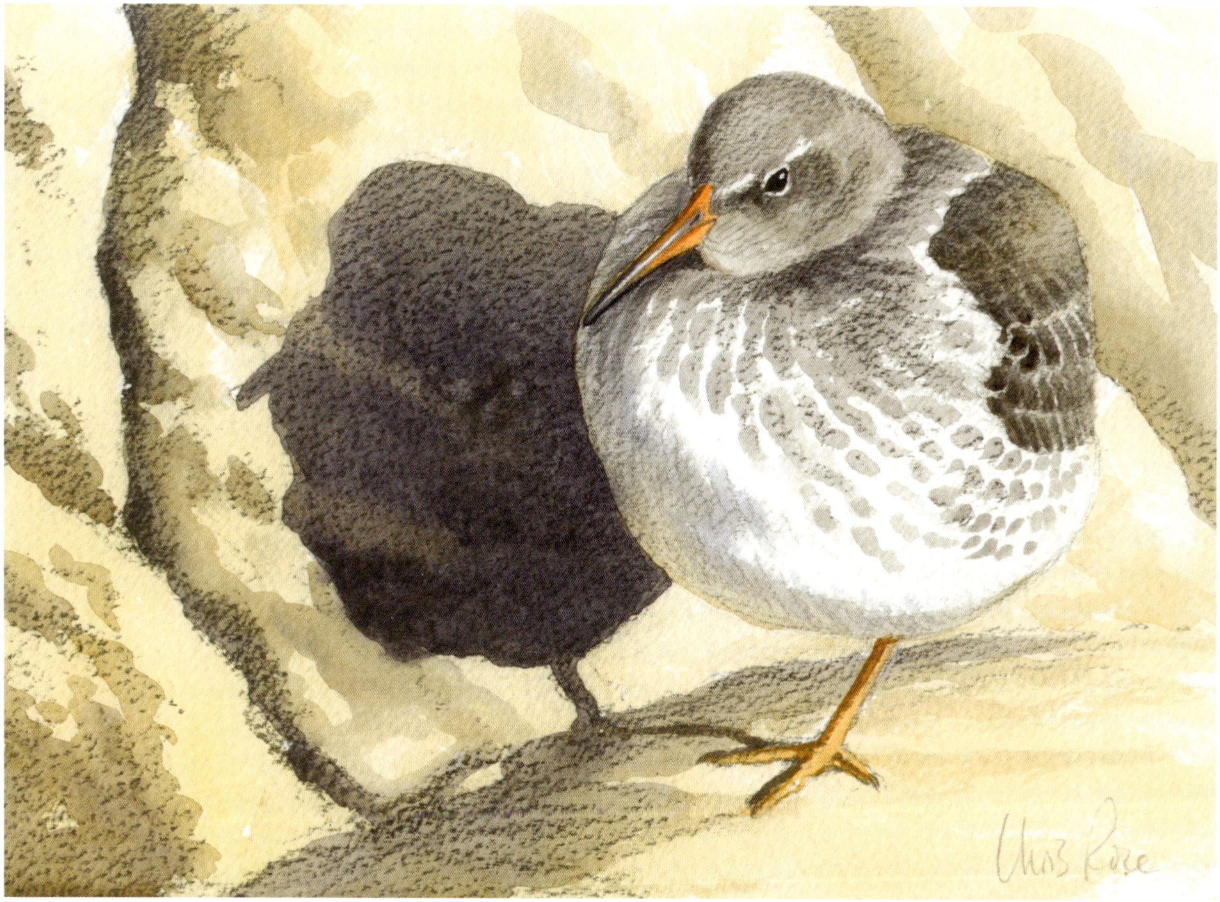


*Purple Sandpiper,* mixed media on paper

This bird was originally sketched at a high-tide roost of Purple Sandpipers on a rocky outcrop at Bamburgh, on the Northumbrian coast. In the cold weather they assume such wonderful, tennis-ball shapes that they are irresistible.

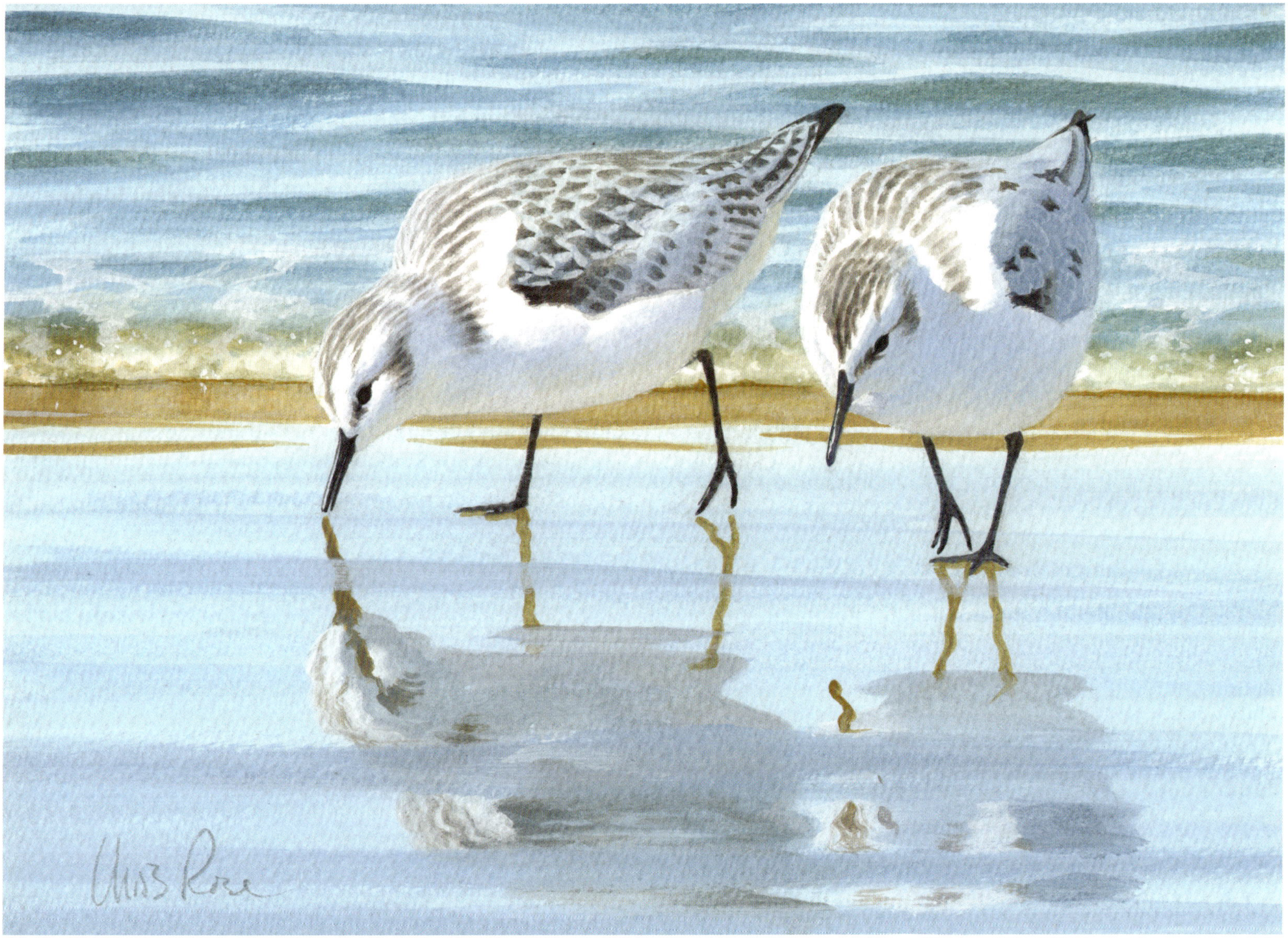

*Sanderlings,* mixed media on paper

These Sanderlings were sketched on the sands at Lindisfarne as they scurried in front of the incoming tide. I used this and similar sketches to create a large oil painting called *Beachcombers* of a group of Sanderlings feeding amongst stranded seaweed on the shore.

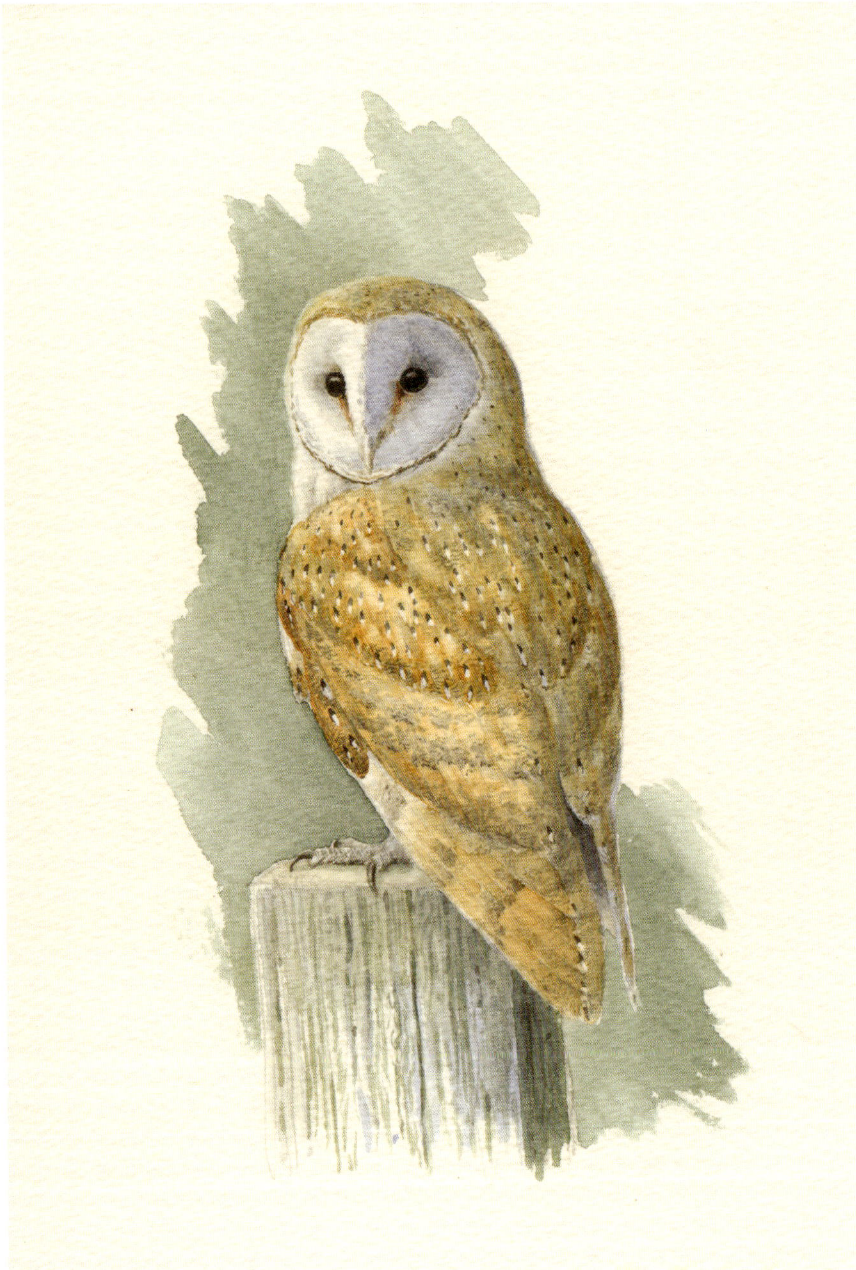

# Andrew Stock

*Barn Owl*, watercolour

I've been watching a pair of Barn Owls for a couple of weeks now (March '13). One cold morning one of the pair continued to hunt in broad daylight, occasionally perching on a fence post alarmingly close to me as I sat huddled in a hedgerow. This is a watercolour of the sketches made.

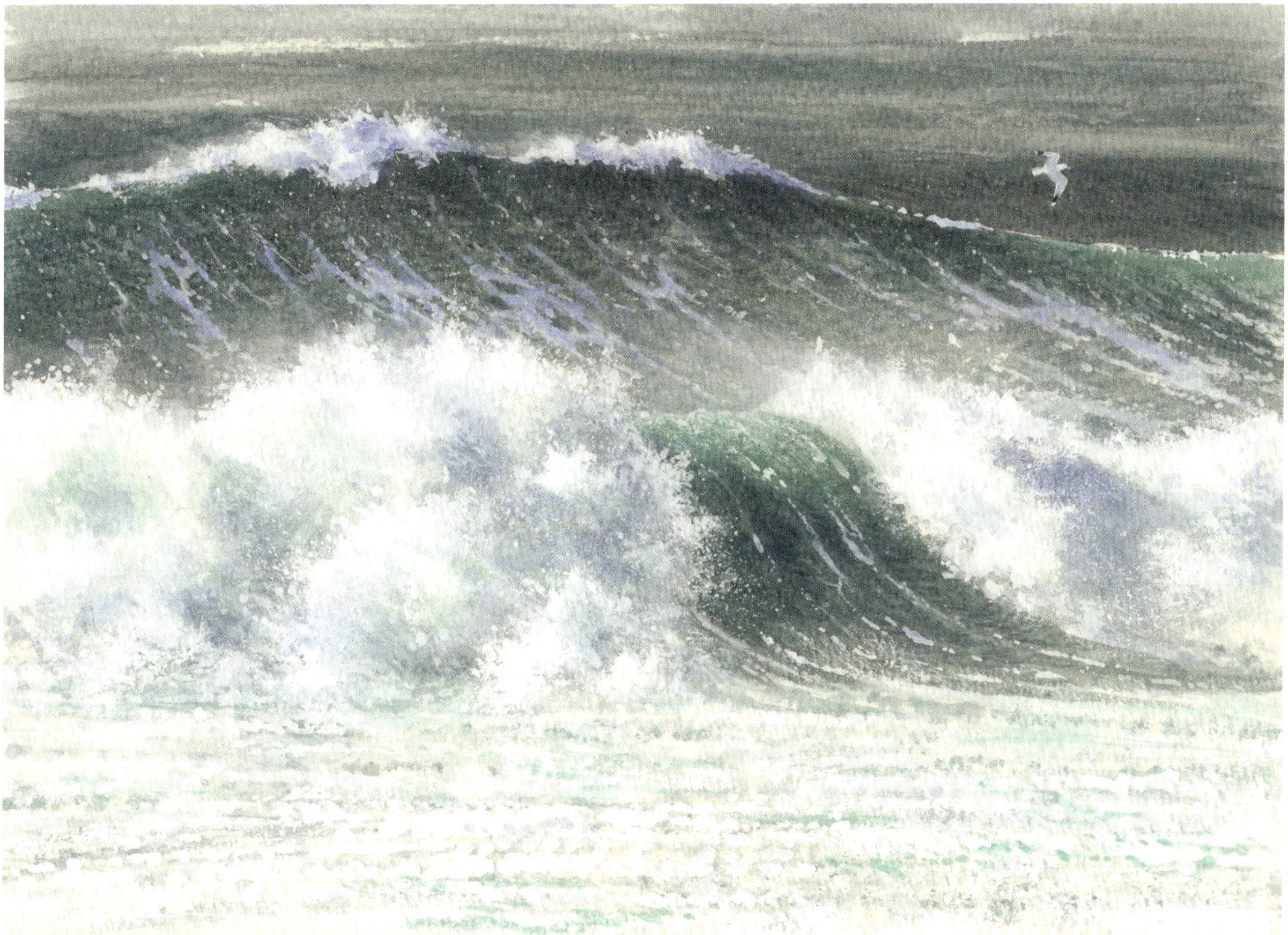

*Ose Point Rollers,* watercolour and gouache

In recent years I have spent a fair bit of time in the Outer Hebrides. Watching the sea from the shore or a boat has become a significant part of these visits and attempting to paint the often spectacular, churning seas, a continuing challenge.

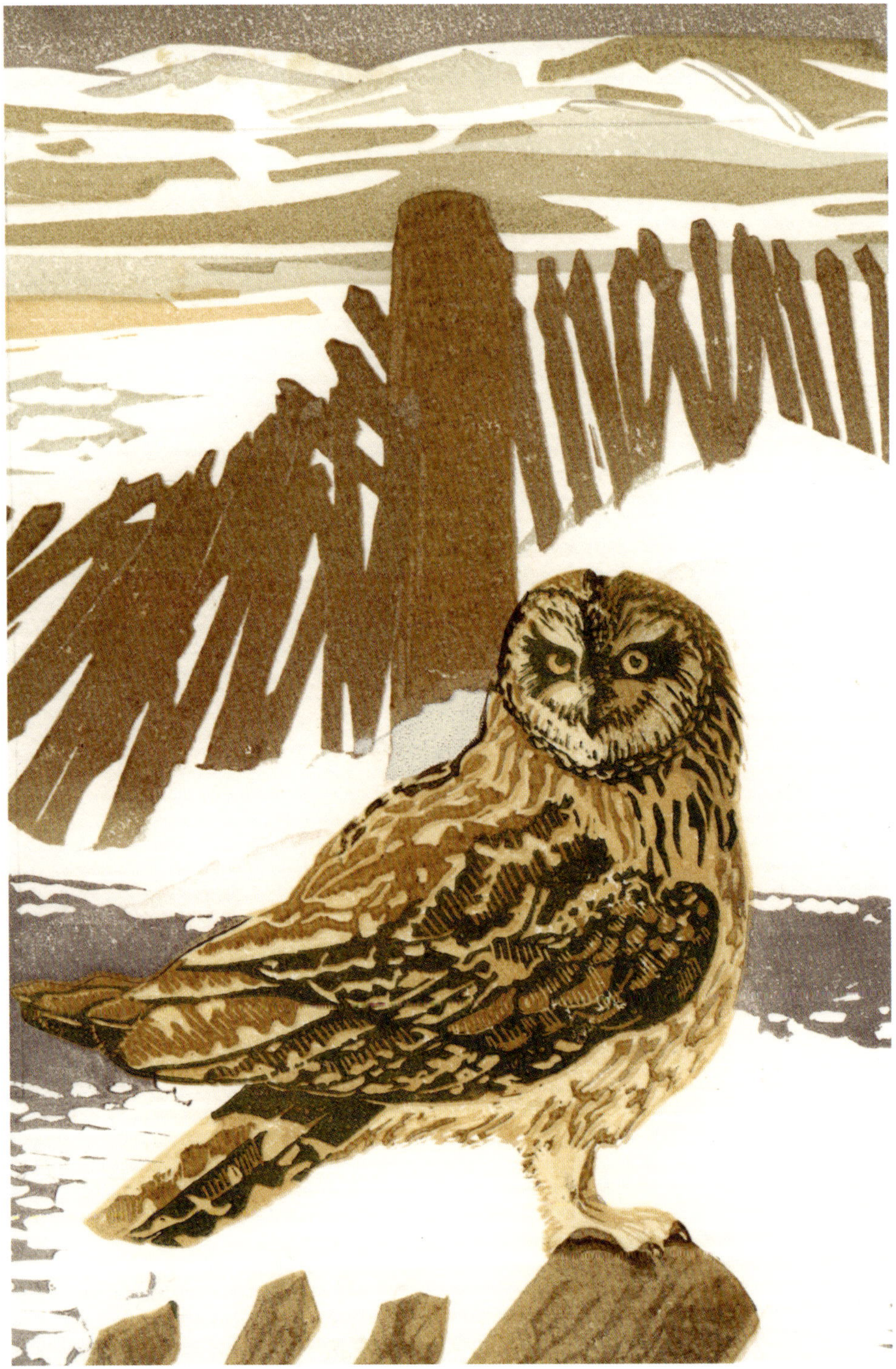

# Thelma Sykes

*The Drifter,* detail, linocut proof

Part of a late-stage proof; the title reminds me of the Short-eared Owl's floating flight and of its vagrant lifestyle, ready to move on when prey is scarce. The staggered fences hold back snowdrifts; man's attempt to keep this high moorland road open. Despite the snow, this is May and the owl is on its territory. I watched it circling in wing-clapping display.

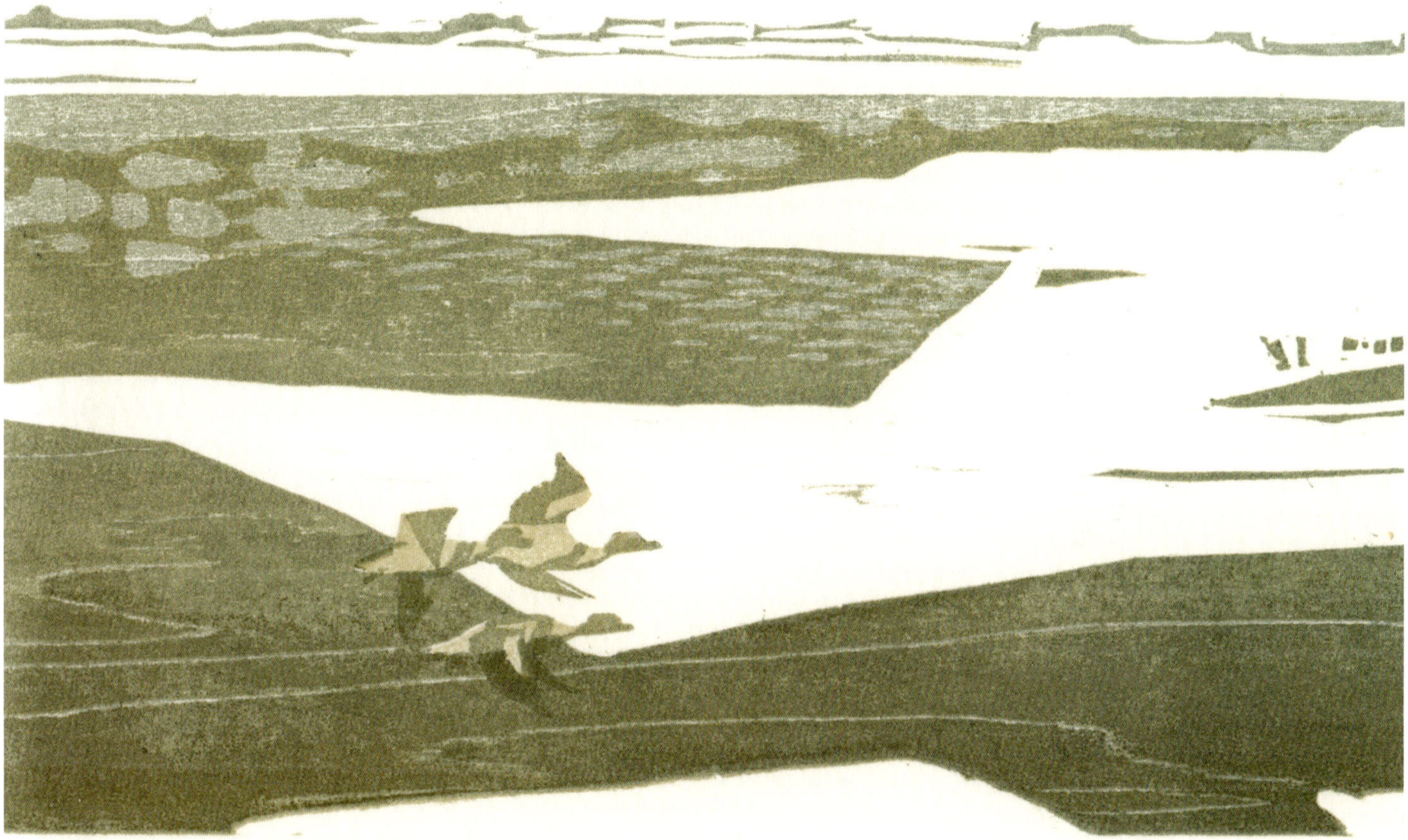

*Estuary,* woodcut proof

They are wet, windswept and wild, yet I love estuaries and live near one. What's the fascination? Is it the quality of the reflected light? A distant shore, fractured, shimmering, floating? I have a feeling of anticipation. There's nothing to see? Wait – and watch. The grain of my block describes fluid lines that add watermarks to the print and help shape my composition.

# Barry Sutton

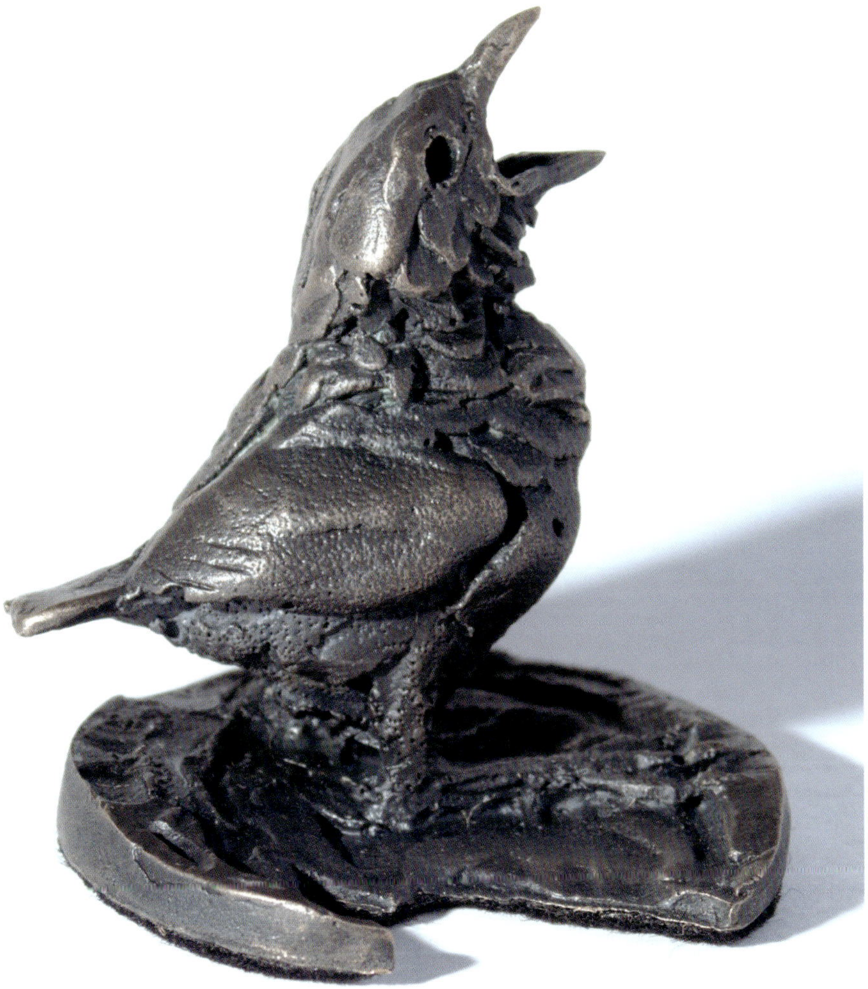

*Fledgling Wren,* bronze

This bronze sculpture of a fledgling Wren was originally made to compliment some adult Wrens but it works rather nicely as an individual piece. I'm rather taken by *Troglodytes troglodytes*; they are stroppy little characters as they scurry around like mice, investigating and defending their territory. They are a frequent and welcome sight in my unkempt garden.

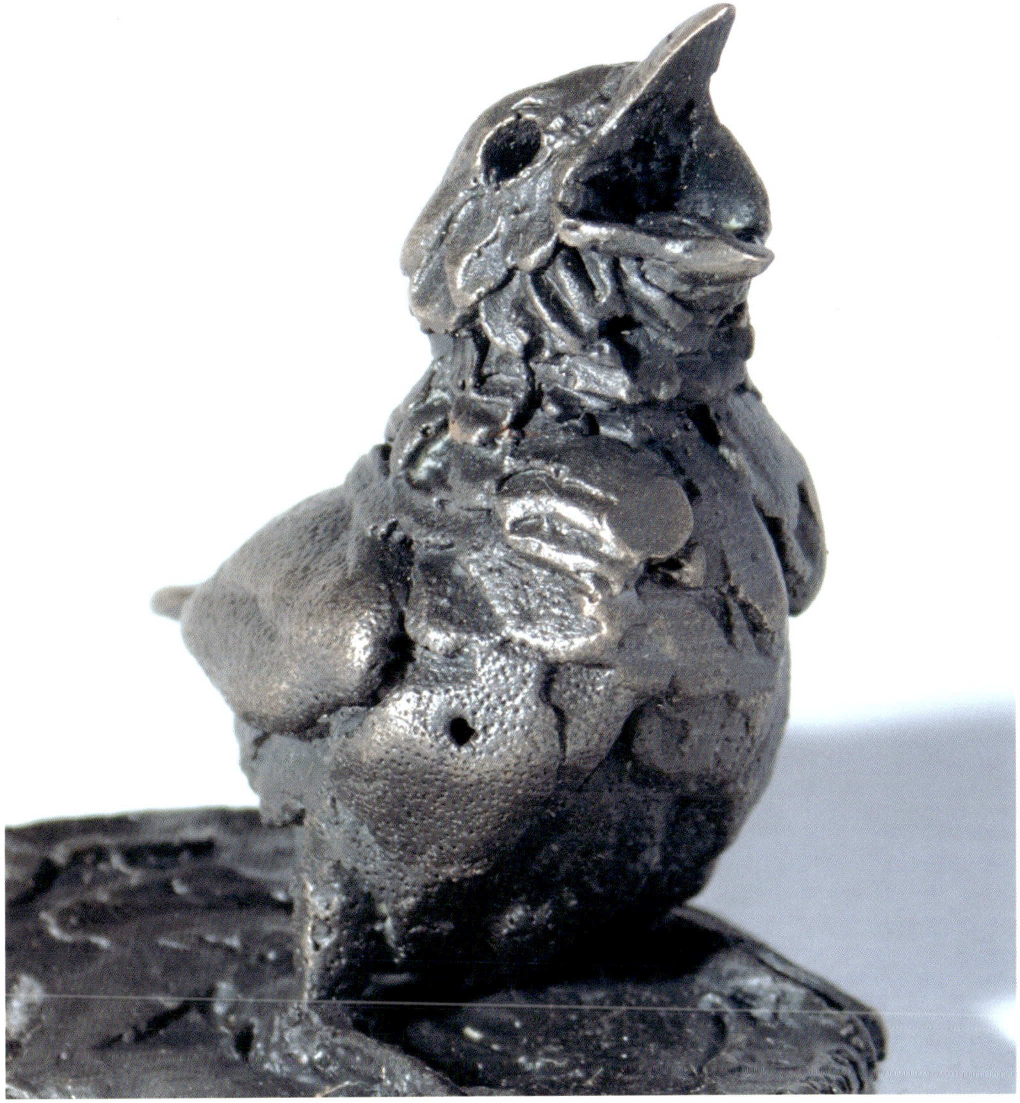

*Fledgling Wren*, bronze

# John Threlfall

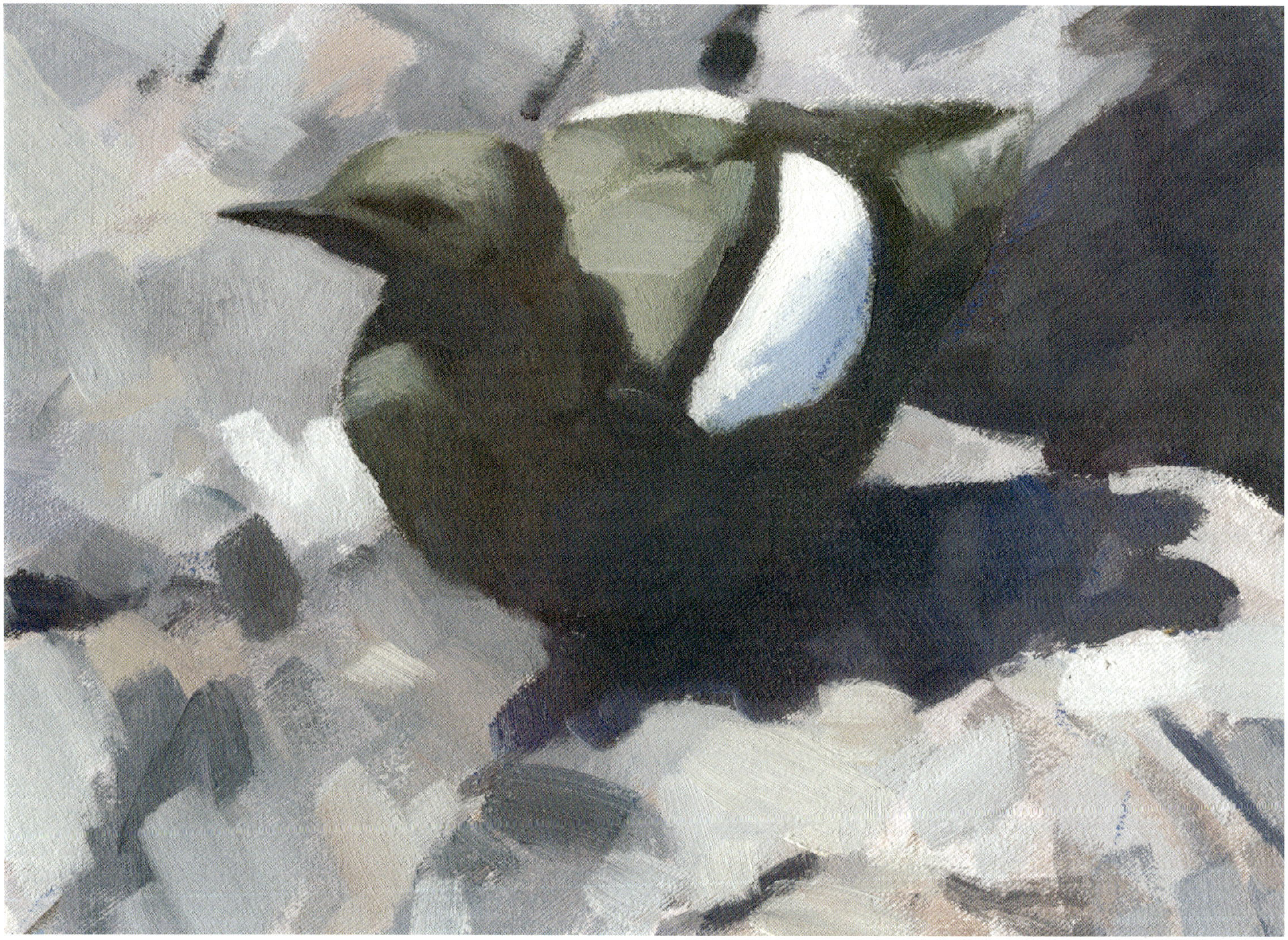

*Black Guillemot (Tystie),* oil on canvas

Balcary Heughs, Dumfries & Galloway. There are just one or two pairs of Black Guillemot breeding here, down towards the base of the cliffs. I can never predict what colour they're going to be in the sun.

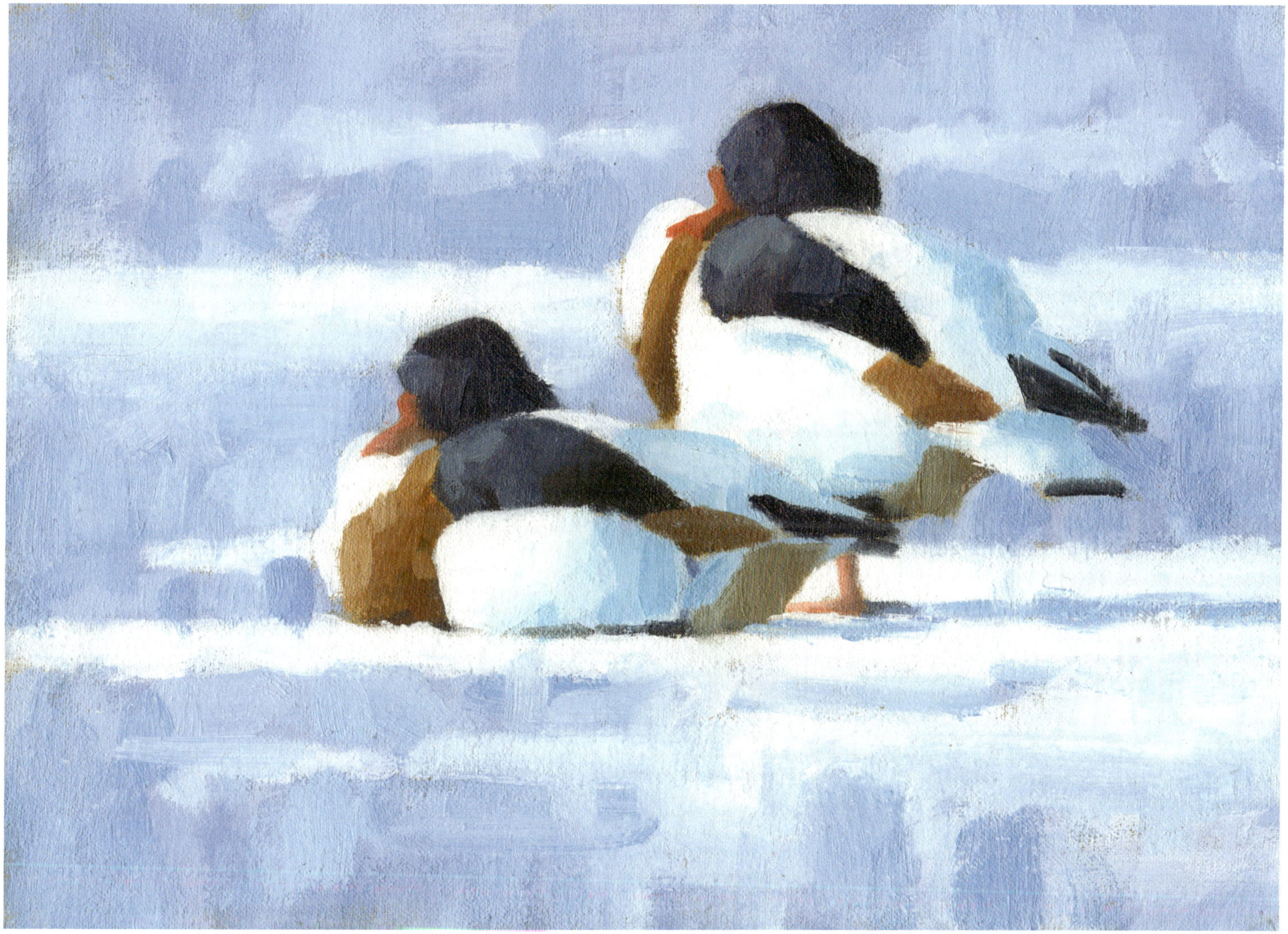

*Midwinter Shelduck*, oil on canvas

Martin Mere, Lancs. It was one of those hard to resist combinations of boldly interlocking jigsaw shapes, of bright white lights and deepening velvet darks, of sun-warmed colours and shadowed colds, where bird blue was colder than snow blue.

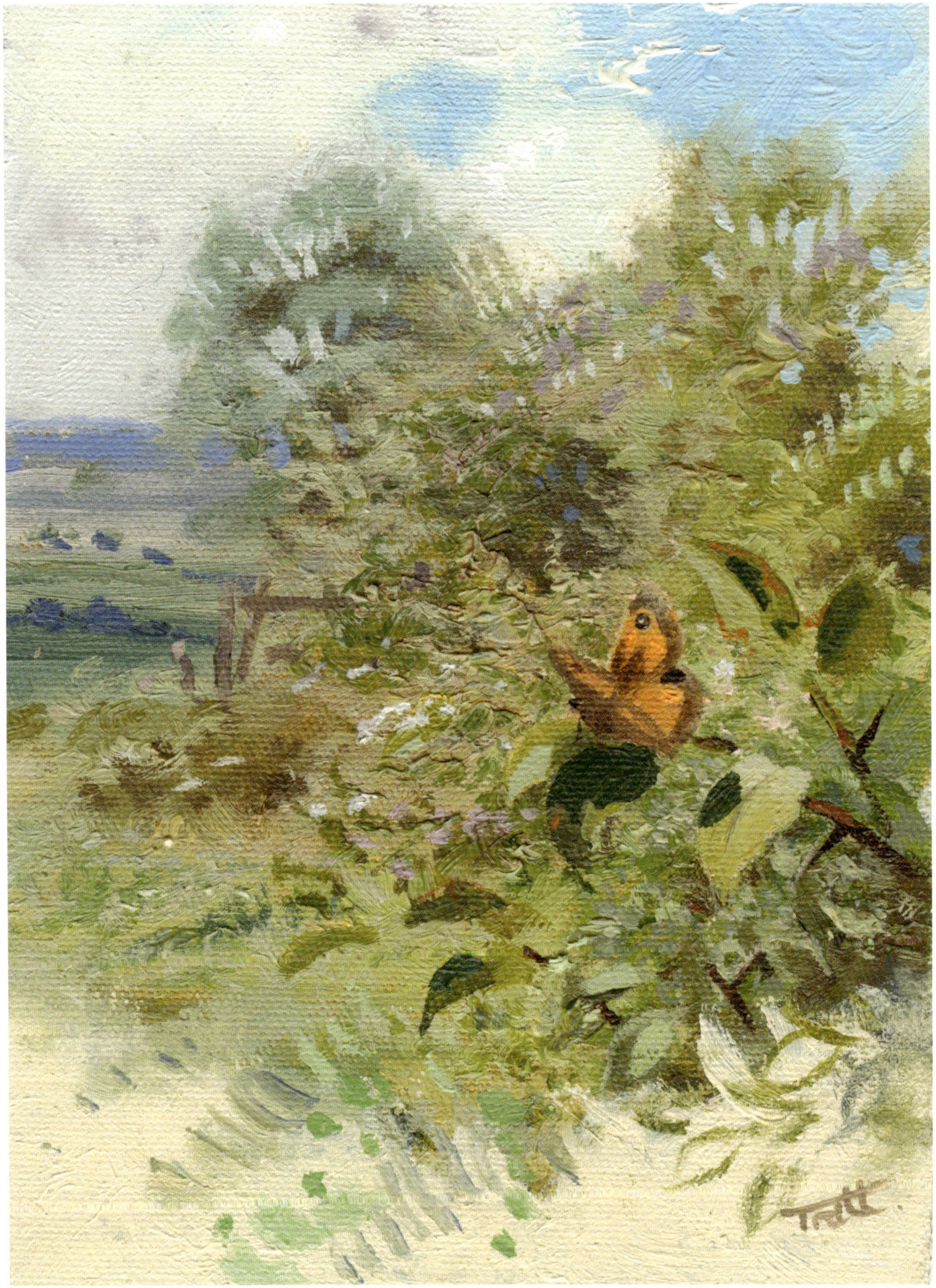

# Richard Tratt

*The Gatekeeper*, oil on canvas

The wings of the Gatekeeper are a rich orange-brown with the dark eyespot of the 'browns' family. I found this male butterfly sunning itself in its preferred hedgerow habitat. I look forward to seeing this butterfly in my garden and surrounding farmland from mid July to late summer.

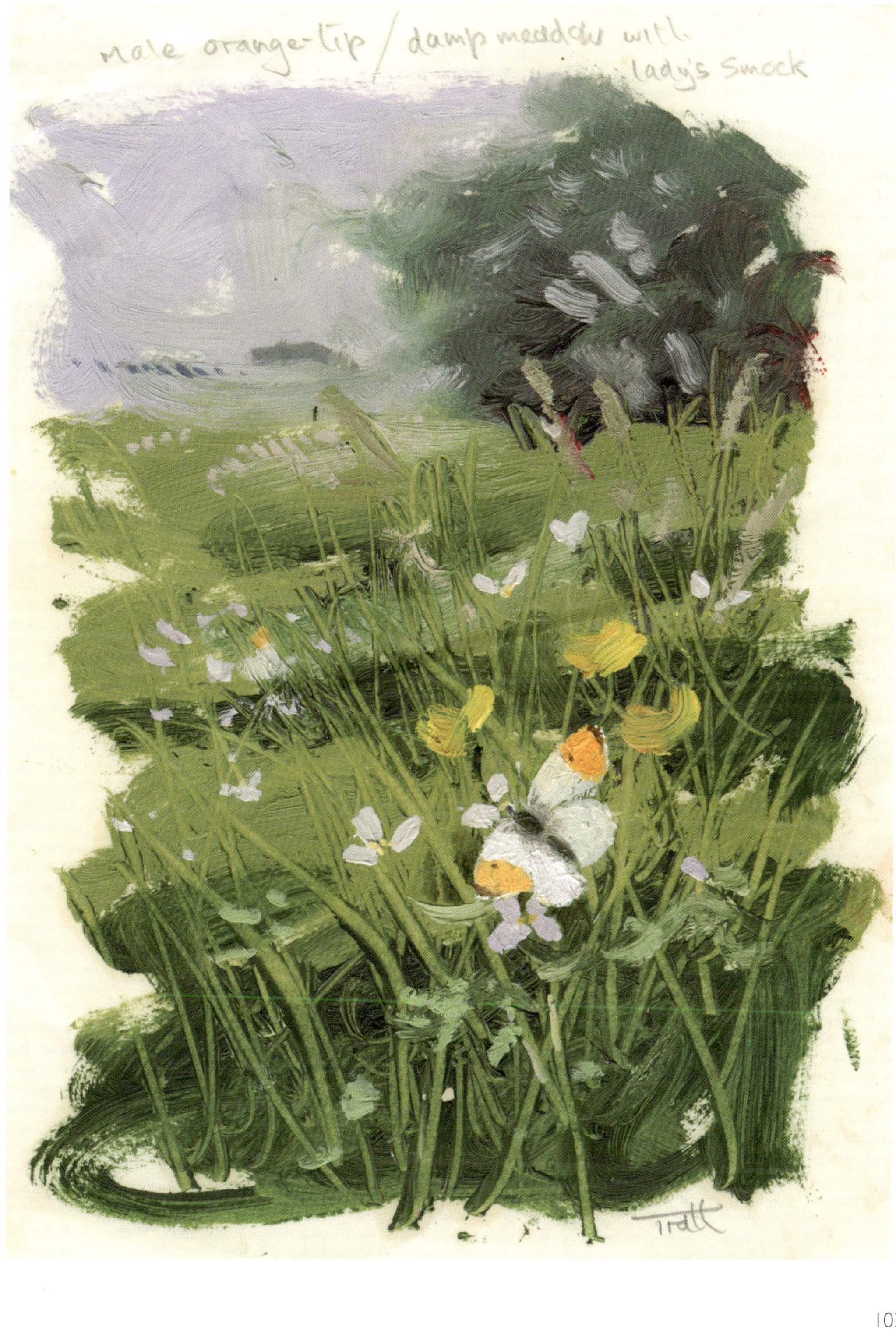


*The Orange Tip*, oil on paper

I'm always thrilled to see the first Orange Tips of the year. They emerge with the welcome warm sunshine of late spring. Only the male has orange forewings, which makes it distinctive and immediately recognizable in flight. This butterfly is found in rural areas along country lanes, in damp meadows and often strays into gardens.

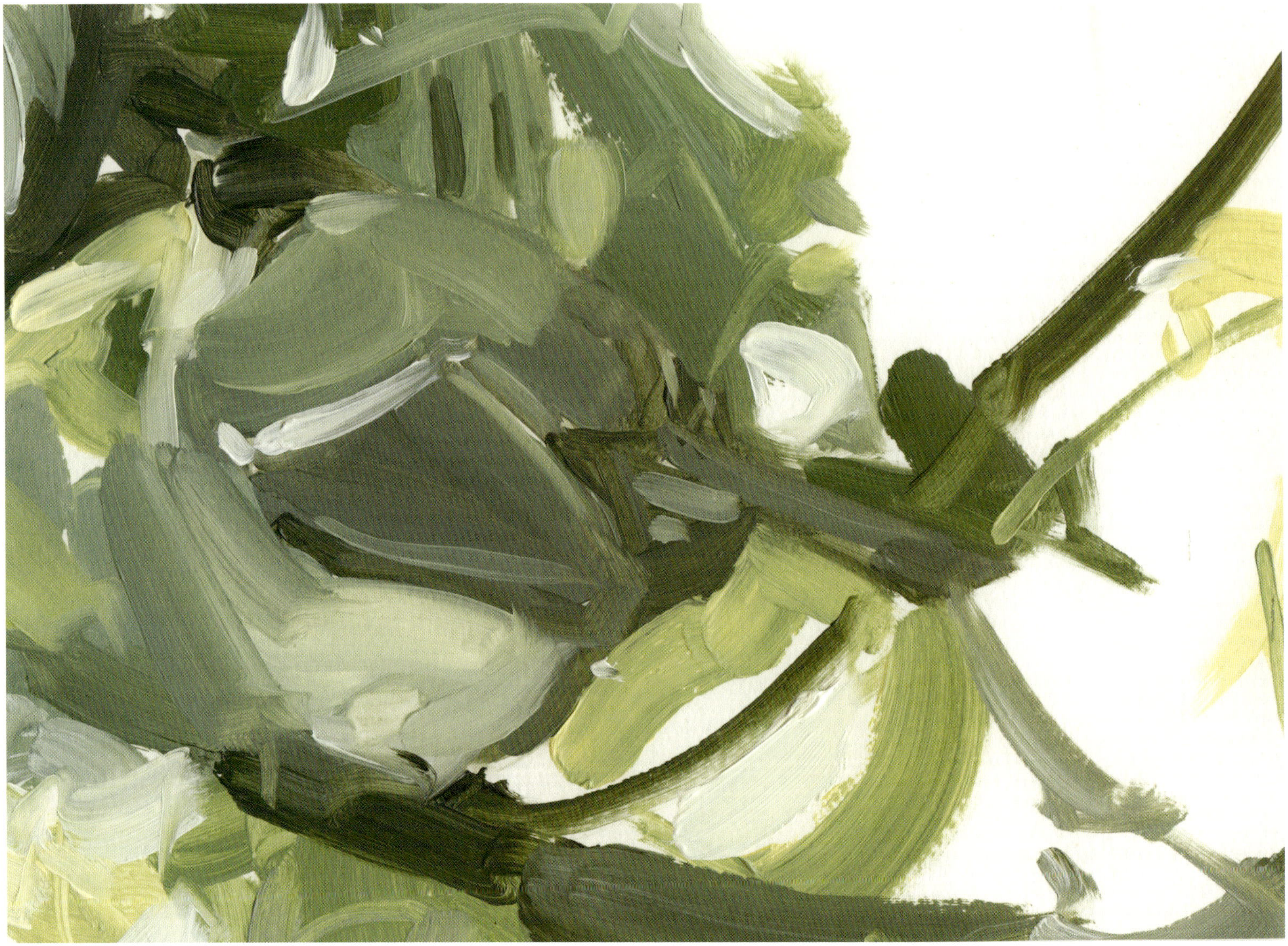

*Great Tit,* oil on paper

# Esther Tyson

The spring light is caught in leaves and the fledgling Great Tits disappear time and again so perfectly amongst the foliage that I am in wonder, how could these colours be better matched? There again, in the lower reaches of this scrubby woodland, the light is shaded and colours subdued, these birds become their surroundings then reappear as though they never left.

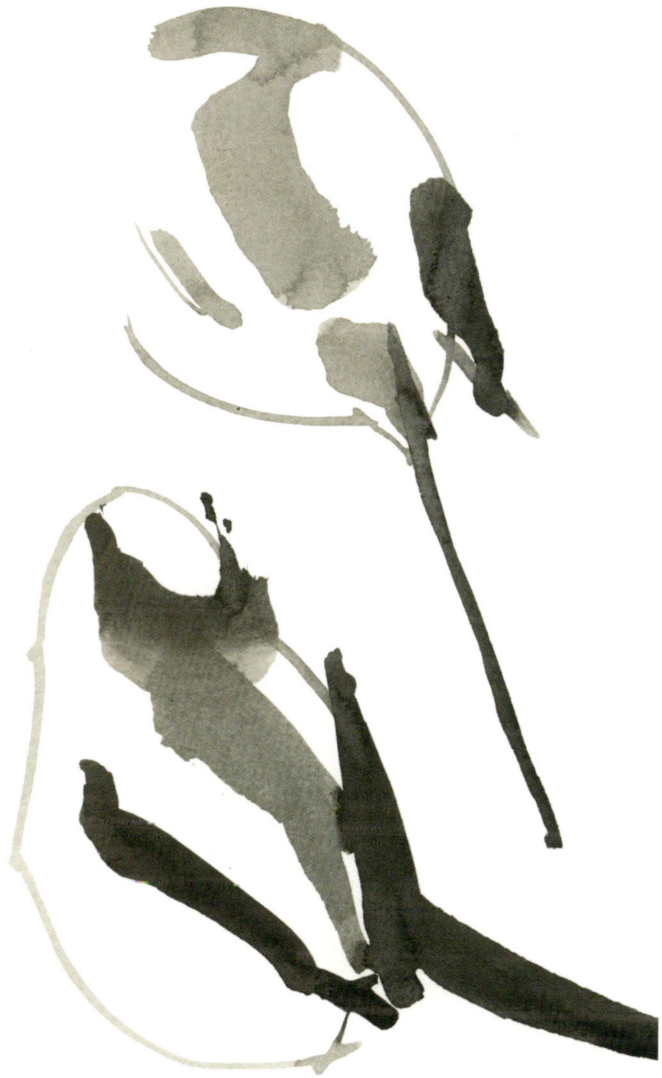

*Long Tailed Tits*, ink on paper

The feeder hangs on the wall opposite my kitchen window making washing up less painful. A shape catches my eye; a shadow, round body, long tail... I dart for my paper and ink, how many months has it taken to entice these birds into the back garden? Now it's as though time stands still. Three Long tailed Tits. I make small drawings, repeat and again.

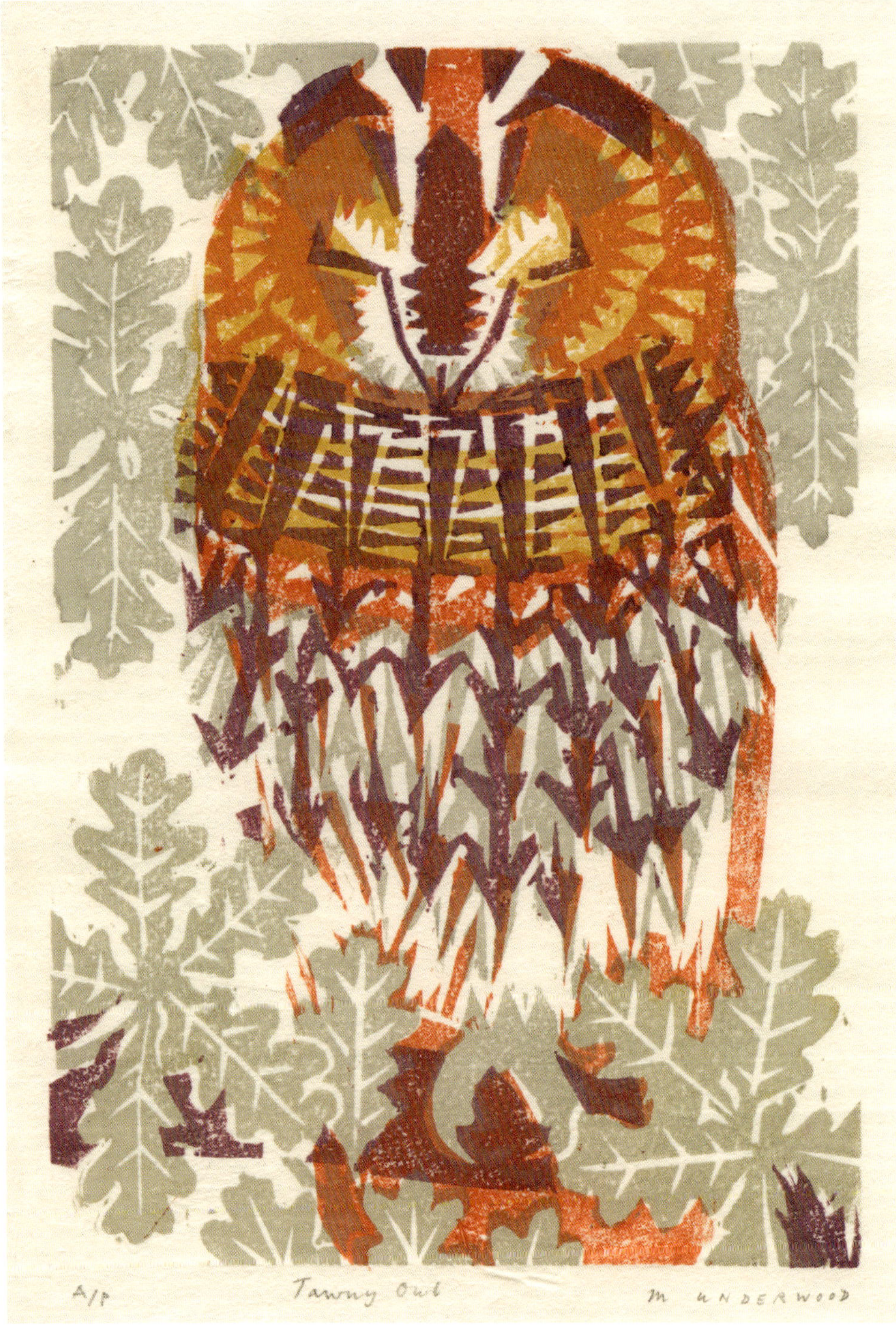


# Matt Underwood

*Tawny Owl,* woodblock print

Wandering off a track in the woods recently, I walked straight into a sleeping Tawny Owl roosting about six foot from the ground. We were both startled to see each other and after a few moments, the owl half fell, half flew away.

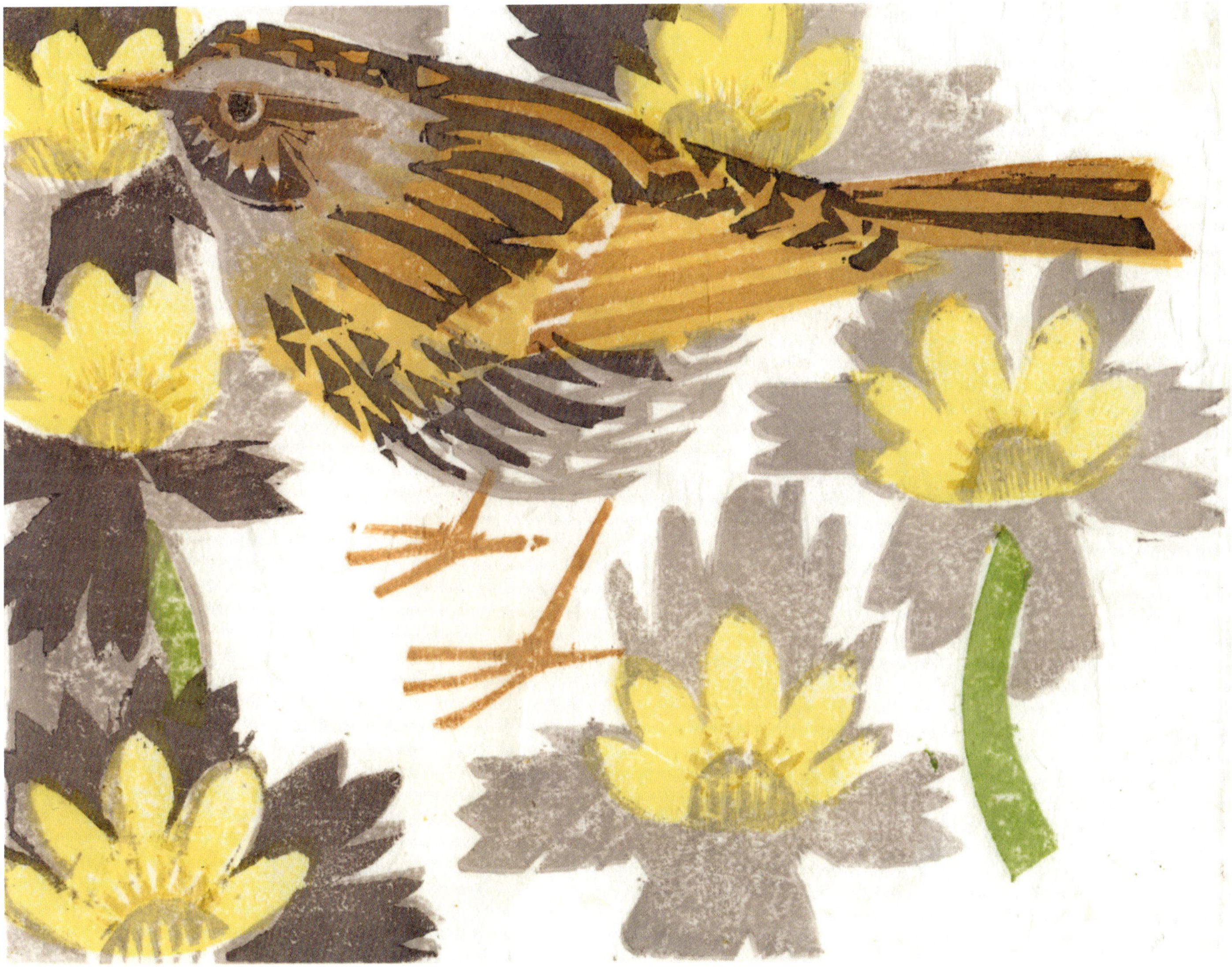

*Dunnock and Aconites,* woodblock print

I look forward to seeing Winter Aconites. They seem to burn their way through lying snow; their petals curled, unfurl in the warm sunshine.

# Simon Turvey

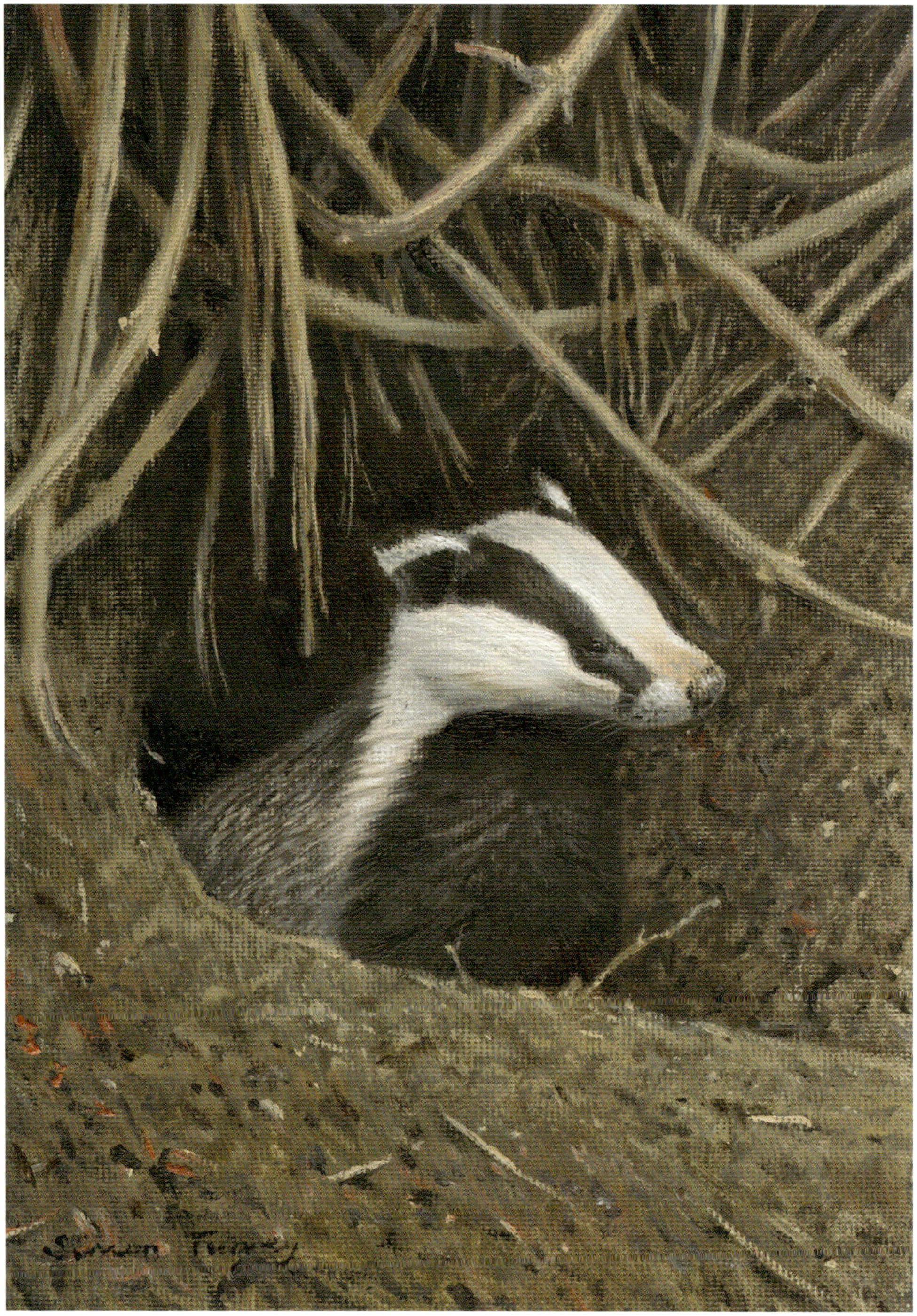

*Badger,* oil on paper

British mammals are a subject close to my heart. I still remember years ago, my first view of a badger as it emerged from its sett deep in a Kentish wood on a September evening.

# Ian Wallace

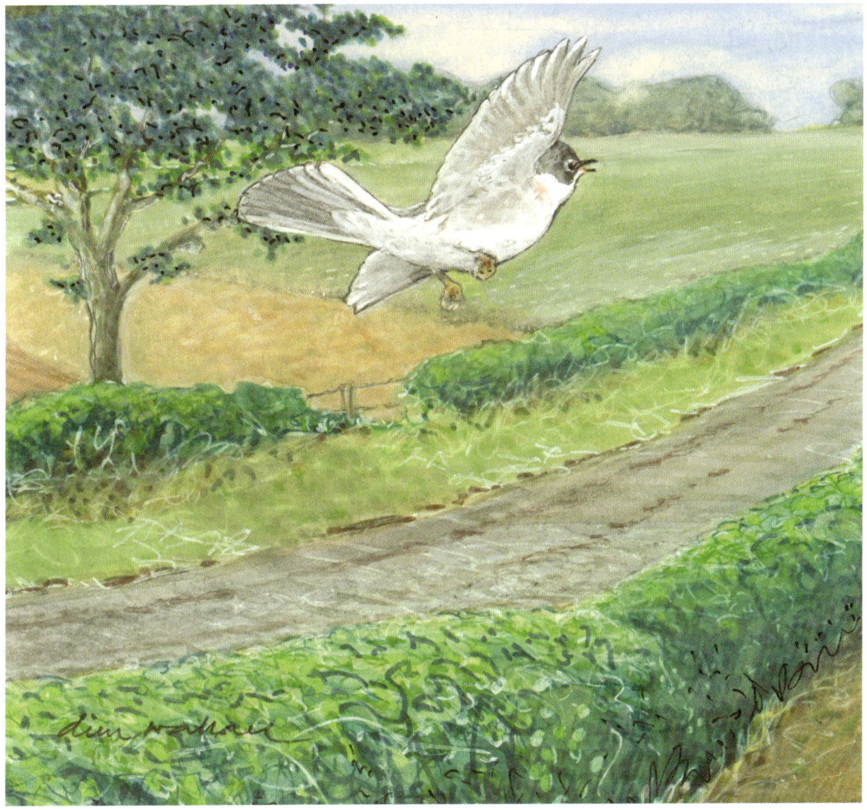

*The Sprite of Bushton Lane,* watercolour

The Sprite of Bushton Lane is a Common Whitethroat. In its lean years it survived in my Staffordshire patch only in a few still successful cells. One of these was the double-hedged lane from Anslow to Bushton where now a least four males bounce about in spring song flights. Even better their young have filled up many other hedges.

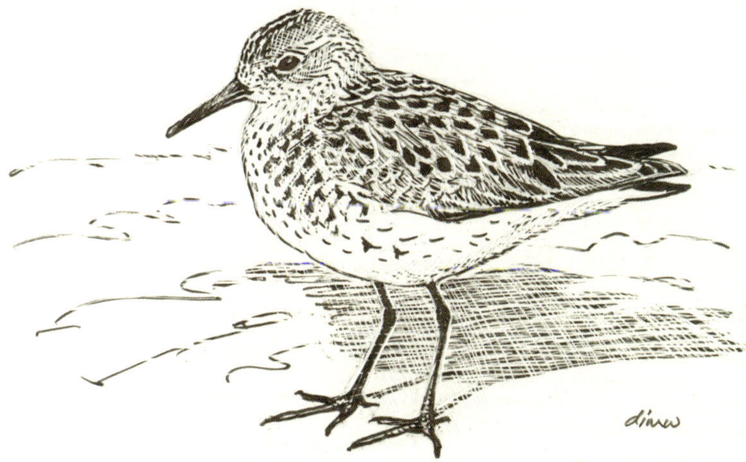

*Western Sandpiper,* scraperboard

Never at ease with pen and ink, I discovered that the medium of scraperboard allowed instant correction of mistakes and good printed definition.

# Michael Warren

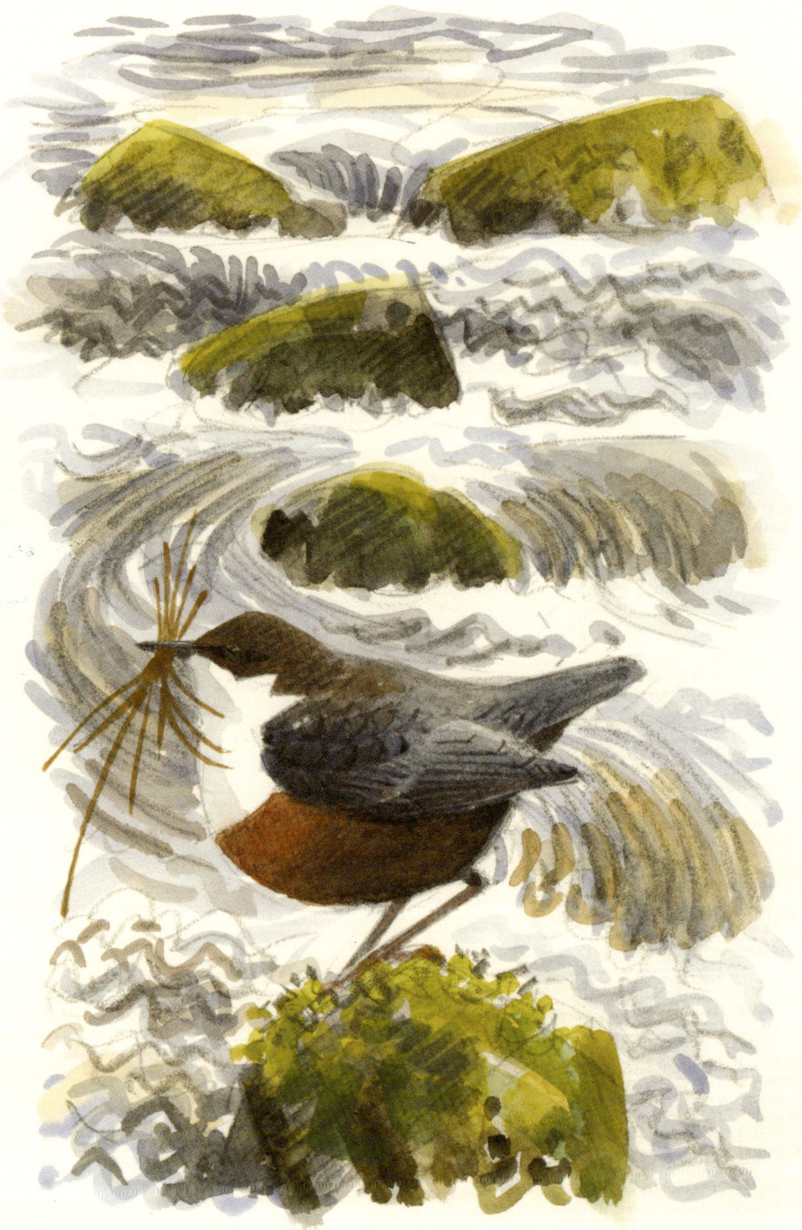

*Dipper,* watercolour

A Dipper briefly perched amid rushing waters. This bird watched in April is collecting nesting material. I sketched this particular individual in Yorkshire, the mossy stones in the stream glistened sharp yellow and green against the colours of the water.

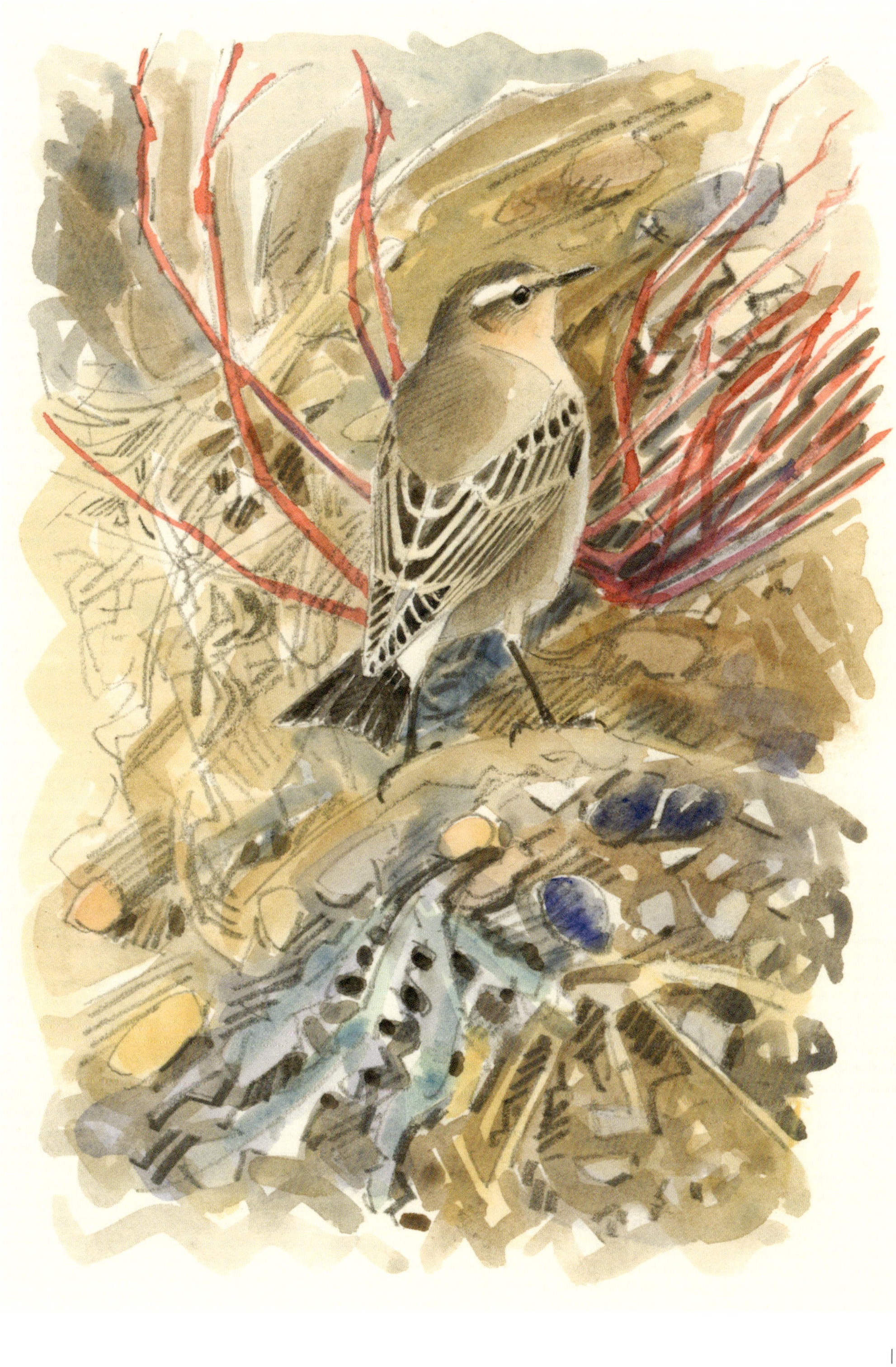

*First Winter Wheatear,* watercolour

A smart bird observed at my local patch in Nottinghamshire. Typical early October migrant to enliven the day. The colours of the Wheatear echoed the gravel pit background, with red plant stems for contrast.

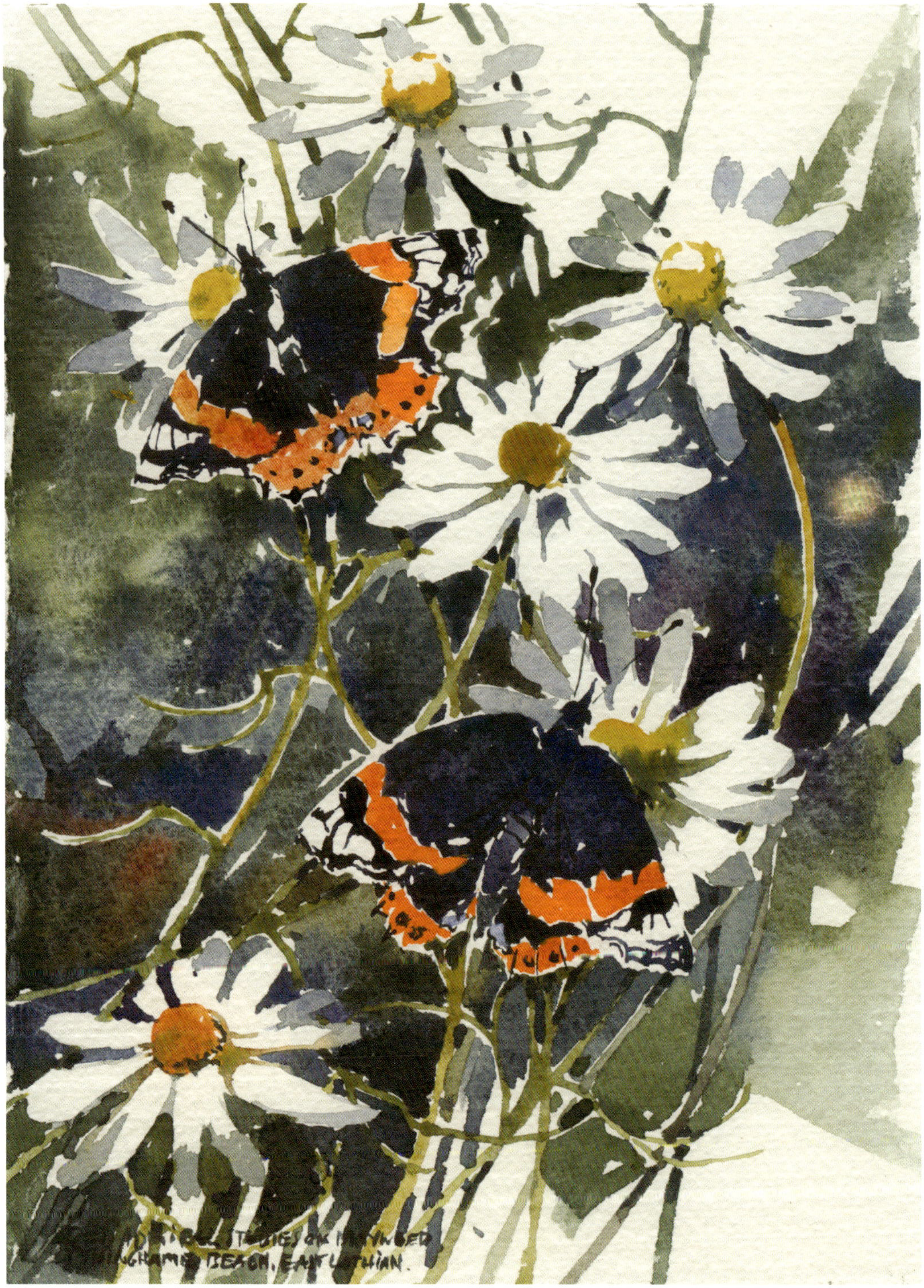

# Darren Woodhead

*Red Admiral,* watercolour on paper

Red Admiral butterfly feeding on Mayweed, Tyninghame beach, East Lothian. September seems to be following a pattern in recent years here, and the first two weeks has been bringing warm weather and wonderful opportunities to paint butterflies among the Mayweed that borders the tideline here. Seldom do their patterns fit exactly to books.

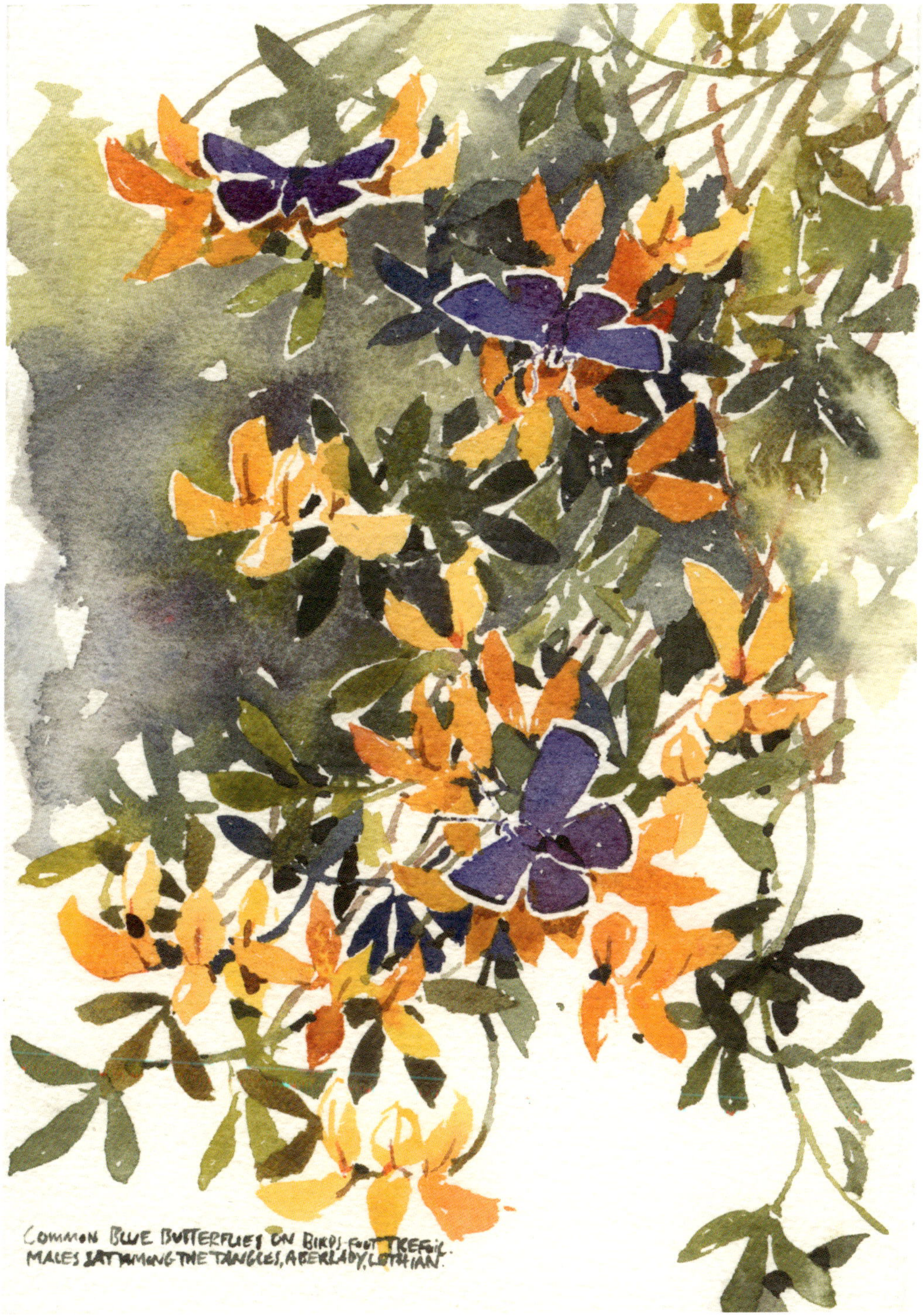


*Common Blue,* watercolour on paper

Common Blue Butterflies on Birdsfoot Trefoil, Aberlady Bay, East Lothian. After what seemed an eternity waiting for good butterfly days, at last a bloom happened, and the trefoil held once again, the dazzling blue of male Common Blues. Very special.

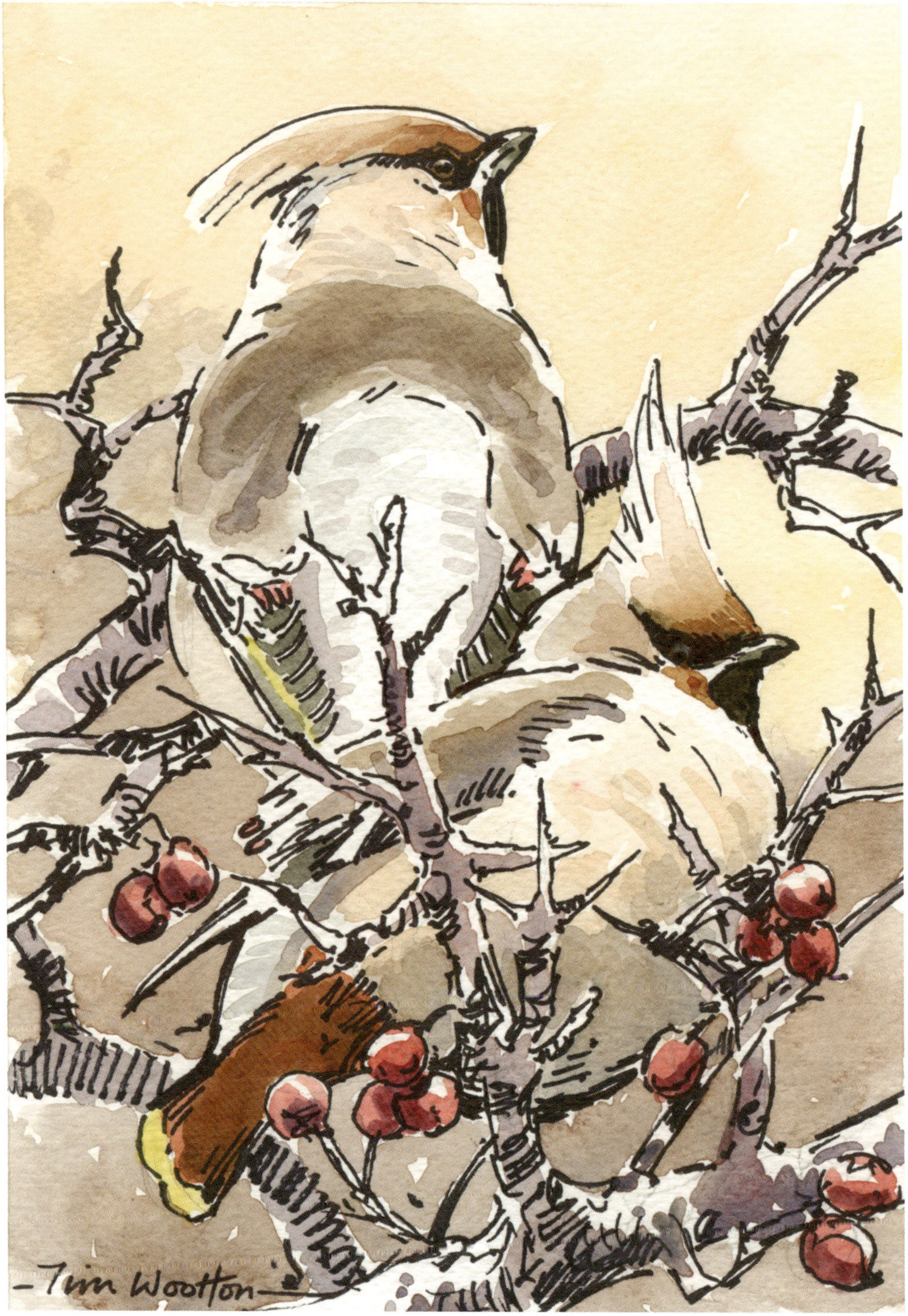


# Tim Wootton

*Waxwings*, pen and watercolour

If Britain gets Waxwings, they come to the Northern Isles first but usually they overfly my cottage and continue down the coast to Stromness. But this winter two birds came to our garden and, lured by apples on canes and Rosa rugosa hips, I managed to hang on to them for five weeks. Their melodic jingling trilling calls brightened up my dark winter daily chores of dog-walking, mucking out ponies and chicken feeding.

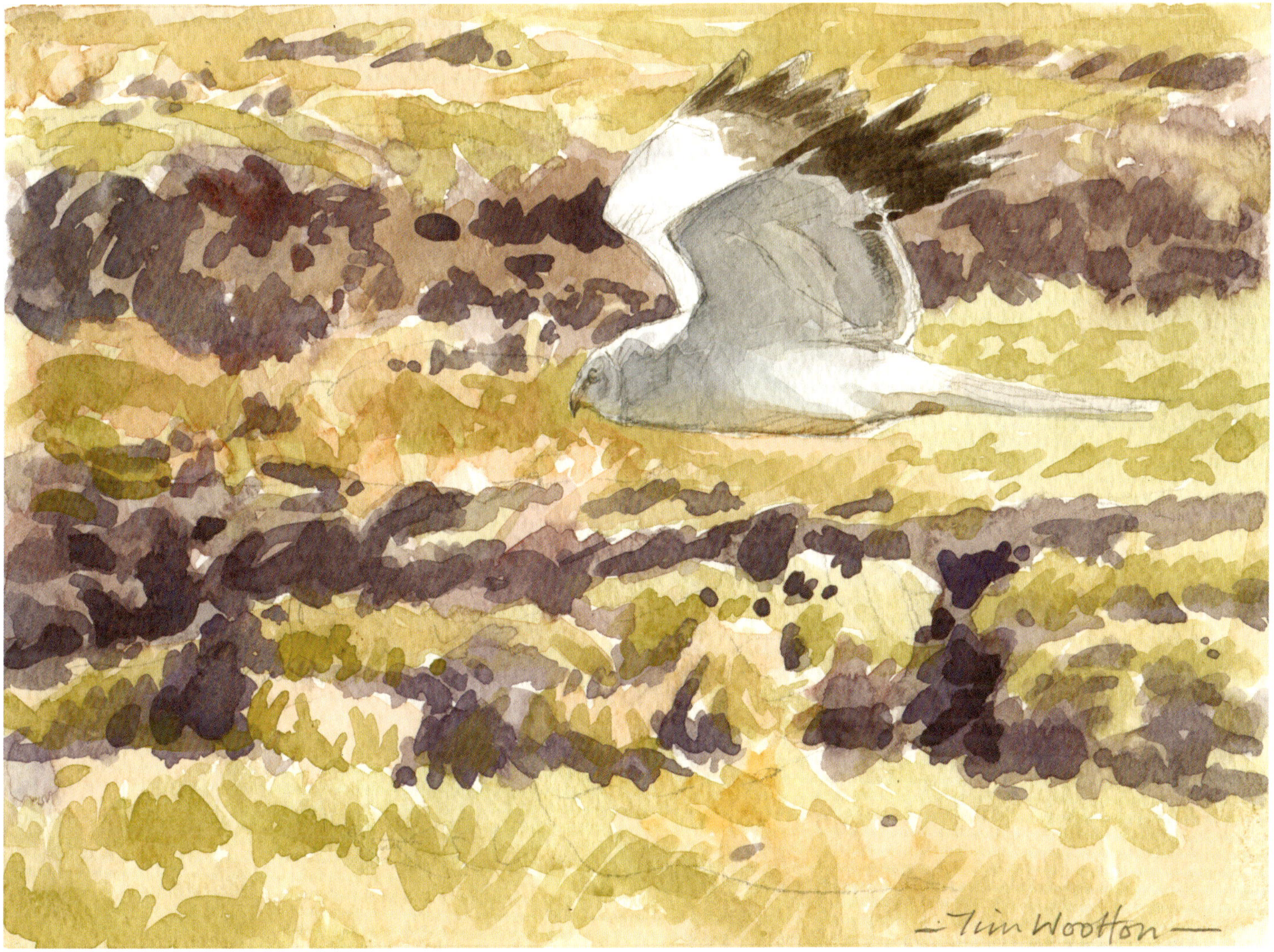


*Hen Harrier*, watercolour

Orkney has a healthy population of Hen Harriers. I live on the edge of an upland heathery breeding territory and males and ringtails are regular birds through my land; scattering Starlings, sparrows, Greenfinches and pipits on their visits. I watched the male drifting slowly across the hillside at the back of the cottage; the light flaring off his plumage.

# Index and Full List of Members



## Associate Members

# The Society Of Wildlife Artists

The Society of Wildlife Artists is a registered charity that hopes to spread the message of conservation and celebrate the natural world through all forms of fine art.

Not only do we offer our bursaries, but in our attempts to discover and encourage talent at an early age, the SWLA collaborates with the Royal Society for the Protection of Birds with their RSPB Wildlife Explorer's annual *Wild Art* competition for children. Winners have their pictures displayed at the annual SWLA exhibition at The Mall Galleries in London.

The Society's annual exhibition, The Natural Eye, featuring all art media (not photography) is held in October/November at the Mall Galleries, London. It is a showcase for the very best of art inspired by the natural world and includes members' work from the UK, mainland Europe, North America and Russia.

Any artist whose work is inspired by nature is eligible to submit - although you don't have to be a traditional wildlife artist or a naturalist, simply showing knowledge and understanding of your subject is the imperative. This knowledge combined with exciting art will take precedence during selection. If the natural world has moved you to create incredible work, the Society would like to see it.

Many Society members are happy to visit schools to help nurture new talent and encourage an interest in their natural environment. Please contact the Society for details. www.swla.co.uk

*The Natural Eye is considered the foremost event in the British wildlife art calendar.*

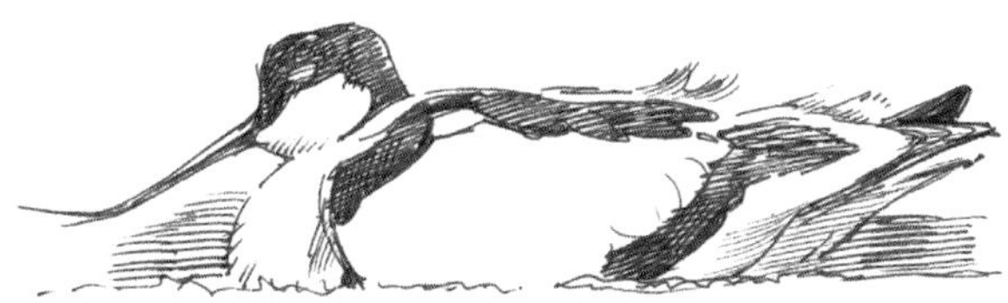

*Sleeping Avocet*, Robert Gillmor.

# The SWLA Bursary Scheme

Did you know our SWLA Bursary Scheme offers up to £750 to artists?
And you don't even have to be a member!

Anyone can submit for our annual exhibition. We take work in a wide variety of mediums (not photography) that is inspired by the natural world. The selection committee is looking for work that captures the spirit of the subject or conveys a sense of place. All work goes through a selection procedure. Artists that have work selected of a consistently high quality and who regularly exhibit are then invited to become members.

Our current bursaries of up to £750 are aimed at helping emerging artists with a project, course costs, travel or materials. We have allocated over 60 Bursaries in the last 20 years and many of the recipients have gone on to become full members of the Society.

We are currently offering places for artists of any age to attend the inspirational John Busby Seabird Drawing Course in Scotland.

Further Bursary opportunities will emerge over time. An example of a recent opportunity open to any artist was the Wildlife Trusts' Undersea Art Award. This Bursary ran for 5 years and gave an artist the chance to learn to scuba dive and then go underwater off the UK coast in order to produce work inspired by the experience and help raise awareness of the amazing habitat off our shores. The work was exhibited at The Natural Eye and at venues for the Wildlife Trusts.

We also have a portfolio day during The Natural Eye so that artists can get feedback and advice from leading members.

Our Bursary Schemes offer a range of opportunities. So if your art is inspired by nature and you feel you have a valid project worthy of a bursary, please contact us. For more details and examples of past bursary winners, please visit our website.

www.swla.co.uk

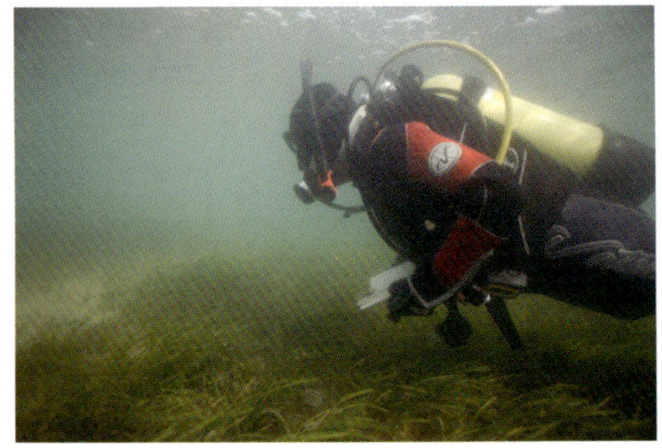

Esther Tyson, winner of the 2010 Bursary sketching underwater at Studland.

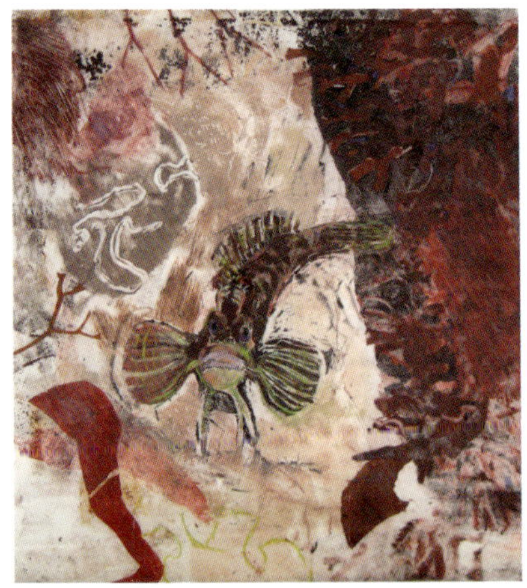

*Tompot Blenny* by Kim Atkinson, winner of the 2007 Wildlife Trusts' Diving Bursary.

# Become a SWLA Friend

If you'd like to be more involved in the SWLA you can easily sign up and become a Friend. You don't have to be an artist; many of our Friends simply want to know more about what we're up to, and of course, the special offers given to Friends. As a Friend you will receive:

• A special Friends' lunch at the Mall Galleries, which allows you a sneak preview of the exhibition before it opens to the public or private view. You can mingle with the artists and take your time to see the exhibition without the crowds. And of course you're able to buy before the doors open.

• You can win £200 to buy art in our Friends' Prize Draw, and you don't even have to do anything! As a Friend you are automatically entered into the draw and the winner is announced at the Friends' Lunch.

• You will be kept up to date with projects and publications and fundraisers, such as the Original Artwork Draw, so that you can buy tickets in advance.

• Friends receive the members' biannual illustrated Newsletter, featuring articles about latest artists' projects, exhibitions, how artists work, new bursary opportunities and general insightful knowledge into the artists' world.

• Free entry to annual The Natural Eye exhibition at the prestigious Mall Galleries.

• First hand information about our regular tours of the annual exhibition with the President and other member artists.

But perhaps more importantly, being a Friend means you are helping us to continue to offer our bursaries to help emerging artists. With the Friend's subscription fees, we can continue to explore collaborations with conservation organisations and charities so that the talent of our artists can help champion conservation.

CURRENTLY OUR SWLA FRIENDS ANNUAL MEMBERSHIP FEE IS ONLY

£17.00

BUT PLEASE VISIT OUR WEBSITE FOR FEE UPDATES.

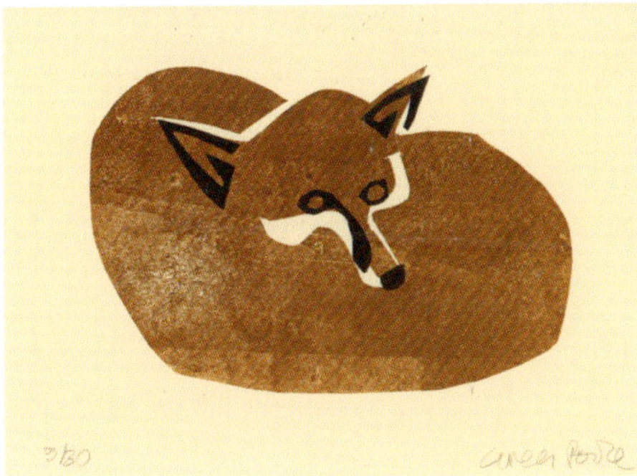

*Fox*, screenprint, Greg Poole.

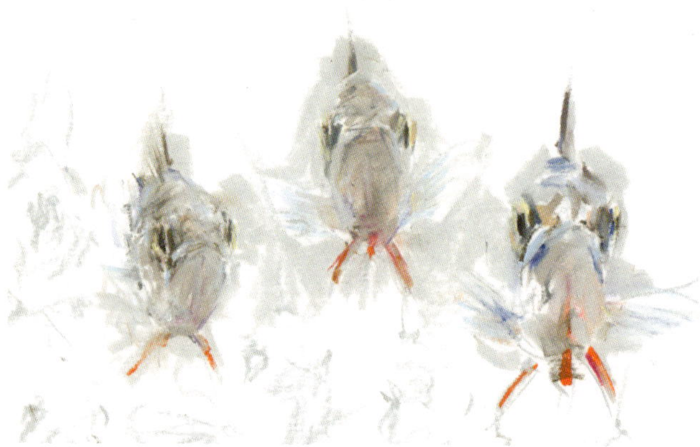

# Acknowledgements

The biggest thank you has to go to the SWLA artists. Without their generous donations of time and art this book simply would not have existed.

Harriet Mead, Bruce Pearson, Robert Gillmor & Chris Packham for their work on this book.

Jody Lawrence for the photography of artwork. www.jodylawrence.co.uk

Swallowtail Print for all their help. www.swallowtailprint.co.uk

Red Hare Publishing Ltd www.redharepublishing.co.uk

WildSounds for their help with sales. www.wildsounds.co.uk

Chris Andrews and Kate Risley for letting us use their photos, pages 9,11, & Jeffrey Taylor, ARPS, page 7

Joy Parsons for her legacy.

And finally thank you to the anonymous donor - you know who you are!

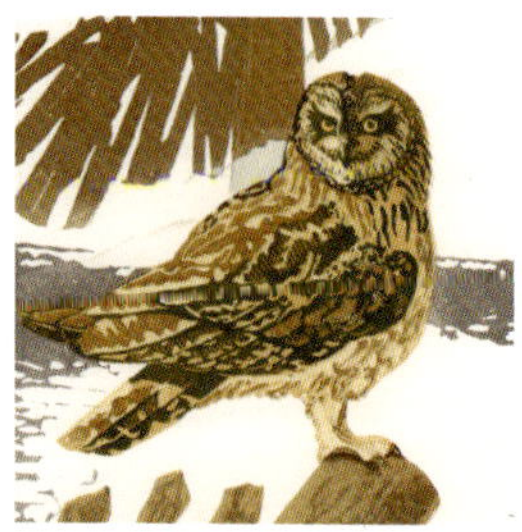